Lodge
"Himalayan Brotherhood"
No. 459 E.C.

Also from Westphalia Press

westphaliapress.org

Lodge
"Himalayan Brotherhood"
No. 459 E.C.

Minute Books and Correspondence

compiled by G. Reeves-Brown

WESTPHALIA PRESS
An imprint of Policy Studies Organization

Lodge "Himalayan Brotherhood" No. 459 E.C.
All Rights Reserved © 2014 by Policy Studies Organization

Westphalia Press
An imprint of Policy Studies Organization
1527 New Hampshire Ave., NW
Washington, D.C. 20036
info@ipsonet.org

ISBN-13: 978-1633910270
ISBN-10: 163391027X

Cover design by Taillefer Long at Illuminated Stories:
www.illuminatedstories.com

Daniel Gutierrez-Sandoval, Executive Director
PSO and Westphalia Press

Devin Proctor, Director of Media and Publications
PSO and Westphalia Press

Updated material and comments on this edition
can be found at the Westphalia Press website:
www.westphaliapress.org

LODGE

"HIMALAYAN BROTHERHOOD"

No. 459 E.C.

being

EXTRACTS

FROM THE

MINUTE BOOKS AND CORRESPONDENCE

From the Foundation of the Lodge on May 19th, 1838 to the 30th May 1927.

with a Nominal List of Members.

Compiled up to the end of the year 1908

by

The Late Wor Bro. E.O.W. Wilsey

and

Re-Edited and Extended to the year 1927

by

Wor. Bro. G. Reeves-Brown.

(P.D.G. Chaplain Punjab)

Printed under the Authority of D.G.L.

Liddell's Press, Simla.

LODGE

" HIMALAYAN BROTHERHOOD "

No. 459 E.C.

being

EXTRACTS

FROM THE

MINUTE BOOKS AND CORRESPONDENCE

*From the Foundation of the Lodge on May 19th, 1838 to the
30th May 1927.*

with a Nominal List of Members.

Compiled up to the end of the year 1908

by

The Late Wor. Bro. E. O. W. Wilsey

and

Re-Edited and Extended to the year 1927

by

Wor. Bro. G. Reeves-Brown.

(P. D. G. Chaplain Punjab)

Printed under the Authority of D. G. L.

———

Wor. Brother R. Watson.
Past Master 1896-97.
P.G.D. (Eng.) P. Deputy D.G.M. (Punjab).

SECOND PREFACE 1927.

To WOR BRO. H. G. RUSSELL,

Worshipful Master, Lodge "Himalayan Brotherhood"

No. 459, E. C.

WORSHIPFUL MASTER,

At the Meeting of our Lodge held on April 12th 1926 the Lodge did me the honour of asking me to "re-write" the Lodge History and to bring it up to date. I accepted this duty and bring you now the results of my labours, or rather the combined efforts of Bro. Adhemar and myself, for without the unselfish and willing co-operation of Bro Adhemar the arduous work of completing the List of Members would have been beyond me.

Some three or four years ago when P. "Z" of our Chapter "Dalhousie" I came across certain old Letter Books of the Lodge which I found "heaved over amongst the rubbish" and which had evidently escaped the notice of the late Wor. Bro. Wilsey and I found much of real interest in them. A reading of the early Minute Books in conjunction with these old Letter Books has induced me to venture to re-write much of the earlier portion of Bro. Wilsey's book and much that he missed down to about 1865 is now for the first time recorded.

An important point that can be noted is the fact that the Lodge warrant was never permanently withdrawn from the Lodge in the critical days of 1849 but was in fact withdrawn from the Master's hand for the space of three months only, during the labours of the Committee of Inquiry in this year, so that we can still claim our date from 1838 and not from the re-opening in 1849 as has been suggested by some.

I can but repeat the words of Wor. Bro. Wilsey when I say that my effort is in no sense a literary production. It is intended for our members only and is meant to place on permanent record the most interesting occurrences in the life of this old Lodge, a knowledge of which will strengthen the ties which bind so many of us to our "Mother in Masonry".

We have been able to complete the records of many of the old members of the early days and the List of Members is now complete to the end of May. 1927.

SIMLA,   G. REEVES-BROWN, P.M.
June 1927.   P.D.G. Chaplain.

FRIST PREFACE, 1909.

Wor. Bro. T. W. Lloyd,

Worshipful Master, Lodge "Himalayan Brotherhood,"

No. 459, E. C.

Worshipful Master,

After I had taken over the duties of Secretary last year and had an opportunity of going through our books and correspondence it struck me that we possessed a mass of information concerning our Lodge which would make interesting reading if collated, arranged, and printed in some convenient form. Besides, it was very apparent that unless something of the sort was done speedily all trace of the rise and progress of one of the oldest Lodges in India, and *the* oldest in the Punjab Masonic district, would be irrevocably lost, as our earlier records were fast falling into decay. I therefore decided to go through all our papers and carefully extract therefrom anything of the least importance or interest, and the result of my labours I now place before you.

This compilation is in no sense a literary production. I have simply made verbatim extracts, and arranged them with a few remarks in chronological order to preserve the sequence of events in as interesting and easily readable a form as possible. The compilation is solely for the perusal of members of the Lodge, and is meant to preserve in a convenient form dates aud incidents in our long history, which otherwise would in course of time be lost to us, and if it answers this purpose and the Lodge will accept and print it, my labour will not have been in vain.

I should mention that when nearing the end of my work, I discovered that a compilation somewhat on these lines was actually sanctioned by the Lodge in 1903, but for some reason or other was never taken in hand. .

I have attached as an appendix a carefully checked list of members from 1838 to the end of 1908, showing dates of joining, initiation, passing, raising, resignation, office held *et cætera,* which I think will be very useful for future reference. Our official register of members I have found to be incorrect in numerous instances.

E. O. WILSEY,

Simla,
20th April 1909.

ROLL OF MASTERS AND WARDENS.

NOTE.—In the following list the year is the year of Installation.

Year.	Master.	Wardens { Senior. / Junior.	
1838	McDonald, Robert Barker	...	W. S. Blackburn.
			D. O'B. Clarke.
1839	Gouland, Henry Godfrey	...	G. Cox.
			D. Seaton.
1841	Giels, J. T.	...	F. W. Porter.
			W. Charde.
1843	Curtis, James Gray William	...	J. T. Giels.
			T. Riddell.
1844	Cox, George	...	W. Charde.
			W. E. Carte.
1845	Dodd, John Beach	...	J. S. Chisholm.
			G. Bouchier.
1846	Marshall, John Samuel ... (Resigned August 1846.)	...	{ P. Innes. / P. Petrovitz.
	Chisholm, John Seton ... (Installed September 1846.)	...	{ J. W. Drummond. / H. B. Riddell.
1847	Chisholm, John Seton	...	H. P. A. B. Riddell.
			I. H. Staines.
1849	Curtis, James Gray William	...	R. B. Wigstrom.
			E. D. Byng.
1850	Bracken, John	...	E. D. Byng.
			H. P. A. B. Riddell,
1851	Ebden, Henry Anderson	...	{ H P. A. B. Riddell. / E. J. Simpson.
1852	Fergusson, James Alexander Duncan	...	G. E. Pool.
			E. C. Thorp.
			E. Oakes.
1853	Mackenzie, James	...	C. E. Davison,
			H. T. Tapp.

Year.	Master.	Wardons. { Senior. Junior.
1854	Jeffrey, George ...	T. Graham. Lord W. M. Hay.
1855	Hay, Lord William Montagu ...	W. A. Hoghton. T. Wood.
1856	Mackenzie, James ...	H. T. Tapp. { D. Briggs. { J. H. Maxwell.
1858	Tapp, Henry Thomas ...	S. R. Beechey. { F. D. Vivian. { A. B Fenwick.
1859	Hoghton, William Alexander ... ... (Installed, 16th May 1859. Resigned 20th June 1859.) Curtis, James Charles ... ... (Elected, 11th July 1859. Installed, 2nd November 1859)	T. Fleming. J. P. Caulfield.
1860	Fleming, Thomas ... ... (Died, 4th January 1861)	F. D. Daly. D. S. Henry.
1861	Clarke, Melville ...	G. N. Cheek. A. L. K. Quigley.
1862		J. C. Hamilton. J. G. Forbes.
1863	Wood, Thomas ...	A. L. K. Quigley. J. Craddock.
1864		W. H. Bishop. C. H. Macleod.
1865	Grant, John Hayes ...	J. E. Cooke. R. Dixon.
1866	Cooke, John Edward ...	G. H. Waller. W. Hill.
1867		A. Lyons. H. R. Cooke.

Year.	Master.	Wardens. { Senior. / Junior.
1868	Bleckley, Thomas McDougall ...	H. R. Cooke. / G. E. Campbell.
1869	Gardiner, Thomas George ...	D. S. Henry. / C. H. Levinge.
1870	Ball, William Edward ...	A. C. Cregeen. / F. D. Daly.
1871	Cooke, Hugh Rowland ...	A. Litster. / W. J. Haverty.
1872	} Litster, Archibald ...	G. Hawksworth. / J. I. Phelps.
1873		P. J. Coyne. / G. C. Caldecourt.
1874	Von Goldstein, Felix ...	C. J. Marsden. / T. Jameson.
1875	Litster, Archibald ...	G. C. Rivers. / J. Robertson.
1876	Robertson, John ...	W. C. Willson. / J. Hopkins.
1877	Willson, William Cater ...	R. Burton. / W. L. Francis.
1878	Rawlins, Thomas W. ...	G. H. M. Batten. / J. L. Walker.
1879	Batten, George Henry Maxwell	J. B. Hamilton. / C. C. Clavering
1880	Phelps, John Isaac ...	W. J. M. Towelle. / W. Ogden.
1881	Freeman, Benson Luke ...	G. E. L. S. Sanford. / G. Eyears.
1882	Sanford, George Edward Langham Somerset...	J E. Myers. / J McDermott.

Year.	Master.	Wardens { Senior. / Junior.
1883	Wolseley, Richard	G. Townley. / E. v S. Cullin.
1884	Freeman, Benson Luke	W. Smith. / R. Watson.
1885	Carson, William Patterson	J. Burt. / H. P. Burt.
1886	Burt, Henry Parsall	J. Burt. / Mima Mull.
1887	Burt, John	R. A. English. / A. James.
1888	Carson, William Patterson	Mima Mull, / C. R. Burn.
1889	English, Robert Abraham	E. H. H. Collen. / E Walmsley.
1890	Cullin, Edward van Someren	J. McDermott. / { L. Dennehy. / { F. Leigh.
1891	McDermott, John	R. G. Woodthorpe. / H. Elkington.
1892	Collen, Edwin Henry Hayter	W. G. Bowyer. / B. G. Wallis.
1893	Elkington, Henry	W. G. Bowyer. / F. G. Wigley.
1894	Burton, Richard	Sir A. E. Miller. / B. E. French.
1895	Miller, Sir Alexander Edward	F. G. Wigley. / W. Alves.
1896	Watson, Richard	G. H. C. Andersson. / A. E. Harris.
1897	Patterson, Alexander Bleakley	H. Bower. / H. J. Marcoolyn.

Year.	Master.	Wardens. { Senior. / Junior,
1898	Alves, William ...	G. E. Money. W. F. Stowell.
1899	Sandbach, Arthur Edward ..	G. H. C. Andersson. G. Curtis.
1900	Andersson, George Henry Crawford (Died 4th November 1900.) ...	C. P. Lukis. H. R. Arthur.
1901	Lukis, Charles Pardy ...	T. G. Sparkes. E. E. Clarke.
1902	D'Silva, John Bower ...	Earl of Suffolk. E. O. W. Wilsey.
1903	Wilsey, Edward Owen Willasey	A. W. Warden. F. R. Rennick.
1904	Leigh, Frank ...	A. J. Ruegg. A. R. D'Silva.
1905	Heard, Richard ...	A. J. Longridge. J. McGregor Cheers.
1906	Longridge, James Atkinson ...	J. Faletti. R. E. Holland.
1907	Faletti, John ...	R. E. Holland. G. T. Fillingham.
1908	Lloyd, Thomas William ...	E. W. Andrews. W. H. Jenn.
1909	D'Silva, Albert Robert ...	E. W. S. K. Maconchy. A. F. Humphreys.
1910	Lukis, Charles Pardy ...	E. R. Abbott. O. C. Sullivan.
1911	Maconchy Ernest William Stuart King ...	R. Tharle-Hughes, R. T. Waugh.
1912	McMahon, Arthur Henry ...	A. F. Humphreys. S. E. Bird.

Year.	Master.	Wardens. { Senior. Junior.
1913	Humphreys, Alfred Frederick ...	C. J. Prior. C. J. Knowles.
1914	Holland, Robert Erskine ...	E. B. Higgs. F. von Goldstein.
1915	Prior, Charles James ...	H. R. Phelps. W. G. Dollman.
1916	Higgs, Ernest Bertram ...	C. J. Knowles. P. C. Mukherjee.
1917	Knowles, Charles James ...	H. F. Cleveland. F. L. Milne.
1918	Cleveland, Henry Francis ...	G. Reeves-Brown. H. Hussey.
1919	Reeves-Brown, Gerald ...	P. H. Marshall. B J. Robertson.
1920	Marshall, Percy Harold ...	W. G. Dollman. H. Brown.
1921	Dollman, William George ..	B. J. Robertson. B. C. W. Otto.
1922	Robertson, Bertram James ..	F. von Goldstein. G. R. Parker.
1923	von Goldstein, Felix ..	R. Line. J. W. B. Gardner.
1924	Brown, Harry ..	G R. Parker. F. R. Evans.
1925	Tinson, John ..	A. E. Higgins. C. E. Wills.
1926	Parker, George Robinson ..	J. W. B. Gardner. H. E. Bloodworth.

GENERAL RECORDS.

1838. LODGE "HIMALAYAN BROTHERHOOD" came into existence on the evening of the 19th May 1838, and the record of our first meeting is simplicity itself, being in the following terms :—

"Pursuant to the Dispensation granted by Lodge "Light of the North" at Kurnaul, the Lodge was opened in the first degree by Brother R. B. McDonald by virtue of his previous election as Master of the Lodge.

Present.—Bro. Jacob. L. Hoff.

,, W. S. Blackburn.

,, D. O. B. Clarke.

,, J. W. Caplain.

,, J. Lemon.

,, J. S. Chisholm.

The Wor. Master having laid the Dispensation before the Lodge, appointed the following Brethren to be office bearers.

Brother Blackburn ... Senior Warden.

,, Clarke ... Junior Warden.

,, Chisholm ... Secretary.

and invested them with the insignia of their respective offices. Brother Caplain was then elected to be the Treasurer of the Lodge, and was likewise invested with the insignia of that office."

One can imagine many weighty matters being discussed and settled by this small company of seven Brethren, but there is nothing to shew what was done this evening beyond what is recorded above, except the reading of an application for initiation from Mr. Charles John French, after which the Lodge "was closed in peace and harmony at half past 9 P.M."

The above minutes were confirmed at a Meeting held on 31st May 1838, on which date our first candidate, Mr. French, the father of our present well-known and esteemed Hony. Member was initiated.

No record is found of the preliminary Meeting at which Bro. R. B. McDonald was elected as First Master but Wor. Bro. J. J. L. Hoff as the only Past Master among our Founders — he was P. M. of Lodge "Humility with Fortitude" Calcutta — must have been the Father of the Lodge.

Writing to Wor. Bro. and Ex. Comp. G. Jeffery on Oct. 6th 1851 R. Wor. Bro Hoff who was then Dy P. G. Master for the N. W. F. P. tells us that he gave the Lodge it's name. He says "I was a member in 1838-39 when it was first established and I had the privilege of giving it the name it now bears. I might have been the first Master of that

Lodge, but my then official avocations would not allow of my accepting the Office".

The very first thought that occurs to us on reading the early Minutes of our Lodge is that there is no where any note of its Consecration and on closer examination the fact is revealed that our first minute book cannot be the original!. In this very small company there was soon apparently a split. Bro J. S. Chisholm had been appointed Secretary at the first meeting in May, but it is evident that something upset him at an early date, for we find that he was absent from the meeting in June and the fourth meeting on July 2nd when the Minutes record that " owing to the absence of the Secretary, the confirmation of the Minutes of the last Regular Meeting was deferred till the next Meeting".

Bro. Chisholm evidently removed himself and his books together as we now note that the whole of the Minutes for the five meetings that had been held are written in the handwriting of Bro. French and that at the Meeting on August 2nd "were again read and confirmed" and were signed by the W. M. on this date.

Thus early did Bro Chisholm introduce into the Lodge a spirit which was, to say the least, unprofitable.

At the meeting on the 2nd August Bro. Chisholm was present, but not as Secretary; he was given the office of Tyler and in the record of the meeting the following paragraph appears: —

"Read likewise Bro. J. S. Chisholm's application to be allowed to withdraw himself from being a member of the Lodge, and to resign his office of Secretary. The Worshipful Master on behalf of himself and the rest of the Brethren, expressed regret at the secession of so worthy a member, and assented to Brother Chisholm's request and accepted his resignation."

Brother French was then appointed Secretary, and was at the same time elected Treasurer in the room of Brother Caplain who had left Simla.

The Lodge had opened with enthusiasm, and applications for initiation and joining were plentiful. At the sixth Meeting (Aug. 1838) Bro. Thomas Conlan "late of Lodge No. 26, held at Meerut under a warrant from the Grand Lodge of Ireland" applied for membership — This Lodge was that attached to H. M's 26th Regt. of Foot the Cameronians and was one of the Irish Military Lodges. Irish Masonry, therefore, was introduced into Upper India even at this early date.

The enthusiasm was infectious and on Sept 21st Bro. Alexander Burnes and Bro. John Taylor, who had visited the Lodge at the previous meeting presented respectively "a donation of Rs 100, one half to be applied for Lodge furniture and the remainder to Masonic and charitable purposes", and "a donation of a set of Officers Jewellry".

On 21st September, the minutes record that "the Brethren under the degree of Master in the Chair having been desired to withdraw, the Lodge was opened in that Degree and Bros. H. T. Tapp, C. J. French and G. W. Hoff readmitted and installed in due and ancient form".

This is the first occasion of many, as will be seen later, in our History on which the ceremony of opening and closing the Lodge in the Installed Masters Degree is recorded and the Degree of "Master passed the Chair" conferred. The Degree was prohibited in 1840 although our records show it being worked at a later date and the Brethren thus installed were not recognised as regularly Installed Masters.

On the 29th of the following month the accounts were considered and discussed, after which the entire Lodge placed themselves on the absent list until the revival of the Lodge in the approaching year, and closed "in peace and harmony at 8 o'clock p.m."

1839. Lodge re-opened on the 19th April 1839, when Wor. Bro. R. B. McDonald "was re-elected as Wor. Master and Bro. C.J. French as Treasurer for 1839", but on the 8th June following, McDonald resigned "owing to the onerous duties of his vocation".

At the meeting held on Sat. 8th June, Bro. John Wood, who had that evening taken his M. M. Degree and Bro. D. Seaton "were subsequently required to retire and the Lodge being opened in the Degree of Master of Arts and Sciences were re-admitted and installed in due and ancient form. The Lodge was opened in the 3rd, 2nd, and 1st degrees and the Brethren without were called in."

At this meeting Wor. Bro. H. G. Gouland applied for membership and was at once unanimously elected an Honorary Member, "in testimony of his high merits as a Mason, and for the many and valuable services rendered by him towards the Institution of Masonry in several parts of India, and particularly in his capacity as Master".

That, by being able to receive Bro. Gouland so soon after opening, the Lodge received a Brother of great Masonic experience is shown by the fact that he came to us as a P. S. W. of old "Humility with Fortitude" Calcutta (1835) P. M. of Lodge "Independence and Philanthropy" Allahabad (1836) and P. M. of Lodge "Freedom with Fraternity" Agra (1837) as well as being P. Scribe "E" of old Chapter "Holy Ascension" attached to Lodge "True Friendship" Calcutta (1835) We are able to trace his activities after he left Simla for Agra again where, in 1845, he was Sovereign of "The Knight Companions of the Magnaminous Order of the Red Cross of Babylon" then working attached to Lodge "Faith, Hope and Charity" there. The following is a copy of an old Certificate of Qualification issued by Lodge "Faith, Hope & Charity" No. 737 (old numbering) of Agra. It is of particular interest to us not only because it is signed by Wor. Bro. Gouland as "Sovereign" and issued to Bro. Blackburn who was our original Senior Warden, but also as showing the wonderful activity of the old pre-Mutiny Lodges in India. Lodge "Faith, Hope and Charity" was constituted in 1844, but had but a short life, being finally erased in 1858 (it had ceased working some years before).

H. G. Gouland,

Sovereign.

To The Knights Companions of the Magnanimous Order of the Red Cross of Babylon Greeting.

Whereas our Trusty and well-beloved Companion William Samuel Blackburn was admitted by us as a Member of our Assembly or Encampment attached to Lodge Faith Hope and Charity No. 737; having previously proved himself to be a duly qualified Knight Companion of the Magnanimous Order of the Red Cross of Babylon on the 30th May 1845.

And Whereas the said William Samuel Blackburn has petitioned us for a Certificate of Qualification;

Now, therefore we, the Sovereign of the above named Assembly, in virtue of the authority in us vested, do grant unto the aforesaid William Samuel Blackburn this Certificate, in testimony that he is a duly qualified Knight of the order and as such we commend him to all our Loving Companions round the Globe.

Given At Agra, this 22nd day of October in the year of our Lord 1845 and of Masonry 5845.

By Command of the R. C. Sovereign.

A. D. Johnson.   C. F. A. Kelly,

R. C. Chancellor.   R. C. Scribe.

A week later Wor Bro. H. G. Gouland was elected and installed as Wor Master, after the Lodge had been "opened in the 2nd, 3rd and Past Masters Degree". At this meeting it was "Resolved further, that with a view to give Wor. Bro. McDonald a more substantial proof of the esteem and regard in which he is held by the members of this Lodge some appropriate Masonic token be presented to him—the expense of which to be defrayed by voluntary subscription." This token took the form of a "medal" which was supplied by Messrs C. J. Pittar & Co., Calcutta, at a cost of Rs. 318-0-0! .

The Practice of presenting a Jewel to the out-going Master, a practice which we have been following for very many years past as a means of showing appreciation for good government, was thus established in this early year.

In this year we have recorded the first attendance of the Brethren at Divine service. It was decided at the meeting on 8th June that a deputation composed of the Wor. Master and the Wardens should wait on the Chaplain of Simla, "and solicit his aid in performing Divine service on that day" (St. John the Baptist's day, 24th June). He, however, refused but our ancient Brethren were determined to celebrate this day and another clergyman, the Revd. Mr. Tucker, was asked and agreed to perform the service. Accordingly on Monday, 24th June, all the Brethren except three (the total number of members had now risen to 21), with four visitors, assembled in the Lodge, which was opened in the 3rd degree, and marched thence in procession to the Church, led by the Viceroy's Band, who were given a donation of Rs. 50 for their services. After the service the Brethren marched back to the Lodge in the same way, and after recording a vote of thanks to the Revd Mr. Tucker, the Lodge was closed. It is recorded that Mr. Tucker preached an eloquent sermon, taking as his text the 17th verse, 2nd Chapter of the 1st Epistle General of St. Peter: —"Honour all men; Love the Brotherhood; Fear God; Honour the King." The collection on this occasion amounting to the respectable sum of Rs. 245, was made over to Mr. Tucker for disposal, and he informed the Lodge later on that he had given Rs. 145 to the "new dispensary at Simla" and the balance to the Church Poor Fund at Ludhiana. Evidently the service was held late in the evening, for the Lodge was not closed till 10 p.m.

This is our first celebration of the Patron Saint of Masonry, for the date was on the Feast of the Nativity of St. John the Baptist.

The London Freemasons Quarterly Review describes the occasion as "the first public Masonic procession ever seen on the Himalayan Mountains" and in the evening there was a banquet, "at which Bro. H. W. Torrens (I. C. S.) sang a song composed by himself."

The following letter to the "Englishman", Calcutta, and dated June 1839 is taken from the "Freemasons' Quarterly Review" for that year and makes interesting reading for us today.

Calcutta: – To the Editor of the Englishman. — Sir,—As I observe that any little scrap of Masonic intelligence which is published in your paper, is afterwards republished in the " Freemasons Quarterly Review" in England, probably the following account of our doings in this remote corner, may not prove uninteresting to the Brethren in England, as well to those in the Indian metropolis.

In May, 1838, about five or six individuals of the Masonic Fraternity, who happened then to be congregated at Simlah, applied for and obtained a dispensation from Lodge "Light of the North" at Kurnaul, and commenced operations forthwith, under the direction of Brother R. C. McDonald, as Worshipful Master. The initiation of some, and the admission of a few, continued gradually to increase the number of members, until November, 1838; when the departure of the Governor-General from the Hills taking away a majority of the Brethren, put a stop to further proceedings, until his Lordship's return in March last. In April the Lodge reopened with brighter prospects: a considerable accession of members has since taken place; and the Lodge now musters twenty-one; as great a number, I believe, as usually, on an average, contained in any Calcutta or Mofussil Lodge. The following is a list of the Officers of the Simlah Lodge, "Himalayan Brotherhood" for the current year.

H. G. Gouland, (late Master of the Lodge of Agra), Master; R. C. McDonald, Past Master; Jacob L. Hoff, Past Master of Lodge, No. 279, Fort William; G. Cox, Senior Warden; D. Seaton, Junior Warden; W. S. Blackburn, Past Senior Warden; D. O. B. Clarke, Past Junior Warden; E. Webb, Past Warden of Lodge "Freedom and Fraternity", at Agra; C. J. French, (the first Mason made on the Himalaya Mountains) Treasurer and Secretary; J. H. Staines, Senior Deacon; H. W. Torrens, Junior Deacon; J. Wood, Tyler.

I may as well add that our Chief Magistrate (Colonel Tapp) is a member of the Lodge; though, I regret to say, from "continued indisposition", that Worthy Brother is unable to grace the Lodge with his presence, as he did last year. Our Present and Past Masters are of the new school, they having derived instruction from Brother Curtis, who, on his return from England, brought out the correct mode of work, as is practised in the British Lodges, and freely imparted his knowledge to all who sought for it.

Monday last, being St. John the Baptist's Day, the Brethren assembled at 10 A.M., at the Lodge-rooms; and, preceded by the G. G.'s band of music (which was kindly lent to them by that obliging gentleman, the Hon. Captain Osborne, Military Secretary to the Governor General), walked in procession to the church; where an appropriate sermon was preached by the Rev. Mr. Tucker. We are sorry to observe the Rev. gentleman labouring under indisposition — yet, his discourse was excellent; the leading topic of which was Charity in its widest sense. A collection was made after the sermon, in aid of the funds of the Hospital and the Asylum for the Poor, &c., at Simlah; which, I understand, amounted to upwards of 200 Rs. In the evening, there was a goodly gathering of the "Sons of Light" and their friends, at a dinner prepared for the occasion, where good humour, combined with every delicacy that Barret and Co's stores could produce, contributed to enliven the festive scene. Music alone was wanting to add to the hilarity of the evening; but that was not come-at-able! Several Masonic toasts were drunk with appropriate honours; and a song written for the day by Brother H. W. Torrens., Civil Service, was sung by himself, which elicited great applause. Among the toasts was one which, if this letter should meet the eye of the Editor of the "Freemasons' Quarterly Review", will not fail to be duly appreciated, as a tribute rendered to his merits, from his Brethren, at the distance of half the globe; the toast I allude to, and which was proposed by the P. M. of No. 279, was that of Bro. Doctor Crucefix, that philanthropic man and Mason, who is ever foremost in every charitable work; and to whose indefatigable exertions may be ascribed the success of the "Asylum for the Aged Masons" in England, which was drunk with all the honours due to so excellent a Brother. I believe the establishment of this Asylum is not generally known to the Brethren in India, or they would unite in contributing their mite towards it. With this view, if the suggestion of so humble an individual as he who writes this letter, can be of any avail, I would recommend that the full accounts regarding "The Asylum for Aged Masons" which have, from time to time, appeared in the "Freemasons' Quarterly Review", be prominently brought forward in every Lodge; so that if every Mason in India were to contribute, say only Rs. 10, it would not impoverish any, however limited his circumstances in life may be, while it would enrich the funds of the institution considerably. Will the Brethren of "Humility with Fortitude", in Fort William, take the hint, and lead the way in this labour of love?

A Wandering Mason.

Simlah,
June 29, 1839.

At the meeting of July 5th. the repeated absence from Lodge on the part of certain brethren was taken notice of, and we find that "a gentle admonition be conveyed to Bros Tapp, Clarke and G. H. Cox for their systematic absence from the several meetings of the Lodge, and that they be asked to show greater punctuality and a better inclination towards the calls of the Institution". All three sent in their apologies and excuses. Bro. Tapp's however were not considered quite satisfactory "it having been asserted in open Lodge that the state of his health does not prevent him from going to all parties and places of public resort, though it prevents him from attending the meeting of the Lodge". Tapp, who was Col. Tapp, Chief Magistrate and later on Political Agent at Subathu, was not to be corrected, however, and he resigned at the next meeting.

At the regular meeting held on the 2nd August 1839, the important part of the proceedings was the trial of a Brother for unmasonic conduct. He was a clerk, was proposed, balloted for and initiated at an Emergent Meeting held on 7th September, 1838, and passed to the F.C. Degree on the 17th May, 1839. He was to have been raised to the 3rd Degree on the 12th July following, but the Wor Master having heard that there were reports in circulation very prejudicial to this Brother, caused him to be informed that his advancement would be postponed, and at the meeting on that date the correspondence in the case was produced and the Lodge appointed a committee, composed of the Wor. Master Wor. Bro. Hoff, I.P.M., the Wardens, past Wardens and the Secretary to enquire into the matter. The committee (W. M. as President, and 8 members) met on the 30th July; Wor. Bro. R. B. McDonald was the prosecutor. There were two charges against the accused : —

"1.   For having been in such a state of continued intoxication from the 24th June last to the 9th or 10th July instant, as to have been incapable of attending to his public duties.

2.   For having, while in the above named state of intoxication behaved to his sister, in a harsh, unmanly and unmasonic manner in the following instances, *viz* : — threatening her with personal violence and finally turning her out of doors."

Both charges were fully proved. In his defence the Bro. had admitted the charge of intoxication, "merely denying the extent of its duration" and begged to be forgiven; but on the 2nd charge he would say nothing beyond what he had stated in a letter received from him shortly before the "trial" *viz*: "that the Lodge should refrain from interference in a matter arising out of family difference". The committee recommended that this Bro. be called upon to resign, failing which he should be excluded, but the Lodge unanimously agreed to a proposal by Bro. Torrens that the Brother be severely reprimanded and suspended for six months. What became of him we do not know; he is never mentioned again, and as a matter of fact a few months after this affair the Lodge closed and did not meet again for nearly two years. I have noted this case somewhat in full as it is quite a unique incident in our history, if not, indeed, in the annals of Freemasonry.

16th August. "Opened the Lodge in the 2nd, 3rd and Past Masters Degree, Bros J. Wood, J. Horn, J. Christie, J. Sheetz and C. W. Linstedt were duly installed as Master Masons past the Chair".

Sept. 26th.   Three brethren "Passed the Chair"

Oct. 15th.   Lodge was opened in "the Degree of Master Mason passed the Chair" when three brethren "were installed in due form"

Oct. 18th.   Opened the Lodge in the 3rd and Past Masters Degree when two brethren " received the degree of Master Mason passed the Chair, the Lodge being then closed in the P. Ms. 3rd and 2nd Degrees".

At the meeting of Oct. 15th a medal was voted to Wor. Bro. Gouland as a token of high esteem. The accounts were audited and passed and showed a Cash in hand of Rs. 188-12-8, and outstandings amounting to a further Rs. 230; these small balances did not, however, deter Bro. Torrens from proposing and the Lodge resolving unanimously that Rs. 200 be given to the victim of the unmasonic brother referred to in August. "it having been represented that she was in distressed circumstances".

At the end of this year prior to the departure of the brethern "in the Governor General's camp on the approaching march" a Lodge of Instruction was formed under Wor. Bro. Gouland and some fifteen of the brethren joined, including Bro. C. J. French, who "is about to quit Simla".

*Bro. French received the thanks of the Lodge—so well earned—for his work as Secretary and Treasurer.

The Lodge was then closed "for the season" at 11 p.m. The minutes were probably fair written next day, and a note is added signed by the W. M. "I attest these minutes as a correct record of our proceedings, but they will have to be confirmed in the usual manner on the reopening of the Lodge". The Lodge did not meet again till the 26th August, 1841, and the foregoing minutes were never confirmed.

In the light of subsequent events it will be of interest to note here the names of the members of the Lodge from its foundation to the date it closed in 1839. They were :—

R. B. McDonald ...	...	These were the founders of our Lodge.
Jacob L. Hoff ...	...	
W. S. Blackburn ...	...	
D. O.'B. Clarke ...	...	
J. W. Caplain ...	...	
J. Lemon ...	...	
John S. Chisholm ...	...	
Charles John French.	Archibald Campbell Gordon.	
George Benjamin Hoff.	Thomas Conlan.	
James Christie.	George Hamilton Cox.	
John Wood.	H. T. Tapp.	
Henry Godfrey Gouland.	James Sheetz.	
William Edward Carte.	Edward Webb.	

*We may note here that Bro. French continued a keen and energetic Mason for years in Agra. He joined old Lodge "Freedom and Fraternity" and became Worshipful Master thereof, and it is interesting to record his Demit from this Lodge dated Agra December 27th 1847—shortly before it vanished from Masonry. The Lodge was numbered 647 and like other Lodges at this time had it's own seal in wafer form. This old relic of Pre-Mutiny Masonry is in the writer's possession. Writing in the Madras Freemasons Herald in Feb. 1849 a correspondent says : —"In another month I hope to be able to send you a few items of interest : at present I have nothing worth communicating. Lodge "Freedom and Fraternity" has finally closed. "Star of Hope" and "Faith, Hope and Charity" are in abeyance. In Sept. last, however, a few good and worthy Brethren met, formed a new lodge, obtained a Dispensation and commenced working. They had many difficulties to contend with but these have been overcome and the Lodge has been established on a firm basis, which I trust will not be easily shaken. At the third Meeting a candidate was admitted to the Light and I am happy to say two more applications are before the Lodge. The name of the Lodge is "Good Feeling" and its regular nights for meeting are on the second and fourth Thursday of every month.

The Office Bearers as they stand at present (1848) are as follows :—

Wor. Bro. Chas. J. French, Master.
Wor. Bro. George Forrest, I. P. M.
Bro. A. D. Johnson, S. W., Bro. Francis Marshall J. W.

Thus did the Sons of our old Lodge help to spread the Light of Masonry through India in those early days.

Richard Edward Conlan.

James Gordon Caulfield.

George Powney Thompson.

George Bruce Michell.

John C. Hoff.

Augustps Burke Morris.

William Wilson.

Johan Horn.

George Carr.

John Taylor (Honorary Member)

George Cox.

James Henry Staines.

Douglas Seaton.

Charles William Lindstedt.

William Henry Woodcock.

Henry Whitelock Torrens.

George Mython Hill.

Robert Lee Burnett.

Total 36 (Excluding the Honorary Member).

Of the above, there is a definite record of two having resigned (Chisholm and Tapp), and one was suspended. So that the Lodge on the close of this, the first stage of its existence, consisted of 33 members.

At this last meeting the Lodge decided "that the Surplus available Funds of the Lodge, after having reserved Rs. 50 to be expended by Wor. Bro. McDonald for Lodge, furniture and Rs. 20 on account of two Lodge guests at the ensuing Masonic Dinner, be remitted to England on behalf of the Asylum for Aged Masons".

This Masonic Charity was the one which had just recently been organised by that fine old Mason Dr. Crucefix and, although in the early days maintained in the face of the greatest opposition from the then Grand Master, has since developed into our present splendid Masonic Charity the Royal Masonic Benevolent Institute for Aged Freemasons and widows.

1840. The year 1840 saw the Lodge in abeyance owing, no doubt, to the absence of most of the senior members being on tour with the Governor General, and it is interesting to note here the names of the brethren who, in the march down from Simla, formed our first Lodge of Instruction under the Preceptorship of Wor. Bro. Gouland.

Wor. Bro. H.G. Gouland.

   ,,   Jacob D. Hoff

Bro. W. S. Blackburn.

,, E. Webb.

,, H. W. Torrens.

,, C. J. French.

,, J. H. Staines.

,, J. Horn.

Bro. J. Wood.

,, J. C. Hoff.

,, J. Sheetz.

,, C. W. Lindstedt.

,, G. M. Hill.

,, G. Carr.

,, W. Wilson.

and we can imagine the simple but helpful meetings that must have been held during and after this march down on tour.

1841. When dealing with the History of any Lodge in India for the years now under consideration, it is very necessary to try and realize the conditions which faced our brethren. The civil population of Simla in the 40s was a very small one, and permanent residents must have been few and we find that by far the great majority of our early candidates and members were military officers who, in those days, came up to Simla, on leave. The following letter taken from the London "Freemasons Quarterly Review" of 1838 gives us some little idea of the almost insurmountable difficulties which were met with in most Lodges in India.

The writer referring to our old Lodge says:—

" A Candidate was initiated on the 31st of May last (*this was Bro. French*) and the application of another is now under consideration. There are no doubt, a great many of the Brotherhood at present located on the hills ; but either from ignorance of the existence of the Lodge amongst them, and from their time being observed in business or amusements, they do not show a disposition to lend their aid in bringing this infant Lodge (the first that has been established on these remote hills) to maturity. Of the Worshipful Master's skill, there can be no doubt, from the proof he has already given at the several meetings which have been held.

Freemasonry in India, since the departure of the Marquis of Hastings has gone out of fashion. In those glorious days, persons of all classes were eager to join the Masonic standard ; but since that period it has devolved on the middling classes ; and is only kept up by those who are still devoted to it from a conviction of the excellent principles it inculcates, and the salutary effect it has on all who make it their study to act up to them. Out of eight Lodges that were formerly in existence at Calcutta, we believe there are only two in active operation at present. The Brethren of one of these two Lodges (Humilitude with Fortitude) should this article meet their eye, will not fail to recognise among the names given above some of their old members ; who though separated several hundred miles from their Mother Lodge, carry their Masonic spirit where ever they go "

At the beginning of each year, the Lodge was faced with the fact that the majority of the previous year's members had not returned to Simla, and with no Hall of their own and little or no furniture it was often, in the early years, difficult indeed to form a Lodge, and we can never adequately thank the old stalwarts for their love for Masonry and the Lodge which enabled them to carry on against difficulties, which resulted, so very often, in the decay and death of so many Lodges in India.

The Lodge reopened practically as a new Lodge on the 26th August 1841, nearly two years after the last meeting in 1839 the proceedings of which, as already stated, were not confirmed. The minutes of the 26th August 1841 are headed "Proceedings of a special and emergent meeting of Lodge Himalayan Brotherhood, and such of the fraternity as felt disposed to assist in opening the Lodge, convened by Wor. Bro. R. B. McDonald * * *". At this meeting only three Members out of the 33 borne on the rolls at the end of 1839 were present, *viz.* Wor. Bro. McDonald and Bros. Clarke and Christie, but at the meeting on the 16th September one more, Douglas Seaton, who is recorded as then attending as a visitor, claimed being a member of the Lodge, and, " it being the opinion of the majority of the Brethren that he ought still to be considered as much, Bro. Seaton was accordingly received and acknowledged as such ". There is nothing to show what occurred between the 18th October 1839 and 26th August 1841 ; to my mind there must have been a disagreement of some sort. That there were more Brethren in Simla on the latter date besides the four named above is quite certain, for at the last meeting of the season, on the 18th November 1841, it was resolved unanimously "that all who were at any time admitted members of this Lodge, and who have not formally and regularly withdrawn from it, be still considered members ; that immediate intimation be conveyed to them that the Lodge is working, together with an extract of the by-laws on the subject of contributions by absent members, to such as may not be present in Simla   *   *   *   that all such as may be present in Simla be considered subscribing members and called upon for their contributions "

Whether this resolution was ever acted on it is impossible to say, but if it was the Brethren in Simla must have been considerably surprised. It is strange that the Lodge should have waited till their last meeting to come to the decision they did. They started as quite a new Lodge, save in name and number, there is not a word about the old members, although the Lodge was in possession of all the former proceedings ending with those of the 18th October 1839, and their action in the case of Seaton, who must have been well known to Wor, Bro. McDonald, is so peculiar that one is forced to the conclusion that the resolution of 18th November 1841 was quite an afterthought, prompted probably by Seaton.

At the meeting of August 26th 1841 Wor. Bro. J. F. Geils was elected Master and one of the first of his activities was the consideration of the By-Laws. The By-Laws of Lodge "Hope" Meerut dated 1832 were adopted with certain amendments. Unfortunately no trace of these By-laws is to be found anywhere today, as it would have been of great interest to us to know the Rules which then governed our Lodge.

One of the alterations adopted, however, reads " Proposed also that the punishment of fines be applied only to cases of non-attendance when excuses are not offerred, and never to exceed Rs. 1 to be paid into St. John's Box", while another was "That Absent Members be requested to pay a monthly contribution of Rs. 1 to be paid into St. John's Box ".

It is evident, therefore, that the Charity Box of our Lodge has been with us ever since our constitution in 1838.

Certain furniture was at this meeting ordered to be obtained including "Pedistals for the W M., S. W. and J. W. a cushion for the East Pedistal and an Altar for the Holy Scriptures".

Did we follow the old Irish and Ancient Grand Lodge custom of having an altar in the centre of the Lodge?.

The Lodge closed on the 18th November 1841 and did not meet again for some 18 months.

To preserve the connection between the events up to this time and those which follow, it is necessary to record here the names of the members of the Lodge when it closed in 1841.

These were:—

Wor. Bro. R. B. McDonald .. ⎱ Founders.	
Bro. D. O'B. Clarke ⎰	
James Christie	Re-joined 26th August 1841.
Douglas Seaton ...	Re-joined 16th Septr. 1841
Wor. Bro. W. H. Hewitt ... ⎫	
,, F. W. Porter ... ⎪	
,, T. J. Geils ...	
Bro. G. Harriott ... ⎬ Joined on reopening of Lodge	
,, W. Charde ... ⎪ on 26th Augt. 1841.	
,, A. Beecher ... ⎪	
,, J. Anderson ... ⎭	
,, Peter McDonald ...	Initiated 2nd September 1841.
,, J. R. Lumley ...	Joined 16th September 1841.
,, Edward Campbell ...	Ditto Ditto
,, R. R. Brooke ...	Honorary Member, 16th September 1841.

Total 15 only, including the Honorary Member.

1843. There is no explanation as to why the Lodge did not meet in 1842, and it was well into the season of 1843 when, on the 19th June Wor. Bro. Geils (who had been installed as Master on 2nd September 1841) with his Secretary and Treasurer (Charde), Bro. Christie and some visitors opened the Lodge once more and entered upon what promised to be a prosperous career, but which unfortunately came to a sudden and somewhat dramatic termination on the evening of the 18th August 1847.

Among the *visitors* recorded as present on this opening night were, it is interesting to note, Wor. Bro. H. B. Gouland, Bros. W. E. Carte, J. H. Staines and J. W. Caplain, all members of the Lodge on its close in October, 1839. The very first business after confirming the minutes of the 18th November 1841 was a motion by the Worshipful Master that such of the visitors as were desirous of joining the Lodge should give their names and late Lodges to the Secretary, whereupon Gouland, Carte and Staines claimed their right to be considered members of the Lodge and were at once accepted. Bro. Caplain, on the contrary, ignored his connection with Lodge Himalayan Brotherhood, although he was one of the founders and had been Treasurer in 1838 and he was actually ballot-ed for, at a later meeting, as joining from Lodge "Light of the North," Kurnaul.

Caplain's action is inexplicable and certainly seems disingenuous. As he left Simla some time in July 1838, he was probably unknown to any of the Brethren of the Lodge present on this occasion.

At the next meeting on June 28th amongst other brethren Wor. Bro. Capt J. G. H. Curtis was admitted a member and at the same meeting elected Worshipful Master, a fortnight later, after opening the Lodge in the 2nd, 3rd and Past Masters Degrees, being duly installed.

Bro. Curtis who joined the Lodge at this critical period was a Mason of out-standing eminence and was, indeed, one of the most prominent Masons in the East. Initiated in Lodge "Fortitude and Old Cumberland" No. 26, the Lodge which in 1717 met at the Apple Tree Tavern, and was No. 3 of The Four Original Old Lodges which formed Grand Lodge in 1717, Bro. Curtis, then Lt. in the 37th Bengal N. I. came to Calcutta at the close of 1831 with a letter of recommendation from the Grand Lodge to the Lodges in Calcutta, recommending him "as a brother thoroughly versed in the three degrees of Craft Masonry, and consequenly capable of communicating the mode of working as practised in the London Lodges".

Bro. Curtis attached himself to Lodge "True Friendship" and was elected an Honorary Member of Lodge "Humility with Fortitude" on Dec. 1st 1831. On April 19th 1832 this Lodge presented him as their instructor with a gold medal "as a token of Gratitude for his unwearied exertions to benefit this Lodge by instructions imparted to the Master and officers in the new and proper mode of work as practiced in England"

We find him imparting his great Masonic knowledge in Agra in 1837 when the *Agra Akhbar* of that year had the following :—

"At the last regular meeting of the Masonic brotherhood at the station.........
the working in the F. C and M. M. was rendered somewhat interesting from the circumstance of Bro. Curtis and MacDonald having been invited to preside in the Western and Southern Chairs on the occasion, in order to enable the Brethren to compare the present with the former mode of the working up the Degrees ; Major MacDonald having brought out the former and visited the several Lodges lying on his route from Calcutta, in order to introduce the requisite alterations in the same manner as the latter was done by Bro. Curtis under the order of Grand Lodge a few years ago".

Wor. Bro. Curtis was indeed a mountain of strength to the Lodge for many years. As will be seen later he was President of the Committee of Inquiry on the conditions of the Lodge in the great crisis in 1849 and it may be that it was his presence and his influence at that time which enabled the Lodge to retain their Warrant, the sentence of suspension removed, and the Lodge reopened to be carried on until today.

He was one of the Founders and First Principal "Z" of our Chapter Dalhousie in 1850, and it is of great interest to remember his credentials from Grand Lodge as an expert exponent of Masonic procedure when reading, to us, the remarkable decision given in 1845.

1843. At the Meeting of July 28th Stewards are appointed for the first time, and this year the By-Laws are finally approved of and ordered to be printed.

"It being the general wish of the Brethren that they should walk in procession to lay the foundation of the new Lodge Rooms it was resolved to apply for the necessary Dispensation," and on Tuesday Sept. 21st a Special Meeting was held, the Lodge opened in the 1st, 2nd and 3rd Degree and "the Brethren having been marshalled in proper form" by Bro. Charde, Master of Ceremonies, they proceeded in procession to the site of the new Lodge where the foundation stone of our first Hall "was laid in due form and a suitable oration delivered by the Worshipful Master".

1844. On the 21st June 1844, George Cox, also a member in 1839, was present in Lodge and was duly acknowledged as a member, and almost exactly a year later, J. S. Chisholm, who resigned in August 1838, apparently on account of some unpleasantness while Secretary, was balloted for and re-admitted.

Wor. Bio. Curtis handed over the Mastership to Bro. George Cox And the Minutes record an Installation which would not be valid today after opening the Lodge in the *1st* Degree "The Worshipful Past. Master (who was Wor. Bro. Curtis) and Wor. Bro. J. Valiant and Adam Bell, *R A.* retired with the Master Elect and Bro. G. Cox was installed as Master in due form. "We see here for the first time in our records the recognition of the standing of a Royal Arch Mason as one who, having passed the Chair, was eligible to form one of the necessary number to form a Board of Installed Masters. This will be recalled when considering our records for 1845.

1845. At the meeting dated June 20th the Lodge "was opened in the Past Masters Degree and Wor. Bro. J. B. Dodd duly installed" as Master.

It was a year of great Masonic activity, no fewer than 15 meetings being held between June and October. At one of the meetings the W. M. was constrained to remark "on the impropriety of any of its members appearing in Lodge otherwise than in respectable and gentlemanly apparel, and trusted that henceforth no Brother would overlook this essential characteristic of all Masonic Lodges and, as he hoped, of Lodge H. B. in particular". The By-Law referring to St. John's Box was this year amended.

The Lodge Charity had up to now been supported by voluntary contribution from the active members and Rs 1 from Absent Members.

It was proposed and adopted "That St. John's Box directed solely to charitable purposes is supported by voluntary contributions from the Brethren at large, and a monthly subscription of One Rupee from all Absent Members, in addition to this sum, one Rupee from monthly subscription of each subscribing member".

Bro. Christie, who had been Secretary for the year, was voted an Honorary Secretary Jewel to be obtained from Mr. Acklam, Masonic Jweller, London. Rs. 50 was voted from Lodge funds the balance of the cost to be defrayed from contributions from the brethren which amounted to Rs. 100, and at the last meeting of this year it was proposed that a remittance be made to Bro. Acklam London for the purchase of a set of Craft Tracing Boards. This was our first set of Tracing Boards but they were not with us long as a second set had to be ordered, as will be seen, consequent on the loss of much of our property in 1848.

The activities of the Lodge under the Mastership of Wor. Bro. Dodd was laid before the Lodge when we see that no fewer than 31 Initiations 22, Passings and 9 Raisings have taken place and he leaves the Lodge with 47 members. Here let us record the character of the Lodge at this time. From the Copy of the Returns sent to G. Lodge we see that the Lodge comprised 51 members, of whom no less than 45 were Military Officers in either the E. India Cos. or the Home Service, the remaining 6 being mercantile or uncovenanted service men. It was in these days, therefore distinctly a Military Lodge.

1846. Yet notwithstanding the flourishing condition of the Lodge at the end of 1845, the season of 1846 was opened on Friday 17th April with not a single regular officer present, and with Bro. J. S. Chisholm S. W. as "Acting Master." Two meetings after, however, Wor. Bro. John S. Marshall, P. M. of "Sussex" Lodge Neemuch (a Lodge which like many others perished in the Mutiny) was proposed as a Joining Member, and was elected W. M., although he does not appear to have ever been actually installed.

At a meeting this year it was resolved "that the Brethren feeling it their bounden duty to promote as far as in their power the worship of God, give their cordial assent to the use of the new Lodge buildings to the Chaplain of Simla for Divine Service until the completion of the new Church". And Bro. Charde adverting to the now finished state of the Lodge rooms, placed on record the fact that it was due entirely to Bro. Chisholm's zeal and liberality in advancing the necessary funds required from his own private purse.

Wor. Bro. Marshall reigned as Master for only three months and, leaving Simla at short notice, left the Lodge on Bro. Chisholm's hands again. He, although not an Installed Worshipful Master, carried on, working all the degrees and signing the Minutes as Officiating W.M. until at an Emergent Meeting on August 26th he was elected to the Chair. "In consequence of some of the Brethren not being aware of the previous election having taken place", however, a re-election was taken at the next regular Meeting at which he was again chosen Master. There not being the requisite number of Installed Masters available in the Lodge to install him, it is evident that a letter was addressed to Wor. Bro. Curtis for advice, and the reply received from this eminent Brother is on record in the next Minutes.

" Read V. Wor. Bro. J. W. G. Curtis' letter, ordered to be read at the next Regular meeting and copied in the Minute Book.

Wor. Brother John Faletti, M.V.O.
Past Master 1907-08.
P.G.S.B (Eng.) P.D.G.W. (Punjab).

Kussaulie,
2 Sept, 1846.

Dear Sir and Brother,

 I am in receipt of your letter of the 31st ult. No person can be regularly initiated into the mysteries of Masonry except by a Mason *who has passed the Chair.* If the W. M. Elect be a Royal Arch Mason he has passed the Chair and can therefore lawfully perform on Emergency the functions of W. M. even if not duly installed. 3 Past Masters (or 3 Royal Arch Masons) in a case of Emergency (like the present) would suffice to install the W. M. Elect.

 " When we *three* or *three*, like me, meet and agree" will convey my meaning to any Royal Arch Mason. The W. M. of the past year can continue to initiate, raise etc. until an opportunity occurs of installing the W. M. Elect. I should think however, 3 Royal Arch Masons might be found in Simla.

Yours fraternally,
J. G. W. Curtis.

 This remarkable Ruling from one who had come to India with such strong recommendations from Grand Lodge as Bro. Curtis had, shows us the practice in vogue "in the London Lodges" in the early 1800s and the high position held by the members of the R. A. Degree.

 Our next Minutes show that *two* Worshipful Brethren were found and " after all Master Masons had withdrawn the Lodge was opened in the Past Masters Degree and W. Bro. Chisholm (Royal Arch Mason) duly installed Master in due form".

 Bro. Chisholm himself therefore, in his capacity as an R. A. Mason formed one of the B. of I Ms. in the same way as Adam Bell, "R.A." had in 1844. It is interesting to compare this Ruling of so highly expert a brother as Wor. Bro. Curtis with Gould.

 In his "Concise History" Bro. Gould tells us "The Royal Arch was the first of the "additional degrees extraneous to the system of Pure and Ancient Freemasonry, and the seed was sown from which it ultimately germinated by the alteration of the Master's Creed in 1723, there cannot be a doubt. The Degree was certainly worked from about the year 1740, and presumably from an earlier date. The members of the Royal Arch are described by Dr. Dassigny, in 1744, as "a body of men who have passed the chair". At that date, however, the *degree* of Installed (or Past) Master was unknown, nor is there any evidence of its being in existence, until some years after formation of the Schismatic Grand Lodge of England in 1751. It would appear there that the communication of the secrets of the Royal Arch was the earliest form in which any esoteric teaching was specially linked with the incident of Lodge Mastership or in other words, that the *degree* of the Royal Arch was the complement of the Master's *Grade.* Out of this was ultimately evolved the degree of Installed Master, a ceremony not sanctioned by the Regular (or constituitional) Grand Lodge of England until 1810, and of which we can trace no sign among the "Schismatics" until the growing practice of conferring the "Arch" upon a Mason, not properly qualified to receive it, brought about a *constructive* passing through the chair, which, by qualifying candidates not otherwise eligible, naturally, curtailed the introduction of a ceremony. *additional* (like the Arch) itself to the simple form known to Payne, Anderson, and Desaguliers".

It was in these days necessary to have passed the chair of Installed Master before being eligible for the Royal Arch, and a Royal Arch Mason was therefore in virtue of his rank eligible to form one of the quorum of an Installing Board.

In 1847 something seems to have gone wrong from the beginning. There were only five meetings this year, and the Master at the time was Wor. Brother Chisholm who had been elected and installed the previous year. The meetings were very poorly attended, indeed it is recorded in the proceedings of the last meeting on the 18th August that in consequence of an insufficient number of the Brethren attending on the evenings of the 16th June, 7th and 21st July and 4th August, the meetings for those evenings were postponed. The Wor. Master at the first meeting of the year recommended the Brethren to elect a Master as his own time had expired, but there is nothing to show that this was done, yet at the meeting of 2nd June, Bro. Banks took the chair (Chisholm was not present though he subsequently signed the minutes) and passed a Brother to the 2nd Degree, and at one part of the proceedings he refers to himself as the future Master. At the next meeting Chisholm was present but as Tyler (it is curious to recall that this is exactly the position he held on the 2nd August 1838 when his resignation was considered), and Bro. Banks was again in the chair and initiated a candidate. Indeed on these two occasions Banks acted in every way as Master, although there is no record of his ever having been installed. At the next and last meeting, the 18th August, Chisholm was in the chair and the only other Brethren present were Riddell, Staines, Tapp, Davison, Fortescue and Roberts, the two last named were Entered Apprentices. There was evidently a good deal before the Lodge but almost everything brought up was "ordered to lie over" except Bank's resignation which was accepted. Finally the ballot was taken for a candidate, and it is recorded that during the ballot (not *after*, it will be observed, but *during*) Bro. Tapp was ordered to relieve Bro. Davision who was acting as Tyler, the record then goes on "Bro. Tapp immediately returned and reported the absence of Bro. Davision; in consequence of this dereliction of duty on Bro. Davision's part, the W. M. was compelled to close the Lodge in peace and harmony at a quarter past 9 o'clock, P.M." Thus abruptly ended the second stage of the Lodge's existence, and it is quite certain that there were grave irregularities this year apart from the incident mentioned above. The Proceedings of this meeting are in the handwriting of Tapp, who was acting as Secretary, but they are not signed by anybody, and when Lodge met again two years later, the acting W. M. refused to confirm the minutes "the Lodge having been under interdict by the Dy. Provincial G. M. owing to certain irregularities in its proceedings." The Lodge, at this time No. 673, E. C., was under the jurisdiction of the Provincial (now called District) Grand Lodge of Bengal.

We do not know today who or what Bro. Chisholm was. In the Returns for 1846 which are the earliest we now possess, we find him designated as a "Citizen of Calcutta". A young man of but 26 years of age when he assumed the Eastern Chair under the circumstances already related, a Mason not of the Military Class, it is evident that he was not a popular Master for we see that it was with the greatest difficulty that he carried on. None of the older members, if they were in Simla, gave him their support. Indeed we see from the Returns for 1847 that the Lodge membership had dropped from 51 down to the low level of 13 (7 Army Officers and 6 Civilians).

The Lodge rooms appear to have been very badly built and hardly a year after Bro. Charde had reported on "the now finished state" of the building and had eulogised Bro. Chisholm for his practical assistance to this end, the minutes record that the W.M. brought to the notice of the brethren "the delapidated state of the new Lodge rooms" and requested them to propose some measure to have the same property repaired. Our early Lodge was, like many other buildings in Simla at that time, built with a flat mud roof, and it is probable that a more than severe winter had been too much for it. Nothing, however, was done and at a later meeting Bro. Chisholm "adverted to the state of the Lodge rooms and requested Bros. Banks, Riddell, Barry and others to inspect and report upon the state of the building."

It is possible that the social side of the Lodge life was being developed to the detriment of the Lodge. The Minute books give a list of Lodge Property at the close of 1846 from which it seems that we owned a very large and complete set of Crockery and kitchen ware, from 6 dozen large plates downwards, while the "Wine Cellar" contained amongst other things 40 bottles of Champagne, 31 Claret, 8 of Port, and 4 bottles of Sherry and, incidentally, $15\frac{1}{2}$ seers of candles. Perhaps the state of the building, the absence of control when called off from labour to refreshment, and the general lack of administrative ability on the part of an unpopular Master combined to make this year a disasterous one from the start. The Secretary was hopelessly incapable and unreliable, and at the close of the year Wor. Bro. Chisholm returned thanks to Bro. Tapp, who had taken over the duties of this office "for his exertions in endeavouring to bring the accounts in some measure into an intelligible form".

What exactly happened during the years 1847 and 48 we shall never know but the last recorded minutes show one significant entry— "Bro. Offg. Secretary also reported the receipt of several communications from the United Grand Lodge of England, Pro. Grand Lodge of Calcutta and Brethren *now and formerly* members of the Lodge". All of which must have been of the greatest urgency and importance but which, like most matters at this time were "ordered to lie over"!

Much can be gleaned from an old Letter Book of the Lodge for the year 1850 which must have escaped the vigilant eye of Bro. Wilsey when writing up his book, as to the condition of things in the year 1848 during which year no meetings were held. It is evident that early in the year 1847 some of the brethren appointed a Committee to enquire into Lodge affairs and that the findings of this Committee resulted in a Memorial being sent to the Provincial Grand Lodge. In June 1849 the Deputy Pro. Grand Master Rt. Wor. Bro. A. H. E. Boileau who was resident in Allahabad, appointed a Committee composed of four stalwarts Bros. Curtis, Ramsay, Riddell, and Charde to demand from Wor. Bro. Chisholm the Warrant and all Records of the Lodge and to make thorough investigation into its affairs. The result of their labours is set forth in their Report to the D.P.G. Master, a full copy of which is given in the Letter Book and which is given here in extenso.

To

    Rt. Wor. Bro. A. H. E. BOILEAU,

        Dy. Pro. Grand Master,

            Allahabad.

Rt. Wor. Sir and Brother,

We the undersigned members of the Committee appointed by your letter No. 37 of the 15th June 1849 to investigate and report upon the affairs of Lodge Himalayan Brotherhood, No. 673, beg now to report for your information the result of our labours.

On proceeding to inspect the Lodge Rooms we found the building in a frightfully delapidated state, many of the walls and a portion of the roof had fallen in, other portions of the walls being so greatly bulged, as to render the building unsafe, and all this destruction of property resulting from gross neglect and mismanagement of the late master Brother J. S. Chisholm, who although a resident of Simla and apparently in possession of Lodge funds, failed to adopt the common and ordinary precautions by which the delapidation of the Lodge might so easily have been prevented. We duly furnished to Brothers Chisholm and Tapp copies of your letter No. 37 above quoted and requested those Brethren to deliver over to us the Warrant and Property of the Lodge, and to aid us in adjusting its affairs and accounts. After some delay Bro. Chisholm delivered over to Bro. Charde the Secretary of our Committee to whose zeal and exertions we his fellow members desire to bear testimony, the Warrant and three sealed boxes containing some books and papers belonging to the Lodge.

Among the contents of these boxes we sought in vain for a register of returns furnished to the Grand Lodge of England and Pro. Grand Lodge of Bengal, and were equally unsuccessful in finding any account of the Treasurer's receipts and disbursements of any of those records usually kept in Masonic Lodges. Indeed, it appears that since the Lodge closed its proceedings for the season of 1845, no returns have been sent to either Grand Lodge, and since Bro. Charde resigned the office of Treasurer in June 1846, no regular accounts have been kept! The absence of every document save the Minute Book which could throw light on the confused and mistified state of the Lodge affairs and accounts greatly increased our labours and unavoidably delayed the transmission of our report. We gather from the disjointed memoranda before us and the evidence of Brothers Tapp and Riddell both then members of the Lodge, that towards the close of the season of 1846 the disorder into which the affairs and accounts had fallen called for some active remedy; the Brethren were induced to appoint a Committee in 1847, to investigate and report upon the state of the Lodge funds, and by the Committee so appointed (of which Bro. Riddell was a member) the following painful facts were elicited.

Firstly.—That Bro. Emerson (now of Mer M's. 63rd Foot) who during a part of 1846 held the office of Secretary and Treasurer had proceeded to England, taking with him or having in his possession, when leaving the Lodge a sum of Cos. Rs. 312-12-0 being a portion of the Lodge funds, besides his own dues, no parts of which has to this hour been recovered. Secondly—That Bro. Chisholm though not elected Treasurer had unauthorisedly collected on account of the Lodge a sum of Cos. Rs. 1600 rendering no account of the same and failing even to report the receipt of this large amount. Thirdly—

That Bro. Chisholm was indebted to the Lodge on account of this sum of Cos. Rs. 1600 and other items to an amount aggregating Cos. Rs. 2221-2-7. Fourthly—That on the discovery of this serious defalcation, Bro. Chisholm was called upon by the Committee to refund the money, he paid a portion of the same and gave for the balance (Rs. 1500) a promissary note payable at one month's date, which was negotiated by the Committee with the Simla Bank, but is yet, we grieve to say unredeemed, a balance of Rs. 202-11-9 being still due thereon.

5. The laxity to use the mildest term of Bro. Chisholm has entailed yet further losses on Lodge dues, and fees for 1846 have in many instances remained uncollected and from the departure of some of the Brethren for England and many other causes we fear that but a small portion of these debts will be recovered by the Lodge, and apprehend that Bro. Chisholm, the party answerable for the amount, is not in a position to pay it.

6. Again tho'this Lodge was working during a portion of 1847, there is no record save the Minute Book made over to us by Bro. Chisholm to enable us to discover what is due for that year. So far as we can learn the outstanding dues and liabilities of the Lodge may be estimated as per margin, but the data on which they are prepared are so imperfect and unsatisfactory that discrepancies may and probably will be hereafter discovered.

7. We annex a list of Lodge Properties made over to Bros. Chisholm and Tapp, and regret to observe that the statement of Lodge properties, exhibited in the Minute Book and records, shews several articles which are not forthcoming, and for which Bro. Chisholm is responsible.

8. We cannot refrain from recording our dissatisfaction both with Bro. Chisholm's past conduct and present bearing. Though frequently invited by Brothers Curtis and Charde to come forward, assist us with such information as he could afford, and expurgate himself from the heavy charges which existing appearances give rise to, he has shown no disposition to aid us in our painful investigation or remove from our minds impressions no true man or Mason should hesitate to remove if possible. It may be that the Committee have formed as wrong opinion, but the conclusion they have come to is the only one which in the absence of any explanation from Bro. Chisholm, they could arrive at. A copy of this report shall be furnished to Bro. Chisholm, and extract to Bro. Tapp, and every opportunity of replying to it afforded them.

9. We now come to Bro. Tapp who appears to have been acting Secretary and Treasurer and offg. Steward in 1847, and whom we cannot acquit of great carelessness and laxity in conducting his various duties, but against whom we have nothing besides to urge. We are also bound to record our acknowledgement of the manly and Masonic way in which he has avowed his errors of omission, the readiness and active zeal he has shown in rendering us every information and assistance in his power, the pains he has taken to collect memoranda and explain every point he could elucidate, and the effort he has made to rectify the confusion caused by his careless mode of conducting his various duties.

10. In conclusion we beg to state that we have thoroughly repaired the Lodge rooms and defrayed the expenses by voluntary contributions of members. We have reopened the Lodge under authority conveyed in your letter No. 42 dated 29th July 1849. We have furnished accounts to all apparent debtors. We have also prepared returns of the Lodge for 1846 and 1847 as well as the insufficient records enable us to prepare them, and they shall be forwarded in due course. We shall remit such dues as have been realized for the past seasons when transmitting those for the current year; and shall furnish a statement of such sums as are due by Brethren in England, which I trust the Grand Lodge of England will aid us in recovering.

We are,

Rt. Wor. Sir and dear Brother,
Your f. fully and Fraternally,

G. W. Curtis.

Jas. Ramsey.

H. B. Riddell.

William Charde.

Simla, 26th September 1849.

The importance of this letter is apparant. It shows us that the Lodge was alive in 1847 when the members petitioned the Dy. D. G. Master for assistance. He appointed his Committee of Inquiry on 15th of June 1849 and after authorising the Committee to take possession of the Warrant from the W. M. during their Inquiry, permitted them to *reopen* the Lodge by his letter dated 29th July of the same year.

Our Warrant was not withdrawn from the Lodge and we were under the interdict of P. Grand Lodge during the three months the Committee of Inquiry sat only.

Bro. D. A. G. Secretary, District Grand Lodge, Calcutta, has very kindly supplied the following notes from Provincial Grand Lodge Proceedings for this year which put the matter beyond all doubt.

The Proceedings dated March 21st, 1849 show that our Lodge was still "working" but at the Meeting held on 25th June 1849 the following item appears.

"The P. Grand Secretary reported that Lodge "Hope" at Meerut had been placed in abeyance on account of paucity of members. Lodge "Himalayan Brotherhood" at Simla and Lodge "Fraternity and Perseverance" at Benares were also ascertained to have been dormant for some time past, and their affairs were under investigation by the Officiating Deputy Provincial Grand Master in the North West Provinces."

Four months later, however, at the Meeting held on 25th October 1849 it is recorded that "The P. G. Secretary reported that Lodge "Himalayan Brotherhood No. 673, at Simla, had revived under the auspices of W. Bro. Lt.-Col. Curtis, C.B., as Wor. Master, R. Wor.-Bro. Major James Ramsay, Provincial Senior Grand Warden, and other Brethren."

1849. The Lodge opened again on the 8th Agust 1849 (bearing the same No. 673, allotted to it in 1843) under a dispensation from the Provincial Deputy Grand Master of Bengal, dated 29th July 1849 addressed to the following Brethren :—

Wor. Bro. James Ramsay.	Bro. George Lloyd Williams.
Wor. Bro. James Gray	Bro. William Edward Carte.
William Curtis.	
Bro. R. B. Wigstrom.	Bro. W. Smyth.
Bro. Edmund Dirney Byng.	Bro. William Charde.

and nominating the undermentioned to be the first officers of the Lodge and "to act as such * * * until a fresh Warrant shall be obtained from the P. G. L. of Bengal."

Wor. Master	...	Wor. Bro. J. G. W. Curtis.
Officiating P. M. ...	...	Wor. Bro. J. Ramsay.
S. W.	...	Bro. R. B. Wigstrom.
J. W.	...	Bro. E. D. Byng.

Of those named above, Curtis, Carte and Charde were members in 1843 and there is no record that they ever resigned. Besides these three, the other old members who joined on the opening night were H. P. Riddell, Bagot, Michell, Erskine and Poole ; Riddell and Poole were the only two who had anything to do with the Lodge in 1847 ; Riddell was Junior Warden and attended every meeting that year, except the one on 2nd July which was the only meeting Poole attended. Considering the large number of members on the roll at the end of the year 1846, it is remarkable how very few rejoined when the Lodge was struggling for life in 1849. In May 1850, C. E. Davison enquired whether he could be still considered a member but he was informed that his resignation in 1847 was on record, "moreover that owing to certain irregularities the Lodge had been placed under ban by the D. P. G. M. in consequence of which the former member had lost their privileges as such." On the 5th of the following month, however, on receipt of a letter of explanation from Davison, his case was referred to the Permanent Committee for opinion and they recommended "that the Brother having apologised for his dereliction (he was acting Tyler at the meeting of 18th August 1847) is eligible to be balloted for as a member." Tapp, another old member, who was Secretary and Treasurer in 1847, was often present in Lodge as a visitor in 1849 and 1850, and seems to have given considerable help in squaring up the accounts, &c., of the old Lodge but apparently he never claimed his rights as Davison did. On 17th October 1850 both Davison and Tapp were admitted as members in virtue of their having been recently "exalted as Companions of the R. A. Chapter attached to this Lodge." The reply given to Davison is hardly reconcilable with the fact that Riddell and Poole who were also connected with the Lodge in 1847 were admitted to the new Lodge without question. Davison it may be mentioned remained a member till the end of 1853 in which year he held the office of Senior Warden. Tapp was a well known figure for many years later, took a great interest in the Lodge and held the offices of Secretary, Warden and ultimately that of Master in 1858, He died, while still a member in January 1865 and was the last of those who belonged to the Lodge previous to its re-establishment on its present foundation in 1849.

Wor. Bro. Curtis, to whom we must ever feel the liveliest sense of gratitude and appreciation for all he did to pull the Lodge together, wrote to the Provincial Grand Lodge, announcing the re-opening of the Lodge, in the following terms which show how hopelessly our young Master had neglected his responsibilities:—

3. On reopening this Lodge, which was, as you were doubtless aware, for some time in abeyance, I found that the Returns for 1846 and 1847 had not been forwarded by my predecessors in the Eastern Chair, the last of whom (Br. Chisholm) has, I grieve to say, not only failed to furnish the Returns or remit the dues even to the Grand Lodge of England, but evinced an utter indifference on the subject of the serious irregularities and heavy defalcations which occurred during his tenure of the Office of Master, and consequently the task of reparing the Returns for 1846, and 1847, has been both tedious and difficult, indeed they have been necessarily compiled from very imperfect data obtained from the Minute Book, irregular entries in loose records, and such information as Bro. Tapp the late officiating Secretary could afford which was willingly and zealously given.

6. The prescribed Returns and fees for the present year as well as for the seasons of 1846, and 1847 have been forwarded to the Grand Lodge of England.

7. In conformity with the addendum to Rule 36 of the Prov. Grand Lodge, I annex a Statement of the Accounts of this Lodge from its resuscitation on the 4th August last to this date, you will observe that so far from this being a balance in hand the sum of Cos. Rs. 270-9-1 has actually been borrowed to make the required remittances to cover the defalcations of my predecessors. It is to be hoped that a portion of this may be recovered from Members whose dues appear not to have been claimed owing to the culpable laxity of those who should have demanded them. A full report of the circumstances will be found in my No. 90 to the Deputy Prov. Grand Master.

8. The Lodge buildings and property have been made over, as per annexed list, to Bro. Charde, the oldest Member of the Lodge at Simla, who besides being Treasurer and Secretary of the Lodge is a permanent resident of the place. The annexed copy of a resolution passed in open Lodge will show the date on which the Lodge can be re-opened.

10. I cannot conclude this letter without recording my grateful sense of the support and assistance I have received from Bro. Charde in adjusting the intricate affairs of this Lodge.

(Sd) J. G. W. Curtis, Master.

At the inaugural meeting of the Lodge in 1849 the Worshipful Master stated " that the Deputy Provincial Grand Master had appointed a committee to report on the affairs of the Lodge ; the committee had obtained possession of the papers and accounts and that some of the property had also been recovered."

Wor. Bro. Curtis brought with him all his usual energy and zeal, and with Bro. Charde as Treasurer and Secretary soon placed the Lodge on a sound basis once again and from now on, with the exception of the critical period of the Mutiny years, the Lodge has continued to flourish.

The following Extract from the Minutes of 1849 shows the very high estimation in which Wor. Bro. Curtis, our W. M. stood : —

" The Offg. Grand Master stated that altho' he did not consider it right to appoint any brother to an office in Grand Lodge who was not resident in Calcutta, yet in consideration of the services rendered many years past in India by Wor. Bro. Lt.-Col. J. G. W. Curtis C.B., (now at Agra), his attainments in Masonic knowledge and practice, he would confer on Bro. Curtis the honorary rank of Provincial Senior Grand Warden in the Province of Bengal".

The gross carelessness in preserving the Lodge property during the past two years is shown by the record telling us that " Bro. Davison sent the Lodge Seal to Bro. Secretary, and discloses the fact that three glass candleabra belonging to the Lodge are in possession of one of the local firms in Simla.

1st October. An emergent meeting was held on this date "to receive with honours Brother Charles Napier" and a banquet followed. This Brother was no doubt Sir Charles Napier, the Commander-in-Chief in India, and the simplicity of this Minute is in striking contrast to our present custom—surely wrong—of introducing military and social rank into our Minutes and Summonses. As Bro. Rudyard Kipling has expressed it in " The Mother Lodge " " We meet upon the Level ".

This Banquet was evidently a sumptuous affair and it is seldom we have been in recent years able to table one like it. It cost Rs. 896 and was shared by 28 members at a pro rata share of Rs. 32 each. As so often happens unfortunately in these days, Bro. Secretary had to waste much paper and ink before he had collected the dues, for the Letter Books of this period are full of reminders calling for these, and the last dinner subscription was not collected until 1851.

3rd October. It was resolved unanimously " that Brother E. C. Vibarts' continued absence from Lodge since his initiation is deserving of censure, and that the disapprobation of the Lodge be manifested by not permitting him to proceed higher in masonry this season."

Vibart was apparently struck off at the close of the year, and although he was present in Lodge on two or three occasions in 1851, he is never again acknowledged as a member.

1850. This was a year of great Masonic activity. The Lodge opened on the 8th May under the Hiram of Wor. Bro. J. F. Banks who although it was recorded that he had resigned at Chisholm's last meeting, we find still on the Roll of Members for this year. Wor. Bro. Bracken who was elected Master reports his election to the Eastern Chair in the following letter to P. G. Lodge: —

30th June-50. To J. J. L. Hoff, Secy. Prov. Grand Lodge of Bengal. From John Bracken, W. M.

" The Lodge now numbers 31 Members, 6 of whom are on the absent List".

" I am also in possession of your letter No. 152 dated the 13th December last to the address of my predecessor in office V. W. Bro. I. G. W. Curtis, and in compliance with the request therein contained I beg to hand you copies of the Returns furnished to the Grand Lodge of England for the years 1846, 1847 and 1849, also copy of W. Master Bro. Curtis' letter to the Grand Secretary dated 11th November last forwarding the above Returns.

I also beg to wait on you with the omitted Quarterly Return of this Lodge to the Fund of Benevolence for the 3rd Quarter of last year or from 8th August to 16th October inclusive the Lodge having worked for that period only. The contributions to the Masonic Fund of Benevolence for the above Quarter amount to Rs. 25 and this amount shall be remitted to you shortly, together with the Subscriptions to that Fund for the closing Quarter.

The Lodge was in abeyance during the whole of 1848 and up to 8th August 1849.

In reply to your enquiry I beg to state that on reference to the Book of Proceedings I find that Bro. John Seton Chisholm was the Master by whom Bros. Elliot and Colebrooke were raised to the 3rd Degree within the period prescribed by the Constitutions and it does not appear from the Books and Records of the Lodge that the Sanction of the R. W. the Pro Grand Lodge or one of his Deputies in the N. W. Provinces was either obtained or applied for to this deviation from the Constitutions of the Grand Lodge of England."

Bro. Charde threw himself wholeheartedly into his arduous duties as Treasurer and the letter book is full of his letters calling for dues which had not been collected since 1846.

In July of this year our Royal Arch Chapter was formed and the first meeting was held on Sept. 16th 1850 with the following eminent Companions as Principals :—

> M. E. Comp. Col. Curtis P. " Z."
> M. E. Comp. Ramsay P. " H."
> M. E. Comp. Jeffery P. " J."

and from this date our Chapter has had a continuous record of enthusiastic working and to how large extent the old Lodge was dependant on the Chapter for financial assistance is shown by the old Account Book of this period. Comp. Curtis and Comp. Jeffery were both old Royal Arch Masons the former being exalted in 1831 in Chapter " Prudence " No. 12 attached to Lodge "Fortitude and Old Cumberland " London and the latter in 1839 in Chapter " Royal Sussex " No. 376 attached to Lodge " Perfect Friendship " Ipswich. Under these two expert Companions the flickering Light of Freemasonry in Simla was encouraged into a flame the brightness of which has not since been surpassed. In connection with the Chapter and subsequently incorporated with the Lodge the Super Excellent Degree, The Ark and Mark Degree (a degree long since lost) and the Red Cross of Babylon Degree was actively worked and in this year therefore Simla became one of the most active centres of Masonry in the East.

1851. In these days of active R. Arch Masonry it is not generally known that in accordance with the Rules in force in 1850 it was necessary to be an active member of a Craft Lodge and to formally apply for a " Recommendation " from that Lodge for exaltation in the Chapter. It is of interest to record here By-Laws No. 13 and 16 of the D. G. Chapter of Bengal, under which our Chapter worked, of this period.

No. 13 reads :—" As every R. A. Mason ought to support Craft Masonry... on his ceasing to be a full subscribing Member of a Lodge, he shall also cease to be a Member of the Chapter to which he he may belong. ………"

And No. 16 has :—A Royal Arch Mason suspended or excluded from a Chapter, ought not to remain, during the period of such suspension or exclusion, a Member of the Lodge to which he belongs."

In this year, therefore, we find the first entry referring to this "Recommendation ", " Read application from Bro. J. C. Smith to be recommended for Exaltation in the R.A.C. " Dalhousie ". This apli-cation was " duly signed by the W.M., Senior Warden, Offg. J. W. and Off. Secretary ".

This recommendation took the form of the following Certificate which is of interest today :—

" Whereas our trusty and well-beloved Brother...............…, a Geometrical Master Mason, and registered in the Grand Lodge Books for more than twelve months past, as appears by his Certificate from the Lodge No. 673 under the sanction of the Grand Lodge of England, hath solicited us to recommend him as a Master Mason, every way qualified for exaltation to the degree of Royal Arch, we do hereby certify, that so far as we are judges of the necessary qualifications the said Brother hath obtained the unanimous consent of our Lodge for this recommendation.

Given under our hands this ....…day of ....… .... A.L. ....… .........A.D. ....… ....

Wor. Bro. Bracken died at the close of 1850 and was followed in the Chair by Wor Bro Ebden who, initiated, passed and raised in The Grand Masters Lodge of Ireland, came to us as Past Senior Warden of Lodge " Cape of Good Hope " (1847).

A certain mysterious occurrence alluded to as " an investigation in the 3rd degree " was before the Lodge in September, but whatever it was, the matter was twice postponed and is never afterwards referred to, so it must have settled itself somehow.

1852. Bro. S. W. Fergusson P.S. Warden of Lodge " Industry and Perseverence " Calcutta (now No. 109 E.C.) was this year installed as W.M. "in due form in the Oriental Chair of King Solomon", and in his year of office the splendid work of Wor. Bro. G. Jeffery was recognised, a handsome fluted Beer Mug with cover, supplied by Bro. Chaunce of Calcutta, being subscribed for by 18 members. It was inscribed :—

Presented to worshipful Past Master G. Jeffery by the Brethren of Lodge Himalayan Brotherhood No. 673 Simla A. L. 5852 A. D. 1852 as a mark of their Appreciation of his zealous services for the benefit of the Craft and of this Lodge and as a token of their esteem for himself as a good man and a Mason ".

The length of time which elapsed between writing to London and receiving a reply therefrom and the great delays which occurred between the Provincial Grand Lodge in Calcutta and the Grand Lodge in London rendered it almost imperative that some system of Local Certi-ficates be used. The issue of these Certificates of the Degrees was, I believe, the practice with most Lodges in India doubtess without any authority from Grand Lodge however.

The procedure adopted in this Lodge is shown in the following letter 17th August 1852. To H. Monckton Esq., C. S. Ferozpoor.

Dear Sir and Bro,

I have the pleasure to forward herewith a Certificate of your having been raised in this Lodge in the margin of which please to sign your name and return to me, when it will be duly signed by the Master, Wardens and Secy. I also beg to send your bill and on your remitting me the amount I shall send you a receipt in full of all demands, with your Certificate duly signed.

(Sd.) J. WALKER, SECY.

None of these Certificates of the Lodge are with us today but the By-Laws of 1853 given as an Appendix to this book give a Copy of them in Chapter IX No. 1 " Form of Certificate ".

1853. Many of our Masters of these early days were Masons of great outstanding merit and of them all our Master of this year, Wor. Bro. James Mackenzie, was one of the foremost. He joined us as Past Master of "St. John's Lodge of Central India" (erased in 1855) and was immediately recommended for the Royal Arch. A meeting of members under the Chairmanship of this Brother is of interest to us in these days of high costs:—

Proposed "That as Mr. Crabb, the contractor for the Mess of the Simla Club had offered to supply Lodge Suppers at one rupee per head and in such style as to insure the approval of the members his offer be closed with". Carried. "That Brandy and Sherry be considered Lodge Wines and the expenses thereof be shared equally among the Brethren present. All other Wines and Beer to be paid for by those ordering the same". Carried.

The later part of the above probably refers to Champagne which we have seen was considered a "Lodge Wine" in Chisholm's time.

In this year we find the first mention in the Minutes of the Lodge of the Side Degrees which were then being worked in connection with the Lodge and Chapter. "Read a letter from Bro. Pool resigning the Lodge and requesting that he might be furnished with Super Excellent and "Ark and Mark" Certificates."

In November Lodge "Jullundur" appealed to the Lodge for funds when it is recorded that "as the R.A. Chapter intends aiding the Jullundur Lodge it is not expedient for the Craft Lodge to lessen its Funds... ... ...".

Thus did the old Chapter grant it's aid whenever called for.

On St. John's Day in December a meeting was convened "in honour of our Ancient Brother St. John the Evangelist" and as it was then and had been for years the invariable custom to have Supper after every meeting the brethren again established the custom of honouring the memory of the Patron Saints of Masonry in 1853. Why has this old Custom been allowed to die?

The Account Books tell us that this year we purchased from Spencer & Co., a Set of Tracing Boards and these are the ones in use in the Lodge today and these Boards are therefore 73 years old. This long association with our Lodge through its many vicissitudes will ensure for them that care and consideration due to almost the oldest relics we have of our early Lodge life.

In the minutes of 2nd May is recorded an important letter from the Provincial Deputy Grand Master portions of which are of interest and worth reproducing. After pointing out several shortcomings in the past the Provincial Deputy Grand Master adds "I may as well enumerate the several points which require to be attended to by the Masters of Lodges:—

"5. A Master elected should not be installed by any other than *bona fide* installed masters. Brethren who have "passed the chair" in former times (prohibited in 1840) are not recognised as installed masters.

"6. No votes by proxy should be recorded at the election of a Master, Treasurer or Tyler.

"11. The affairs of the Royal Arch Chapter are to be kept quite distinct from those of the Craft Lodge.

"13. ASIATICS are not to be initiated without previous sanction."

In the proceedings of the Permanent Committee of 7th May, confirmed by the Lodge on the 16th idem, the following para appears:—

"As many societies possessing accumulating property do not exact any fee or charge for the same but receive presents from their members, it was resolved by the committee that the propriety of suggesting to Brethren becoming members of Lodge "Himalayan Brotherhood" either by joining or initiation, that they should, on thus participating in the already possessed property of the Lodge, make some present of an useful or ornamental nature, be laid before the Worshipful Master."

All the Lodge ever received, however, on this suggestion so far as recorded was Rs. 50 from Brother Swinton and 12 finger glasses from Brother Jervis.

On 13th June the Permanent Committee recommended "that the members of the Lodge meet on the 24th instant for the purpose of celebrating St. John's day by a dinner."

1854—St. John the Baptist's memory was this year again honoured a meeting being held on St. John's Day in June at which "The Worshipful Master read several of the Ancient Charges" and the brethren then adjourned to Supper. The Reading of the "Charges" which after very many years is noted in the year 1912, was heard again, at the September meeting of this year. The Lodge was raised to the 3rd degree when the W. M. "read portions of the Ancient Lectures and then, lowering to the 1st Degree, he read "portions of the Ancient Charges"

A long letter to P. G. Lodge from our Wor. Master J. Mackenzie, calling for a number of Certificates shows that it was then the custom to apply for these after each degree. 10 Master Masons, 2 Fellow-Crafts and 5 Entered Apprentice Certificates are asked for including one M.M. for a brother who had been initiated 20 years previously but had had no opportunity of completing his degrees.

1855—On April 30th of this year The Lord Wm. Hay*, who was away from Simla at the time was written to by the S.W. in charge:— "It is with much pleasure I have to announce your unanimous election to the Eastern Chair by the members ....Wor. Bro Ramsay presided at the meeting and anticipating your assent made the following nominations... .. ..Trusting your election to the Chair and the several nominations will meet with your cordial assent ...." It was evident that Lord Hay did not refuse the honour but it was not until 13 months ater that he was duly installed, the Lodge being run in his absence by the S. W. His installation took place on May 12 1856 as the following interesting letter shows:

"I have the honour to report that on Monday the 12th inst an Emergent Meeting of Lodge Himalayan Brotherhood No. 673 was held for the purpose of installing the Master Elect, and Wor. Bro. Lord W. M. Hay and John Hayes Grant, Master of Jullunder Lodge" J. Mackenzie W. M.

This was the first recorded occasion on which we installed the W. M. Elect of Lodge "Jullunder" now working as Lodge "Wahab".

We have always tried to maintain the Lodge's reputation for good Ritual working and that this tradition has been handed down from the earliest years of our Lodge is evident from the high quality of Masonic experts who from time to time joined and took the Chair and no doubt brought the great advantage of their Masonic experience to bear on the working of the Lodge. We shall see that in 1860 a very serious breach in the harmony of the Lodge was caused by the Worshipful Master bringing into Lodge and using a printed Ritual. Brought up as the Lodge had been under such men as McDonald, Gouland, Curtis, Jeffery etc. this was too much for the members and eventually called forth a definite pronouncement against the use of printed books from P. Grand Lodge. And so it is well to record the admission as member in this year of Bro. Major George Jeffery who had been initiated old " Royal Kent Lodge of Antiquity " No. 20, a Lodge which was constituted in 1723.

---

*Wor. Bro. Lord William Montague Hay who had been initiated in our Lodge in 1853 and exalted in Chapter "Dalhousie in 1859 continued a very active member of the Craft until his death in 1911.

In 1870 he succeeded to the ancient title of Marquis of Tweeddale and in 1894 was invested as Senior Grand Warden of the Grand Lodge of England. He was founder of "The Marquis of Dalhousie" Lodge No. 1159 and first W. .M of the Telegraph Cable Lodge No. 2470.

It is members such as these who no doubt helped the old Lodge to maintain it's working at a high standard, correct to mode and proceedure as practiced in the best English Lodges and to them we must ever owe a debt of gratitude.

1856. Wor. Bro J. Mackenzie was this year chosen for the Eastern Chair for the second time. He was a very sincere Mason as many of his letters show. In reporting his re-election to P. G. L. his letter reveals in to what low waters the Lodge had come. "The officers of S. and J. D., I. G., Tyler and Steward are in obeyance at present there are no Brethren on whom to confer the Appointment. Lodge Himalayan Brotherhood never suffered from such a paucity of members as at present. We are not sufficient number of members to make a Lodge without the assistance of Brethren at the station who are not members of our Lodge."

A very interesting letter dated "Mashobrah, near Mahaseo 21st August 1856 reads :—"I observe in the Proceedings of the Grand Lodge received on the 18th inst. that the Mark Master is to be added to the F. C. Degree : I have by me the working, both of Mark Man and Mark Master given me by Rt. Wr. Bro Birch but it strikes me they are defective………… Is the Ark and Mark to be given with the Mark as formerly ? It is not recognised by the Mason authorities."

J. MACKENZIE, W.M.

How interesting it would be to know what exactly this Ark and Mark Degree was.

We note from the above letter that this old degree the "Ark and Mark" is not to be confused with either the Royal Ark Mariner or the Mark Degree as we now have them. It is evidently an old long since forgotten degree and probably was something akin to the "Ark, Mark and Link" which used to be worked by North Country Lodges in England in the early days of the 19th century. No ritual or details have come down to us although it is evident from notes made by Firminger in his "History of Freemasonry in Bengal" and from the cypher writings said to have been found in Cawnpore after the Mutiny that this degree was worked in other places in India besides Simla.

All lovers of the Chapter (and who amongst those that have been exalted therein are not) will take pride in the practical manner in which it was able in those critical days to assist the old Lodge.

A Permanent Committee meeting held on June 28th in this year deserves recording. "The amount received from the Chapter for Lodge purposes (Building and other) is Rs. 1171-7-7 duly sanctioned at the last Chapter meeting but Bro. Treasurer showing the urgent necessity of a further advance the Chapter Committee assembled the same evening authorised the transfer of a further sum of Rs 527-8-5."

The Committee informed a Mr. Farchnie "that the Lodge rooms would be available for an evening party at a rent of Rs. 50 per night," and the further interesting matters were carried at this meeting :—

" Bro. Tapp as Senior Member of the Ark and Mark, Super Excellent and Red Cross Degree attached to Lodge H. B. No. 673 proposed that the surplus of fees for these several degrees after payment of their necessary expenses be carried to a Fund of General Purposes". Carried.

This Fund was duly opened in the Lodge account book and was used to meet the expenses of entertaining our visitors.

" Also Resolved—That Port and Sherry and the several kinds of Spirituous and Malt Liquors Only shall be considered public and the gross expenditure, on each occasion, be shared, share and share alike, as in the good old times of Himalayan Brotherhood. All other wines etc. to be charged individually according to order " Carried.

On August 18th 1856 Bro. Thomas Wood (an initiate of our Lodge) was duly installed as first Master of Lodge "Triune Brotherhood" Soobathoo* by Wor. Bros. J, Mackenzie, Lord Wm. Hay, P. Innes and E. O. K Gilbert.†

1857. In the year 1857 in consequence of the Indian Mutiny the Lodge did not meet at all and once more there is a hiatus in our history.

The old Bible which still lies open in our Lodge was purchased this year at a cost of Rs. 32. This old volume which was printed in 1829 has therefore represented our Greatest Light for seventy years and should be our most cherished possession.

1858. The Lodge met again on the 15th March 1858 after " having been in abeyance during the late troubles " but the attendance was so poor at this and a few subsequent meetings that on the 5th July it was suggested that "a meeting be called to consider the advisability of closing the Lodge for the present year owing to the paucity of members attending the regular meetings." This suggestion was never acted on and the next meeting, a fortnight later, was much better attended.

From this time onwards matters slowly improved and Lodge "Himalayan Brotherhood" is to-day one of the most thriving and

---

*Lodge " Triune Brotherhood " of Subathu and Kasauli received the old number of No. 984 and worked for upwards of ten years before going into decay and extinction. The present Lodge was constituted in 1885 and is numbered No. 2121.

†The latter Wor. Brother had joined us as a P. M. of Lodge " Star of Hope " Agra and was initated in Ireland in Lodge " Meridian " then No. 12. Lodge " Star of Hope " Agra from which we received several Masons at this period was constituted in 1845 but did not last many years for reasons conveyed in the following extract from the Madras Freemasons' Herald for 1848.

"Agra. We regret to learn that Masonry thrives not on the soil of Agra The energies of " Faith, Hope and Charity " are prostrated : the "Star of Hope " (the Gentleman's Lodge) has hidden its diminished head ; and " Freedom and Fraternity " has ceased to exist...........But wherefore should the Genius of Masonry have fled from the spot why...........because it was infected with the plague spot of Masonic Aristocracy and Masonic Exclusiveness ".

influential Lodges in India. Our progress has been continuous. We have of course in these 50 odd years had our troubles and difficulties, we have had lean years and years of plenty, but there has been no break in our progress and the extracts from our minutes and correspondence which follow are both interesting and instructive.

The Lodge had opened under the Hiram of Bro. H. T. Tapp who was installed in May.

He had a most unsatisfactory year mainly due to his own tactless handling. He was early called upon to explain how it was that he allowed the Lodge to be utilised for a public dance and his letter of explanation and excuse gives us some idea of the Lodge buildings.

"In reply to your communication desiring to know if a party was given lately in our Masonic Hall, I have the honour to inform you that an application was made for the use of the rooms by the Mercantile and Uncovenented Community............Our Masonic Hall was originally built with a twofold intention, for the purposes of our Craft generally and when not so required to be available for public purposes at first on hire and eventually when our funds so admitted gratuitously.

In 1856 a similar party was held and again last year on the occasion of rejoicing at the success of our arms against the rebels ....on the late occasion the dining room was appropriated to the dance ....the Lodge room for refreshment, one room being set apart as the express repository of the paraphanalia of the several Orders of our Craft".

Our Lodge Rooms must therefore have been of fairly good dimensions but yet such was the market value of land and property in those days in Simla that when the Lodge was compelled to sell out in 1870 only Rs. 3,500 was realised for it !

Tapp's unsuitability as Master in the Chair is shown by the gross mishandling of an unfortunate occurrence which took place in October.

His Junior Warden had evidently called himself off from labour to refreshment much too often and a charge was laid against him "that from evident symptoms of inebrity you were incapable of discharging your duties as Junior Warden". Although this brother made full apologies to the Lodge and its members the matter was not allowed to drop with the result that the whole matter was reported to P. G. L. No fewer than copies of 16 letters in connection with the case being sent down to Calcutta

1859. The year 1859 seems to have been a stormy one for there is no record of any work of importance being done throughout the year, while in addition to the final stages of the case mentioned above there were some further unpleasant occurences.

Bro. W.A. Hoghton assumed the Eastern Chair on May 16th but reigned only until June 20th when he resigned "finding myself unable to give that attention to the affairs of the Lodge which they require". He had, just before resigning, to investigate a complaint forwarded to The Pro. D.P.G. Master by a Bro. Elliot, Amballa who accused Bro. H.............; an initiate of our Lodge, of gross unmasonic conduct.

This brother was accused of giving expression publicly to opinions highly inimical to Masonry "that you would never follow up such a vile blasphemous system, that it was horrible to listen to the blasphemous language made use of in the Lodge when you were getting made at Simla that the whole system is rot ....it is nothing more than a swindle.........". Bro. Hoghton in calling for an explanation said" as such language or references to the Society which all true Masons regard as a sacred institution is in direct contraventions of the ancient usages and established customs of the order which require that you shall be cautious in your words and carriage in the presence of strangers not Masons, usages and customs, which you, at your initiation, solemnly promised to act and abide by I have to request .... reasons and an expression of sincere regret.........."

Bro. H ....sent an apology which was not accepted "inasmuch as he merely expresses regret at having hurt the *feelings of the Masons* by abuse of the society but none for the abuse of the Society itself".

A fuller and more complete apology being forthcoming from this brother the Lodge accepted it and his resignation. Cases of this sort are fortunately, so very few and far between and this is the only case of its sort that has ever disturbed the harmony of our Lodge.

No fewer than three brethren were elected to the Eastern Chair during this year namely Bro. Hoghton who was installed on May 16th but resigned on 20th June, Bro. J. Harley Maxwell, elected at the meeting of June 27th but who resigned at the next meeting on July 4th "through his expected early departure from Simla" and Bro. James Charles Curtis who was elected "by acclamation" on July 11th. It was not until Nov. 2nd, however, that Bro. Curtis was installed although the Lodge had met in the interim nine times. At his installation we find the opening of a Past Master's Lodge again carried out in full the Minutes recording that "the Lodge was then opened in the Past Master's Degree in due and ancient form in which Wor. Bro. Curtis, Master of Lodge H.B. No. 673 was installed".

This opening of the B. of I. Ms. in extenso, which was evidently the practice of the Lodge from it's constitution is of great interest to us today in view of the animated debate in and the decision of Grand Lodge just recently reported (1926).

One so seldom hears of the claims of a Lewis being insisted on but on more than one occasion the minutes record such items as this in 1859 "Lord Royston and the Hon. H. Harbord being Sons of Masons took preccedence of the other candidates".

1860. On 20th April 1860 and again on 3rd August 1863, the Worshipful Master elect of Lodge "Triune Brotherhood" was installed as Worshipful Master of his Lodge in Lodge "Himalayan Brotherhood". In 1863 Wor. Bro. Wood, assisted by two others performed the ceremony and he mentioned that "the pleasing duty of installing Wor. Brother Fergusson was enhanced by the fact that the Lodge to which he had been elected Master was the one that he (Wor. Brother Wood) had the honour of founding".

20th June. P. G. L. Circular No. 51 read containing an important ruling that "a Past Master has no right to rank amongst the Past Master of another Lodge of which he may be a member but must always sit below them ; nor can he take the chair, or rule the Lodge in preference to the Wardens. This, however, does not prevent a Past Master from working a Lodge if requested to do so by the Wor. Master even if he be not a Past Master of the Lodge".

It seems probable that this Ruling was obtained from P. G. Lodge on a question of the legality of the action of our Senior Warden of this year Bro. Fleming who, although not an installed Master occupied the E. Chair and conferred degrees in the absence of the Worshipful Master and signed the Minutes as "Senior Warden".

3rd September. A letter was read from the Officiating P. G. M. on the subject of using books or manuscripts in the working of Lodges, a practice which he highly disapproved of and ordered to be discontinued in Lodge "Himalayan Brotherhood". At the same time Right Wor. Brother Hoff remarked that it was not correct for Wor. Brother Wood to discuss before visitors the fact of the Wor. Master using a book.

1862. In April 1862 Wor: Brother Wood was elected Master. He was a merchant and was initiated in the Lodge in 1853 and it is clear he took a great interest in the Lodge and a very active part in the working, there being very few meetings at which he was not present from 1853 till he finally left the Lodge about the end of 1867.

Shortly after his election another regretable occurrence took place which upset the harmony of the Lodge. A meeting called for the 19th May 1862 was countermanded and at an emergent meeting held on the 26th June "the Wor: Master stated that owing to the late lamentable occurrence in the Lodge he had felt it his duty to temporarily close the Lodge until he had obtained the advice of the R. W. Prov: Grand Master as to the best course to be adopted to restore the harmony of the Lodge (Wood's letter to the P. G. L. and the reply dated 12th May, neither of which is on record, were then read). The Wor: Master then went on to say that in compliance with the request of the Prov: Grand Master a special committee composed of Wor: Brother General Innes as President, R. W. Brother Elliott and himself as members had been appointed to enquire into the matter. Within 10 days of the receipt of the letter from the R. W. the Prov: Grand Master the special committee met when a document was placed in their hands recording the finding of a Jury (which finding had been confirmed by the Deputy Commissioner of Simla) the purport of which implicated Brother................... in certain monetary transactions which were viewed by the Jury with the gravest suspicions and mistrust and were looked upon as of a fraudulent nature. The special committee after reading this document and taking fully into consideration that three out of the five members of the Jury were R.A. Masons, could only come to the decision that Brother ....should be suspended from his Masonic privileges until the matter was satisfactorily cleared up, or until the views of the R.W. the Prov: Grand Master were ascertained. The committee were further urged to this decision from the knowledge of the fact that several members had expressed their determination not to sit in Lodge with Bro: ....from other causes besides that above stated.

"R. Wor: Brother Elliott then read portions of the finding of the Jury and expressed himself strongly on the necessity of Masons upholding the dignity and respectability of the Craft and that they would fail in their duty as Masons if they allowed the outside world to believe that they countenanced discreditible acts............ ....The Wor: Brother then brought to the notice of the Lodge the fact of his having been informed that Brother................... had some time previously induced Wor: Brther Innes to become security to a Bond for Rs. 14,000, evidence being now in existence which proves that Brother............... knew at the time of the signing of the Bond that Wor: Brother Innes would be involved in great pecuniary loss by the transaction. The R.W. Brother then proceeded to state that he himself had been witness to several exhibitions of unmasonic feeling on the part of Bro:............... in the Lodge and though he and other members of the special committee could not unveil the privacy of the ballot they had a moral conviction in their minds that the Brother in question had taken a part in that which had lately given so much offence to the great majority of the Lodge.... ....The Wor: Brother then alluded to the obligation of secrecy enjoined upon all Masons and regretted to have to state that these obligations had been violated in more than one instance". After one or two others had spoken, and Wor: Brother Graham and Brother Henry as "members of the Jury" had agreed with what had been said it was finally propose and "carried with one dissentient that Brother ....be suspended until the matter be satisfactorily cleared up or until the decision of the R.W. Prov: Grand Master be ascertained."

It nowhere transpires what the result was of this curious mixing up of Masonic matters with some judicial proceedings, nor is there a word to show what became of the Bro: in question who never appeared in Lodge after the 5th May 1862. That the row this year was more serious than the above extracts would lead one to suppose is evident from a note made in the proceedings of the first meeting held in 1863. On this occasion a letter was read from Wor: Brother General Innes expressing his regret at his inability to attend Lodge "as it was his intention to propose the re-election of Wor: Brother Wood to the Eastern Chair, feeling convinced that through that Brother's judicious ruling the Lodge had been saved from abeyance" Wood was re-elected Master in 1863 and was Master again in 1864 which made three years in succession.

16th September. It was proposed by the Wor: Master and unanimously carried "that the San Francisco Ministrels (four of whom were brethren) who on recent occasions by their musical and vocal talents had voluntarily contributed much toward the harmony of our meetings, should be requested to give a concert under the special protection of the Masons in Simla". What the result was does not appear. At this same meeting it was recorded that the sum of £26 the equivalent of Rs. 262 had been subscribed by the Masons of Simla towards the relief of the "distressed Lancashire Weavers".

20th October. A curious procedure at this meeting is worth noticing. Wood was not in the Chair and had probably left Simla for the winter. After Lodge had been regularly closed at 9 P. M. it was at the suggestion of Wor. Brother Tapp " again opened in the first degree for the purpose of proposing ....·...........·· for initiation". Immediately afterwards the Lodge was closed again.

1863. 20th July. An organist (Bro. F. S. Cockburn) was appointed for the first time and apparently received some consideration for his services (he was I know a professional musician) but he did not treat the Lodge well and resigned two years later. In the minutes of 14th August 1865 the following para. appears "Considering the favourable terms conceded to Bro. Cockburn the Wor. Master felt compelled to say that his conduct throughout the season had been in distinct contravention of his engagement and that it was a satisfaction and relief to the Lodge to receive his resignation". On this evening Bro. Elston, a well known personage in Simla to-day, joined the lodge and on the proposal of the Wor. Master "the freedom of the Lodge was conferred on him" and he was appointed Organist. Seven years later all this was forgotten and Cockburn was again admitted to the Lodge and appointed Organist and on the 2nd September 1872 he was elected an honorary member "in consequence of certain pecuniary difficulties under which Bro. Cockburn is labouring". This was certainly a novel reason for doing a man such an honour especially one who so little appreciated it, for early next year it was decided (21st April) to write to Bro. Cockburn and tell him that his frequent absences caused inconvenience. On this he promptly resigned, doubtless to the "satisfaction and relief" of the Lodge once more.

On St. John's Day in June a Bro Macleod "made an application on behalf of himself and a few of the brethren for the use of the Lodge rooms for the purpose of a Ball" which was granted. Was this the first of our Masonic Balls?

1864. At the first meeting this year our number was changed to 459, up to this time we were 673.

21st September. A very largely attended meeting, held almost exclusively for the purpose of installing Wor. Brother John Webb as Master of the Lodge at Agra. This makes the fifth occasion on which the installation of Masters of other Lodges has been carried out in Lodge "Himalayan Brotherhood".

1865. 8th May. Wor. Brother Grant was elected Wor. Master of the Lodge and although he was actually installed on the 29th May, he was not balloted for and elected a member till after the installation ceremony that evening.

It was decided at this meeting to purchase a photograph of R. W. Brother J. J. L. Hoff and have it "suitably framed with the view of having the portrait placed in the banqueting room of the Lodge as a means of perpetuating the memory of an eminent Mason".

If the photograph was ever purchased it has long since disappeared which is very much to be regretted as R. W. Brother Hoff was not only an eminent mason but one of the small party of seven Brethren who founded this Lodge. Towards the end of the year Hoff took seriouly ill and speaking on the 2nd October R. W. Brother the Rev. Dr. Smyth said.—"It has pleased the T. G. A. O. T. U. to lay that great and good mason on a bed of sickness from which humanly speaking he would in no long time be released by the hand of death, but one who had so nobly laboured in the field of masonry as that Brother, could trustfully wait for the summons from this sublunary abode to ascend to the Grand Lodge above".

Hoff lingered on for some months after this as he did not die till early in the following year.

A Special Meeting of the Lodge was held on June 24th this year it being "the anniversary of St. John the Baptist's Day" and at the regular meeting held the following week July 3rd a "handsome silver testimonial" which had been voted by the Lodge was presented to Wor. Bro. Wood for his past services to the Lodge.

An interesting discussion at this meeting arose out of the reading of an Appeal received from the Royal Masonic Institution in England. Bro. Cooke proposed "that the Charity of the Simla Lodge should be centred on local objects instead of being applied to distant schemes and that the purchase of Exhibitons at the Jutogh School would be a proper measure for the nature and education of masons' orphans".

Wor. Bro. Wood who supported mentioned "that a favorite project with him for a long time past had been the institution in Simla of Almshouses under the shadow of the Lodge where superannuated Masons might end their days in comfort". Both projects of truely Masonic inspiration which alas did not materialise. Will the Simla Brotherhood ever be in a possition to carry Bro. Wood's idea into effect ?

At the first meeting in 1866 (16th April) the Worshipful Master elect (Worshipful Brother J. E. Cooke) addressed the Lodge to the following effect "R. W. Brother J. J. L. Hoff's services to masonry in general were well known by some of the Brethren present. It was a melancholy coincidence that the proceedings of our last meeting which had been confirmed to-night contained a high tribute to Brother Hoff's masonic qualities ....
Notwithstanding that Brother Hoff was unknown personally to the rising generation of masons the knowledge of his worth would not perish but would be cherised and perpetuated with a loving gratitude for the benefits which he had secured to the interests of masonry. Brother Cooke had been in Calcutta at the time of R. W. Brother Hoff's death and had been present also at his funeral. He had besides been a witness to the feeling exhibited in several Lodges in Calcutta on the night of their first meeting after Brother Hoff's death, and by the Brethren in Calcutta, but few of whom had ever seen the deceased Brother. One Lodge in particular "Humility with Fortitude" took a melancholy pride in its name of Brother Hoff's Lodge, but the Simla Lodge had a better title to it for although Brother Hoff never presided here yet he assisted in the founding of the Lodge, conferred upon it its name and ever watched its progress with solicitude. Of a lowly station in life he invariably preferred the valley to the hill top, his career was marked by silent and unobtrusive well-doing and strongly exemplified the influence of masonic principles in his every day life ; but although he had courted and maintained lowliness of lot and preferred throughout duty to distinction yet he descended to the grave with more honours than are frequently paid to favourities of fortune and his memory was cherised with a proud regard that might be coveted by those occupying the highest stations in life."

A memorial was erected in Calcutta to R. W. Brother Hoff to- ward which the Brethren in Simla subsribed, but on the death of the Treasurer, some two years later the Worshipful Master at a meeting held on the 25th October 1868 " referred to the extraordinary circums- tance of it not having been found possible to trace any clue to the whereabouts of the sum of Rs. 120 subscribed by the Lodge to the Hoff Testimonial Fund " and it was not till the 20th June 1870 that it was decided to make good the money " so soon as it can be spared by the Lodge."

It will be appropriate to record here a few remarks and extracts regarding Worshipful Brother W. H. Hoff, the son of R. W. Brother J. J. L. Hoff. He was initiated in his father's Lodge " Humility with Fortitude " and was first admitted a member of our Lodge on 16th August 1849 by general acclemation "being the son of our worthy and Worshipful Brother the Provincial Grand Secretary of Bengal" the position held by his father at that time. He probably left Simla at the end of that year when he was, I suppose, struck off and evidently he did not revisit Simla till 1864. At the meeting of the Lodge on the 6th June of that year he was proposed as a joining member and being " a very old and highly esteemed mason" he was elected an honorary member by acclamation. At the next meeting on 4th July after confirming the previous minutes the Worshipful Master said " it afforded him the greatest pleasure to welcome Worshipful Brother Hoff and he was sure the whole of the Brethren present joined him in so doing. Not only on account of his own long and distinguished services in the Craft was Worshipful Brother Hoff entitled to a hearty welcome amongst masons wherever he might go, but he was the son of one of the most enthusiastic masons which India had ever produced. He alluded to R. W. Brother J. J. L. Hoff. Past Dy. Provincial Grand Master of Bengal."

At the meeting of 2nd October 1865, at which Worshipful Brother McAlpin the Master of Lodge " Humility with Fortitude" was an honoured guest, R. W. Brother Dr. Smythe in the course of an address to the Lodge said. " It afforded him peculiar gratification that night............................and to see Worshipful Brother Hoff. Worshipful Brother Hoff had earned a lasting claim to the gratitude of masons in India by his able editorship of the masonic magazine to which he had devoted his private hours for so many years with such marked success. His efforts had certainly advanced the cause of Masonry and they were the more honourable to him from the humble and unostentatious way in which they were bestowed, but although he sought no reward beyond the satisfaction of doing his duty as an earnest and intelligent mason, and richly reaped that reward, yet it could not but be a sourse of high gratification to him to perceive that his work and sentiments were quoted with approval in many quarters of the globe."

Wor. Bro. Hoff remained an active member of the Lodge and took the very greatest interest in its welfare until his death on 30th January 1870. The two Hoff's father and son, are intimately connected with our history and their names will ever be held in the greatest esteem by members of Lodge Himalayan Brotherhood.

It may be mentioned here that in September 1865 a letter was received from Wor. Brother McAlpin the Master of Lodge " Humility with Fortitude" expressing a hope that " during his approaching visit to Simla................it would be possible to call a meeting of the Lodge in order that he might have an opportunity of attending and making the acquaintance of the Brethren." We have always considered that "Lodge Humility with Fortitude " has stood *in loco parentis* to our selves as it was entirely due to the energies of members of the former Lodge, one of whom, as already mentioned. was R. W. Bro. J. J. L. Hoff, that Lodge " Himalayan Brotherhood," was founded.

29th May. It is recorded that Wor. Brother Wood had presented the Lodge with Rs. 200 for a harmonium and that a very superior instrument had been secured for the money.

1866. Our unpunctuality so often commented on now seems to have been handed down to us from ancient days. On 11th October 1866 a Brother complained that although the Lodge was convened for 7 o'clock, work did not begin till 8 p.m. and all the Worshipful Master could say in reply was that this had been the case for the last three years !

1867. 10th June A curious little misunderstanding arose. A Brother who had at the previous meeting been appointed to an important office, resigned "on the ground of his having been superseded by a junior in direct opposition to one of the by-laws of the Lodge." At the next two meetings there were hot discussions on the subject, the Master maintaining his right to make any appointment he thought suitable in the interests of the Lodge while the Bro. in question steadily adhered to his contention that the Wor. Master's action was against the by-laws. Ultimately on putting the point to the vote it was decided " with only one dissentient voice" that the Brother's conduct was unjustifiable and unmasonic. Nevertheless on 5th August the Wor. Master proposed the correction of rule 3 of the by-laws to correspond with the constitutions because the discussion in this case had shown that the rule conveyed the impression that *all* the Officers of the Lodge were to be elected instead of only the Wor, Master, Treasurer and Tyler.

15th July. The Wor. Master announced "that it was his intention to have a new order—that of Mark Masons —formed in this Lodge" but apparently the idea was dropped. The Mark Lodge was not formed till 1881 as it is recorded in the minutes of 4th April of that year that a Mark Lodge was about to be opened and worked by Wor. Bro. Goldstein.

1868. 26th May. Brother F. Von Goldstein, father of the well known family now in Simla, brought before the Lodge the question of joining in a petition for the establishment of a D.G.L. for the Punjab.

At the next meeting on 8th June the matter was considered again and although Wor. Brother Hoff spoke against the proposal it was decided by a large majority to support it. D.G.L. Punjab was duly established before the end of the year.

At the meeting held on April 19th 1869 that perennial source of discussion "Refreshments" came under consideration. In the course of the discussion Wor. Bro. Hoff made an interesting statement anent the early custom of the Lodge as regards this matter.

After Bro. Henry had suggested "that a system which obtained at certain clubs would not be out of place to establish in the Lodge and that was that every Bro. should bring his own supply with him of whatever kind of Liquor he considered best for himself" Wor. Bro. Hoff told us "that when he first joined the Lodge the mode of each Brother bringing his flask obtained and those who preferred doing without the flask did so". Imagination can picture the appearance of our Supper Tables today if this "Mode" obtained in the Lodge at the present time. (G.R-B. 1927).

1869. 10th May. An emergent meeting to receive the District Grand Master of the Punjab (Colonel Charles McWhirter Mercer). The following extracts are taken from the summary of his address on this occasion "............ .. and spoke with regard to the condition of the Lodge at the present date and what it was some years ago when there were barely sufficient members to work the Lodge. He also stated that the Initiations, Passings and Raisings exceeded all the other Lodges, with one exception, under his Hiram. He also spoke at length with reference to a new Lodge to be set up in Simla . ... he further remarked that unless good and sufficient grounds were given for the necessity of establishing another Lodge he would never give his support as he was quite certain it would materially injure the Craft.' It would have been interesting if the speech had been give more in detail unfortunately the record is very meagre and sketchy. On the 7th June following, the petition for the forming of the new Lodge was duly presented but on being put to the vote was rejected. Another Lodge was often hinted at in after years but it was not till 1903 that the schism actually took place when the "Kitchener" Lodge was founded.

1870. Financially, however, the Lodge was in anything but a flourishing state in 1869 and in 1870 it was found to be so much in debt that on the 5th May the Permanent Committee reported that it was "simply injudicious to continue in this state, further that only one alternative remains, i.e., to sell the Lodge estate to enable the debts being cleared". Worshipful Brother Daly, one of the members of the Committee, stated "that from years of experience in the Masonic circle he had never met with a Lodge so much embarrassed as Lodge Himalayan Brotherhood.... .... He suggested the establishment of a new Lodge....................he would do all in his power to assist in the formation; that he would apply for a new Charter.... ....and in a few months he had no doubt the new Lodge would be in a flourishing condition and a credit to the Craft which he was sorry to remark was not the case with the old Lodge". Before the end of the year the Lodge estate was actually sold and after 24 years we were once more homeless through, I am afraid, gross mis-management and want of supervision over our funds (See under head "Accounts").

Probably it was due to the Lodge being in such a bad state that not one of the nine Brethren eligible would accept the Eastern chair this year and a deputation therefore waited on Brother Ball, "an old Mason with considerable experience in the Craft and one who takes a great interest in Masonry" to persuade him to take the office. He consented and was duly installed. The Brethren apparently did not know until Ball mentioned the fact himself that this was his mother Lodge although he had not been a member for some fifteen years.

1871. Lodge met for the first time this year on the 5th June in the old "Assembly Rooms" the Temple having been sold for debt the previous year. The meeting was poorly attended owing apparently to the Government offices remaining in Calcutta till very late. Brother Belle was elected Master by a narrow majority, but at the next meeting a fortnight later the Brethren refused to confirm the minutes. Belle appealed to the District Grand Master, Colonel C.W. Mercer (in Lodge on the 3rd July) who ruled that the first meeting of the year must be considered null and void owing to the informality of the summons, the meeting having been convened in the name of the Worshipful Master who was at the time actually on his way to England, and that the "Senior Past Master, the only person in Simla, was the sole legal authority to summon a meeting". A fresh election then took place with the result that Brother H.R. Cooke got eight votes and Brother Belle five In his address at this meeting the District Grand Master congratulated the Lodge in having got rid of the heavy debt it had been hampered with for years and added that "from what he could learn it was now in a good state from a financial point of view and he sincerely trusted it would continue so". Speaking in Lodge later this season (18th September) the District Grand Master said "he was glad to find that the Lodge was in such a flourishing condition, for whereas formerly the Lodge had been in debt, there was now, he was gratified to learn, a fair balance at the bank and the number of members had increased from 18 to 30................. ...further that the prosperous condition of Himalayan Brotherhood under its present Master had very nearly induced him to alter an opinion which he previously formed, *viz.* that owing to the migratory population in the Hills, hill Lodges never could work with any satisfactory result.................... ".

1872. 2nd September. A "Masonic Ball" was mooted for the first time. At the next meeting the matter was discussed again and for want of support the proposal was about to be dropped when a Brother asked permission " to make one more effort to carry out the project". Evidently, however, it failed, and it was not till four years later, *viz.*, on the 22nd September 1876 that the first ball was held and it is recorded in the minutes of 2nd October 1876 that it was a " great success." In the following year the ball must have been a still greater success as it is mentioned in the minutes of 15th April 1878 that the balance of the ball fund account, Rs. 325, was given to the Punjab Masonic Institution. From this time forward the ball has, I believe, been held annually with more or less success financially, up to the present day and it has become one of the most brilliant and distinguished social functions of the Simla season.

The Punjab Masonic Institution is referred to for the first time this year. In the minutes of 16th September 1872 the following paragraph appears. "Read, a letter from Worshipful Brother Adlard soliciting some further (sic) support from Himalayan Brotherhood on behalf of the Punjab Masonic Institution. Resolved, that the whole of the papers connected with this question be circulated for the consideration of the members of the Lodge". On the 21st October, following, the Lodge made evidently their first donation to the Punjab Masonic Institution and that was Rs. 50 only from St. John's Box.

27th December. A special meeting in commemoration of St. John's Day. Only one member besides the officers and three visitors were present! There is nothing to show what was done at this meeting beyond reading a letter from the District Grand Lodge, explaining that some free criticisms on the working of Lodges in the Punjab, contained in a recent proceedings of District Grand Lodge did not apply to Lodge Himalayan Brotherhood the working of which during 1872 was considered to be "highly satisfactory."

1873. We sometimes see in these days of hustle a certain amouns of impatience shown by some brethren if, by any chance, our meetingt today are extended beyond the usual time or if more than one Degree appears on the Agenda. The Agenda for the meeting held on 14th April 1873 shows this was not so in earlier days. The meeting was called for 7-30 p.m. the "work of the evening" being:—1. To elect the W. M. and Treasurer for the current season. 2. To ballot for a Rejoining member. 3. To ballot for and to initiate James Bruce Cowmeadow. 4. To pass Bro. G. Douglas and 5. To raise Bro. T. Morris.

Our Brethren certainly "werked" in those days!

1874. It is interesting to note that at the meeting of 18th May this year worshipful Brother C. J. French, who was the first candidate initiated in Lodge Himalayan Brotherhood so far back as 31st May 1838, was elected an honorary member. Worshipful Brother French probably resigned at the end of 1839 on leaving Simla, but his son tells me he returned in 1865 and died here in February 1885. He seems, however, to have been of a restless, roving disposition and was frequently absent from Simla for more or less lengthened periods and it was probably owing to this reason that he never rejoined the Lodge. He was in Lodge at the two meetings immediately preceding his election as honorary member, but he apparently never attended Lodge afterwards and when our Register was written up afresh in 1877 Worshipful

Brother French's name was omitted and he is never again mentioned.

1875. The election of the Master did not take place this year at the first meeting, as usual heretofore from the earliest times, in consequence of a ruling from District Grand Lodge, " that the Master and Wardens, in order to qualify for past rank and privileges, should serve in their respective offices for a clear 12 months." It followed that as the Master had been installed in May 1874 the elections could not take place till April this year, the installation following in May. This practice continued till 1883 when for some reason not recorded the election did not take place till May and the installation in June. May and June have ever since been our dates for election and installation respectively.

17th May. Brother Topple was balloted for but it is nowhere recorded that he was ever initiated, although the Register gives 17th May as date of initiation. Again on the 7th June, Brother Seide was proposed as a joining member, but there is no record of his having been balloted for. Clearly there was something wrong with the Secretary at this time. In addition to the above omissions there is absolutely no record whatever of the meeting held on 21st June 1875, when Bros. Walker, Showell and McRae were raised. The notes of 7th June are very meage (a most unusual thing with Coyne who was inclined to be rather prolix) and two paragraphs were certainly written by his wife, as were also almost the whole of the minutes of the 6th September. I knew the Coynes well and comparing the writing in the above minutes with a letter from Mrs. Coyne still in my wife's possession, there is no shadow of a doubt that the notes were written by her. It is surprising these irregularities escaped the Worshipful Master (Litster) who was to my personal knowledge a very precise and particular person in every way. It is impossible to believe that the minutes of 21st June could have been overlooked by the Worshipful Master, and the Lodge. The minute book is complete and there is no trace of any pages having been torn out, besides part of the minutes of *7th June*, ending with the W. M's. signature, is on the *same page* as that on which the minutes of *5th July* begin, so that the notes of 21st June could never have been in the book. I can only surmise that the notes were recorded and confirmed on a separate sheet of paper which it was intended to paste into the minute book, but which was never done. There is ample evidence in the Register of members that there *was* a meeting on this date but the record of it is certainly not to be found.

The following paragraph in the notes of 5th July is rather amusing and shows how seriously the Worshipful Master used to take matters:—

"With regard to the proposed masonic concert it was proposed that the first five rows of seats in the theatre be reserved for the public and that all members of the Lodge appear in masonic clothing; more, that the members be at liberty to mix with the general community." I can well imagine our pompous W. M. allowing this liberty as a great concession instead of insisting on marshalling the Brethren in two by two like Sunday school children as he dearly would have liked to do.

4th October. A sum of Rs. 100 was placed at the disposal of the District Grand Lodge "for the reception of H. R. H. the Prince of Wales, our Grand Master," now His Majesty King Edward VII.

1876. On the 3rd April following a circular was read from the District Grand Lodge forwarding a copy of the address presented to His Royal Highness at Lahore on the 18th January 1876 and the reply received thereto. It was then proposed, and agreed to unanimously, "that the photograph of the address, the column in which it was contained (a model of one of the pillars of K. S. Temple) and the reply, should be framed and hung in Lodge." It is a thousand pities this unique photograph does not now exist in our Lodge.

18th September. " A question was raised as to the propriety of members wearing in Lodge the decoration sold by masonic clothiers under the name of a Master Mason's jewel. As there seemed to be nothing in the Constitutions to warrant the wearing of such a decoration, and as there was a difference of opinion among the Brethren, the Secretary was asked to refer the question to the District Grand Lodge of the Punjab." Whether District Grand Lodge ever vouchsafed a reply is not recorded. No reply had, anyhow, been received up to the 6th August in the following year, when it was decided to send a reminder and thereafter there is no mention of the subject.

1877. 16th July. The Lodge was regularly inspected this year for the first time and at this meeting the Worshipful Master elect of Lodge " Excelsior " was installed by dispensation as Worshipful Master of his Lodge making the sixth occasion on which we have installed the Masters of other Lodges. A few years later it was ruled by Grand Lodge (see letter recorded in minutes of 23rd April 1883) " that a Worshipful Master elect cannot be installed in any Lodge but that in which he has been so elected to the chair and that no dispensation can be issued permitting him to be so." In this connection it may be noted that in 1902 we were asked to invest the Senior Warden elect of Lodge " Deccan " but District Grand Lodge refused to sanction such a procedure.

This year for the first time a regular convocation of District Grand Lodge was held on 21st September under our Banner and was the beginning no doubt of our now well known " Masonic Week". The ball this year was decided to be held " during the visit of the Right Worshipful the District Grand Master". The Brethren at this period evidently took " Masonic Week " less strenuously than we do now for on 3rd September it is recorded " It was proposed and carried unanimously that as the convocation of District Grand Lodge, the Masonic ball and a regular meeting of Lodge Himalayan Brotherhood fall in one week and would probably be too great a tax on the Brethren, the Lodge empower the Worshipful Master to dispense if possible with the regular meeting."

1878. 15th April. The following extract from the report of the working of the Punjab Masonic Institution for 1877 was read:—

" It has been decided by the general meeting that each Lodge in the Province be asked to appoint a Steward to serve the Charity. He will collect the subscriptions of the Lodge and its members and generally represent its interests; he will be in communication with the Secretary and will be in a position to afford full information as to what is being done by the Institution. At the close of the year an illuminated letter of thanks will be presented to each Steward..............The Committee tender their thanks to Worshipful Brothers Willson and Goldstein................ for their unremitting advocacy of the interests of the Institution". Worshipful Brother Willson was our first P. M. I. Steward

At the meeting of 15th April a Native of India was proposed for initiation for the first time in our history but the ballot taken at the next meeting on 6th May " proved unfavourable." Next year another native was proposed and the ballot in this instance proving unanimously favourable our first Indian Brother was initiated on the 15th August 1879.

1881. 4th April. " Brother Colonel Sanford then explained his views regarding the faulty way in which the budget estimates of the Punjab Masonic Institution were arrived at, and proposed in order to have something to fall back upon in case the actual receipts of the P.M.I. should fall short of the estimated receipts, that a fund should be formed to be called the P. M. I. investment fund of Lodge Himalayan Brotherhood, and that into this fund all monies realised by concerts, theatrical performances, etc., should be paid, the interest on such invested monies being annually withdrawn and made over to the Honorary Secretary of the P. M. I. as a donation from the Lodge in addition to the usual annual subscription of Rs. 12...............That the fund should be started with the proceeds of the concert of 7th October which he hoped would amount to something over Rs. 100." This proposal was approved. Next year Wor. Bro. Colonel Sanford further proposed " that the P.M.I. capital fund be credited to the same account as the building fund and the interest on this portion paid yearly to the P.M.I." This fund is never again alluded to and probably died out shortly after it was opened.

1882. 15th May. With these minutes is recorded for the first time a copy of the " Summons" and it is interesting to note that it was printed by Messrs Cotton and Morris who do most of our printing to this day.

On the 20th June and again on the 28th August, what seems to me to have been a most irregular procedure was adopted for disposal of work and that was to divide the Lodge into two parts and work different degrees in adjoining rooms. It is worth mentioning that on both occasions our present Chaplain Wor. Bro. Watson was, so to speak, the victim. On the 20th June Wor Bro. Watson was initiated in one room while another Brother was being raised in the adjoining room. The notes of the 28th August record—"On resuming work it (the Lodge) was raised to the third Degree. The W. M. then decided, so as to save time, that the M. M's Degree should be given to Bro. Watson in a separate room and for this purpose the following Brethren were passed out to conduct the ceremony and by them Bro. Watson was duly and solemnly raised to the 3rd Degree *   * Lodge was then lowered (i.e., when the above were passed out) to the 2nd Degree   *   *   *   *   (the candidate for that degree) was admitted and in due and ancient form passed to the 2nd Degree *   *   *   Lodge was again raised to the 3rd Degree and then called off. On resuming labour Bro. Watson was called to the Eastern Pedestal when the Wor. Master gave the lecture on the tracing board of that Degree."

Practically therefore, Wor. Bro Watson was raised to the 3rd Degree in a Fellow Craft Lodge, as the action of the Wor. Master in lowering the Lodge to the 2nd Degree when Wor. Bro. Watson and the others were passed into the next room, could not possibly admit of a portion of the Lodge continuing to work in the 3rd Degree. This proceedure was again followed on the 14th September 1885 by Wor. Bro. Carson who, after raising the Lodge to the 3rd Degree, passed out Wor. Bro. Freeman and some others to an adjoining room to raise two candidates, while he himself in his own room solemnly lowered the Lodge to the 2nd Degree and passed two candidates, then lowered it to the 1st Degree and initiated four candidates !

I quote the following paragraph from the minutes of the 11th September for the benefit of some present day Brethren who complain at times at not getting to supper till near 9 p.m. "There being no further work before the Lodge it was closed in peace and harmony at 1 a.m., when the Brethren adjourned to banquet." I wonder if sufficient explanation of this is to be found in the fact that on this night the Lodge was inspected by Wor. Brother E. W. Parker, the D. G. Registrar.

1883. On October 8th, in this year Bro. Robert von Goldstein presented to the Lodge the large Tripod and Perfect Ashlar which still stands in front of our S. W's Pedestal. It is inscribed as being presented by "The only Lewis made in the Lodge up to date". This is not quite correct as we find that as early as 1859 our Minutes record the making of two Lewises. (G.R.B. 1927).

Past Masters of Lodge Himalayan Brotherhood, No. 459 E. C., Simla.

Standing—H. G. Russell 1927-28.   H. Brown P.D.G.A.D.C. 1924-25.   C. J. Prior P.D.G.A.P. 1915-16.
G. R. Parker 1926-27.   J. Tinson P.D.G.J.W. 1925-26.   B. J. Robertson 1922-23.

Sitting—C. J. Knowles P.D.G.S.D. 1917-18.   J. Faletti P.D.G.J.W. 1907-08.   R. Watson P. Deputy
D.G.M. (Punjab) P.A.G.D. of C. (Eng.) 1896-97.   P. H. Marshall P.D.G.S.W. 1920-21.
G. Reeves Brown P.D.G. Ch. 1919-20.

23rd October. A discussion arose in Wor. Bro. Litster's case as to whether a Brother who is not a subscribing member of any Lodge was eligible to be elected an honorary member and on the point being referred to D. G. L. they decided in the negative (see minutes of 9th April 1883) A propos of Wor. Bro. Litster it is worth noting that he did more "resigning" and "rejoining" than any other member in our long history. He joined first in 1862 and resigned in January 1863 ; rejoined in 1865, resigned July 1868; rejoined June 1869, resigned May 1876, elected Honorary Member June 1876; rejoined April 1877, resigned April 1878, and again elected honorary member; rejoined April 1879, resigned May 1880, and was once again elected honorary member in October 1882 but this election could not be confirmed in consequence of the D. G. L. ruling referred to above. On 13th April 1885 Wor. Bro. Litster was again proposed as a joining member but he withdrew before the ballot in May. On 12th July 1886 he was once more elected an honorary member, a ruling in G. L. Quarterly Communication of March 1886 "relative to the election and status of honorary members in Private Lodges" apparently allowing the election. Litster was frequently in Lodge after 1886 and often took an active part in our proceedings but he never "rejoined" again.

1886. At an emergent meeting on 21st July a discussion arose as to whether a Brother who was not mentioned in the agenda of business for the meeting could be raised to the 3rd Degree and the point was referred to the D. G. L. when it was ruled "that the purpose of an emergent meeting must be expressed in the summons and no other business entered upon" :Letter from D. G. L, No. 276 of 9th August 1886—vide notes of 3rd September 1886).

1887. 8th August. It was proposed that the question of a "Masonic Festival" be considered but it was decided to settle this matter out of Lodge and I can find no further reference to it. The "Festival" may possibly have been intended to commemorate the Jubilee of the Lodge in 1888. In the minutes of 10th October 1887 is recorded the receipt of a letter from the Grand Secretary stating "that he did not think the G. M. would grant any badge in commemoration of its Jubilee."

The following extracts are taken from the minutes of the meeting held on 12th September 1887 at which the R. W. the D. D G. M. (Parker) was present officially to inspect—"Wor. Bro Col. Sanford and Bro.—were passed out and Lodge close tyled." After a few minutes Wor. Bro. Sanford was readmitted alone when he asked the W. M. if he would allow him to remove one of the tassels from the Lodge ; this was of course permitted and Wor. Bro. Col. Sanford was again passed out " with the tassel." Immediately after " alarm proved to be Wor. Bro. Col. Sanford and Bro.—(the latter carrying the tassel) who were duly admitted and Lodge close tyled. Wor Bro Col. Sanford informed the W. M. that Bro.—who was carrying the tassel, symbolical of temperance, wished to make a few remarks. The W M. said he would be glad to hear those remark on which Bro.—apologised to the W. M. and the Lodge for having violated the principals inculcated in the symbol he held in his hand and trusted that the Lodge would forgive him and promised that such an offence would not be committed by him again. The W. M. then handed the Hiram to the R. W. the D. D. G. M. who addressed Bro.—on the subject and stated that he sincerely hoped that the lesson given Bro.— would prove beneficial both to him and all the Brethren in the Lodge and that it would be deeply impressed on all their memories for nothing degraded a man so much as excessive drinking." The Bro. concerned was not a member of the Lodge but a visitor on this occasion.

1888. 9th April. A circular, No. 30, dated 26th March 1888, from District Grand Lodge is recorded with these minutes "forbidding the use of any ritual in open Lodge, forbidding the perusal of such works by Brethren below the rank of M. M. and stating that the use of a ritual in open Lodge by any W. M. renders him liable to expulsion from the Order, and the Lodge which allows its W. M. to use a ritual is itself liable to be erased." This was repeated some years later in Cir. No. 7 of 20th July 1898 which will be found recorded with our minutes of 10th October 1898 and a further letter on the subject was received from G. L. in 1900 (*vide* minutes of 12th March) which will be found duly recorded with our important papers.

1890. The notes of 14th April contain a ruling by District Grand Lodge (Circular No. 3 dated 1st April 1890) "that the charge is really part of the ceremony (of Initation) and should not under any circumstances be omitted or deferred."

1891. At the installation of Worshipful Brother McDermott in June 1891, Worshipful Brother Sanford, who was then D. D. G. M. in the course of an address after the installation ceremony "recommended the Brethren cordially to support their Master in his efforts to advance the interests of Freemasonry in general, and of this Lodge in particular, and with a view to enable him to do so he suggested that a subscription should there and then be raised towards St. John's Box.". The Worshipful Master immediately had subscription lists circulated by the Treasurer and Deacons, and the handsome sum of Rs. 300 was collected. A similar procedure was adopted next year at the installation of Worshipful Brother General Sir Edwin Collen, when a sum of about Rs. 380 was collected. Worshipful Brother Lord Roberts, the Commander-in-Chief in India, was present on this occasion.

1892. The case of Sir Alexander Miller is probably a unique one of a Brother having been initiated and passed twice in his life. When Sir Alexander asked to join the Lodge he could give no proof of his being a Mason, nor could we obtain any particulars regarding him from the Lodge in Ireland in which he was initiated some 40 years previously. In referring the case to D. G. L. the Worshipful Master asked whether it would suffice to take an obligation from Sir Alexander Miller that he had been duly initiated and passed in a regular Lodge and then confer the third degree, but sanction to this course was refused, and Sir Alexander was therefore re-initiated and passed and then raised.

1893. The notes of 10th April say that an interesting discussion arose on an objection by Worshipful Brother Freeman to the S. W. in charge of the Lodge signing the minutes in the absence of the W. M. when a P. M. was in the chair. Several Brethren spoke on the occasion and gave their views on the interpretation to be placed on Article 141 of the Constitutions and in the end "the difficulty was finally settled by the P. M. in the chair and the S. W. in charge both signing."

8th May.—The Lodge considered a recommendation by the Permanent Committee that the resignation of no member be accepted until he had paid his dues, but Wor. Bro. Burton pointed out that the D. G. M, who was present at one of our meetings in the seventies, had ruled that "when a member had tendered his resignation the Lodge had no option but to accept whether his dues were paid or not." The suggestion of the P. C. was not, therefore, agreed to.

14th August.—It was decided to initiate Mr. Mansfield as a serving Brother with a view to his ultimate appointment as Organist. This is the first reference to, and appointment of, an Organist for many years, but from this time onwards an Organist has been regularly appointed at every installation.

1894. In November Wor. Bro. J. R. B. Bell, (to quote from our letter of 23rd February 1895) offered to place Rs. 1,000 "with the W. M. of this Lodge as a trust in order that the interest on the said sum may be devoted to prizes for girl wards of the P. M. I. as a memorial to his late wife." Some correspondence ensued on the subject, but beyond the following reference to the bequest in the minutes of 8th April 1895, there is nothing to show what became of this money:—"Brother Secretary was ordered to write to Wor. Bro. Bell intimating that the Lodge concurred in Wor. Bro. Bell's proposals, and that no further action would be taken by this Lodge pending receipt of a communication from D. G. L."

This sum was invested by the Trustees of the P. M. I. and is what is now known as the Bell Scholarship, the interest being yearly devoted to deserving girl scholars. (G. R. B. 1927)

1895. 10th June. Worshipful Brother R. Burton, I. P. M., "brought to the notice of the W. M. (Sir Alexander Miller had been installed at this meeting) the services performed by Brother Walmsley, the outgoing Secretary, not only with reference to the past year but in previous years, and stated that besides having held nearly every office in the Lodge from Tyler to J. W., Bro. Walsmley had been Secretary of Lodge "Himalayan Brotherhood" for four years, viz., 1887-88, 1889-90, 1893-94. and 1894-05, and it was during these last two years of his office as Secretary that the revised by laws had at last been issued, and which, in their present form, would prove a valuable document, especially as regards the record of officers of this Lodge since its formation in 1837 (sic). He therefore proposed that as a token of appreciation of his services the Lodge should present Brother Walmsley with a Secretary's jewel with four bars, the cost not to exceed Rs. 100." This was carried with acclamation.

1897. The following very important decision by the Grand Registrar (Brother R. Horton Smith, Q. C.) is taken from the minutes of the 9th August 1897. A charge of gross unmasonic conduct had been brought against one of our Brethren, and he had been summoned to attend Lodge on a particular evening to show cause why he should not be excluded. Instead of doing so, however, he sent in his resignation the day before the meeting, and actually left Simla on the morning of the day fixed for the meeting. The Lodge nevertheless considered his case ex parte, refused to accept the resignation, and excluded him. Brother Horton Smith's opinion on the above facts is :—" That resignation having been placed in the hands of the Lodge, and being, whether accepted by them or not, sufficient to determine his membership thereof it was beyond their jurisdiction to exclude him, as they did, though of course they were not compelled to give him his clearance certificate until all his dues were satisfied, and then only with a statement of the circumstances under which he left the Lodge. It therefore follows that his exclusion should be cancelled, aud his resignation duly recorded."

1898. The following is extracted from the minutes of 10th January :—" In regard to the resignation of Brother Bowyer. the W. M. (Worshipful Brother Watson was in the chair) said he could not allow it to pass without drawing the attention of the Lodge to the great munificence that had marked his connection with the Lodge. He had now sent a cheque for Rs. 150, of which Rs. 100 had been sent as a donation to the P. M. I., and the remainder, after deducting the small dues of Brother Bowyer, was for the funds of St. John's Box of this Lodge."

1899. 8th May. "It was proposed by the W. M. (Worshipful Brother Alves), and seconded by Wor. Brother Shearer, that owing to the duties being very heavy Rs. 30 per mensem be paid to the Lodge Secretary (in addition to exemption from paying fees) to pay for an assistant if he desired to employ one."

On 14th September 1903 this resolution was cancelled on a motion by Wor. Brother Leigh, but the matter came before the Lodge again on the 9th May following, when Wor. Brother Alves proposed that the minutes of the previous year be rescinded. Brother Faletti suggested, however as an amendment, that the grant be made at the discretion of the W. M., and this proposal was approved, after some discussion, by a large majority of the members present.

Our first and only record of a Masonic funeral is contained in the minutes of the 15th December 1899, which I reproduce almost in full :—

" The W. M. (Wor. Brother Watson presided) after the Lodge had been opened in due and ancient from at 9 a.m., explained the sad occasion which had led to the hurried assembly of the Brethren, *viz.*, the death of Bro. Charles DeCosta, W. M. of Lodge " True Brothers," 1210-E.C., and Companion of R. A. Chapter "St. Paul's," attached to Lodge No. 1210 E. C. On his death bed the aged Brother had desired to be laid at rest by the Masonic Brethren, and in respect to his memory, and in obedience to his last wishes, the Brethren had assembled to accompany his body to the tomb. A dispensation to wear Masonic regalia had been obtained by wire from D. G. L.

"The Lodge having been placed in abeyance the Brethren proceeded to the cemetery, at the gate of which they robed, and marched in procession to meet the funeral party at the other gate. The Brethren then carried the coffin to its last resting place, and the burial service of the Church of England was performed by the Rev. M. C. Sanders, M.A., who then withdrew. (It may be mentioned that the Rev. Sanders was himself a Mason and a member of Lodge Himalayan Brotherhood at the time). Thereupon the Masonic service was conducted in a simple, earnest manner by Wor. Brother R. Watson, and the scroll and white gloves were deposited on the coffin, and the remains of Brother DeCosta left to the care of T. G. A. O. T. U.

"The Brethren then returned to the Lodge. The Lodge was closed in peace and harmony at 11-5 a.m."

Brother DeCosta was never a member of our Lodge.

1900. 9th April. Wor. Brother Craigie then referred to a meeting of P. Ms. who had assembled on 15th March to consider the question of expenditure to which Masters in the past had been put, and submitted the following resolutions, which, after a full discussion. were either accepted or negatived, as noted below :—

" As regards the installation banquet

(a) that the number of official guests be limited to H. H. the Lieut -Governor, I I. E. the Commander-in-Chief, and one staff officer each, the German Consul, and the two leading Press-men in Simla, or a total of 7.   *Carried*

(*b*) That dinner tickets for members of the Lodge and for Masonic guests be still Rs. 10, tickets for non-Masonic guests to be Rs. 12.   *Carried.*

(*c*) That a member of the Lodge be asked each year to undertake the duties of Honorary Secretary and Steward of the Banquet Committee, and that no assistant steward, or other member working on the Committee, have power to incur any expenditure without the written authority of the Honorary Secretary.   *Carried.*

" As regards the Lodge—A proposal to restrict the issue of refreshments, and make the Lodge Steward personally responsible that expenditure was kept within the contributions month by month, was negatived."

13th August,—" Wor. Brother Watson proposed, and the W. M. seconded, that the thanks of the Lodge be tendered to Brother the Most Rev. Bishop Welldon, Pro. G. Chaplain for Middlesex, for his kindness is delivering his recent Masonic lecture." His Lordship was elected an honorary member of the Lodge at this meeting, and his name is still borne on the rolls as such. The lecture was subsequently printed and many copies were sold among the Brethren.

At this meeting it was also decided " that a jewel be presented to Wor. Brother the Hon. General Sir E. H. H. Collen in consideration of his long connection with, and the good work performed by him for, the Lodge," and at the meeting of 10th December it was resolved " that a vote of thanks be sent to Lady Collen for her valuable assistance in connection with the funds of the P. M. I." General Sir Edwin Collen joined the Lodge in October 1888, and was Wor. Master in 1892-93. He was frequently in Lodge, and ever took the most lively interest in its welfare until his retirement from the service in 1900. He resigned the Lodge in December 1907, and was then elected an Hon. Member.

1901. 13th May.—" Wor Bro. Lieut.-Colonel Shearer, D.S.O., I.M.S., proposed, seconded by Wor. Brother Alves, that a standing rule be made that in future any public masonic functions (except such as concern the Craft Lodge only, *e.g.*, the installation of the W.M.) shall be given not in the name of Lodge Himalayan Brotherhood only, but of the Masonic fraternity of Simla, and the heads of every Masonic body in Simla, shall be invited to co-operate. After a lengthy discussion on this proposal, in which Wor. Brothers Shearer, Alves, Watson, Cullin, and Brother Rudolf took part, Brother Lt.-Col. C. P. Lukis proposed as an amendment thereto, which was seconded by Brother Sparkes, that the masonic ball be held as heretofore under the banner of Lodge Himalayan Brotherhood, but that the principals of other masonic bodies in Simla be invited to assist. Wor. Brother Carson then proposed, and Wor. Brother the Rev. M. C. Sanders seconded, as a further amendment that no alteration be made in the arrangements that have been in force for a number of years past." This last amendment was then put to the Lodge, and carried.

1902. 10th February. – "Wor. Brother Carson referred to the many gifts the W. M. (Lieut.-Colonel Lukis) had made to the Lodge during his occupancy of the Eastern Chair. He wished to bring to the notice of the members his most recent gift in having had, at his own expense, the roof of the Lodge room so tastefully repainted, Wor. Brother Carson then proposed, and Wor. Brother Watson seconded, a most cordial vote of thanks to the W. M. for having so beautified the Lodge room. Carried with acclamation.

6th October. – An emergent meeting was held "to present to Wor. Brother Major W. P. Carson a piece of silver plate as an acknowledgment of the great services which he has rendered to this Lodge and to the craft generally during the many years he has been in Simla." The following extracts are taken from the minutes of this meeting:—

"The W. M. (Wor. Brother Watson was in the chair in the absence of the W. M., Wor. Brother J. B. D'Silva) * * * * spoke as to the period of his membership in Lodge Himalayan Brotherhood extending over 18 years, he having joined us from Madras, where he had been doing great good service for the craft, and where, as we know, they had been duly appreciated. The W. M. went on to remark that when Wor Brother Carson joined us the Lodge was working in "Benmore," and the Town Hall was in course of construction. At this time it became incumbent on us to find new quarters, and in the interval between quitting "Benmore" and finally setting down in our present quarters in the Town Hall. Wor. Brother Carson arranged for the meetings of the Lodge to be held in his own house. To him was due the credit of our having accommodation in the Town Hall, as also for the fittings still in our Lodge room ; and further it was mainly due to his exertions that our annual installation banquet had developed into so important a masonic and social event, and that the masonic ball, unknown as an annual fixture until his arrival, had become one of the principal entertainments of the Simla season. But all these facts were subordinate in their importance to the very excellent example he had set as a Mason, and particularly his ability when presiding in the Lodge. In fact, the W. M. went on to remark, there was no more capable, zealous, and energetic Mason in the whole of India. The W. M. concluded by remarking on the extreme regret we felt at losing the Wor. Brother, and then requested R. W. Bro. General Sir A. P. Palmer (the D.G.M.) to make the presentation.

" R. W. Bro. His Excellency General Sir A. P. Palmer said he had very little to add to what the W. M. had said. He remarked that he had always seen in Wor. Brother Carson the moving spirit of the craft in Simla. He thought indeed that he had been a pillar to the craft and that the great name Lodge Himalayan Brotherhood had gained was due in a large measure to the Wor. Brother. It had aways been a pleasure to him and visiting Brethren to listen when lectures were given and degrees conferred by Wor. Bro. Carson".

The inscription on the plate was. " - Presented to Wor. Bro. W. P. Carson by the members of Lodge Himalayan Brotherhood No. 459 E. C., on the occasion of his leaving Simla, as a token of their high esteem, and in recognition of the services he has rendered to Freemasonry during the many years he has been amongst them. 6th October 1902."

Wor. Brother Carson joined the Lodge on 12th May 1884. He resigned on 31st December 1886, but rejoined in April 1888 and thereafter remained a member until his death, which took place in Bedford, England, on the 21st November 1905, just about three years after leaving Simla. He was a most energetic, active member, and untiring in his interest in, and work for, the Lodge and the Craft, as evidenced from the fact that he was twice W. M. (1885 and 1888). Treasurer in 1886, 1894-1897, 1900 and 1901, and P. M. I. Steward in 1885, 1890, 1892, 1895, 1896, 1897 and 1901. When announcing his death to the Lodge at the meeting of 11th December 1905, Wor. Brother Watson said — " It is about 20 years since Wor. Brother Carson first came to Simla, and was at once recognised as a very great acquisition to the fraternity in this part of the country. He promptly joined Lodge Himalayan Brotherhood, and it was not long before the number of members upon our roll was more than doubled, mainly through his instrumentality. He occupied the Eastern chair of the Lodge for two years with great success and unusual ability. At the time when we were actually without accommodation for our meetings Wor. Bro. Carson placed a portion of his residence at the disposal of the Lodge, and it was largely due to his foresight and influence that we found an asylum in the Town Hall (in 1886), where we have been ever since. He was at all times, both inside the Lodge and outside in connection with our important social functions, a tower of strength to those who sought, and never sought in vain, the advice and personal assistance which he was ever ready to afford. Wor. Brother Carson's talents were well known to D.G.L., and they were recognised by the bestowal upon him of the important office of D.D.G.M."

The Lodge gave a sum of Rs. 300 towards the tombstone erected to Wor. Brother Carson's memory in the cemetery at Bedford.

1903. The idea of having another Lodge in Simla, which was discussed so far back as 1869, and frequently hinted at by some Brethren in more recent years, was carried out this year by the founding of the "Kitchener" Lodge.

The petition for the founding of the Lodge was signed by myself and my two wardens (Major A. W. Warden and Major R.F. Rennick) some time in June 1903 at the request of Wor. Brother Col. J. Shearer an old member of our Lodge and P. D. G. J. W. Unfortunately for ourselves it struck none of us in the peculiar circumstances of the case that we should first have obtained, if possible, the approval of the Lodge to our action, and consequently when the matter came before them at the meeting of the 13th July a good deal was said about the irregularity of our procedure. It was very evident that many members of the old Lodge were greatly opposed to the opening of a new one, but the founders of the new Lodge were clearly determined to carry their project through whether Lodge H. B. gave their consent or not, and I am quite certain that if we had not signed the petition the necessary recommendation would have been obtained elsewhere. It is satisfactory to note now that when "Kitchener" Lodge was actually opened (I had the honour of acting as S. W. at the ceremony) some time in the following October all differences were speedily forgotten, and time has proved that the "Kitchener" Lodge supplied a want in Simla, and so far from in any way injuring Lodge Himalayan Brotherhood, it has exercised an influence for good. The two Lodges are to-day working side by side in the greatest unanimity.

With the minutes of the 14th September is recorded an important letter from the Grand Secretary, dated 22nd April 1903, pointing out the impropriety of "publishing the proceedings of Lodges without proper authority, and of publishing things which it is improper for Masons to publish".

12th October. – "Bro. S. W. proposed that a Brother be got to go through all the minute books of the Lodge and extract and print all important minutes, as he (the proposer) thought that they would form a very valuable record, and be of interest to the Brethren. He would be willing to contribute Rs. 50 towards the expenses involved by his proposal. Wor. Bro. J. B. D'Silva, in sounding the proposal, stated that he also would be willing to contribute towards the cost. Wor. Bro. Leigh undertook to do the work provided the Lodge acquiesced. The proposal was then put and carried unanimously". There is nothing to show that this very desirable work was ever taken in hand. Personally I do not think it was, which is much to be regretted because Wor. Bro. Leigh was eminently fitted for it. Probably want of time and ill health made it impossible for him to undertake such a heavy task. In addition to his ordinary avocations Wor. Bro. Leigh accepted Mastership of the

Lodge in 1904, next year as I.P.M. he was also pretty well occupied while in 1906 he was in failing health for many months before his lamented death on 28th July of that year.

The balance credit this year from the ball (Rs, 150) was given as a donation in the name of the S. W. to the P. M. I., thus constituting the S. W. of the Lodge for the time being a life governor of the Institution.

1904. It is worth noticing that at the installation this year of Wor. Bro. Leigh both the Viceroy and Commander-in-Chief were present throughout the proceedings. The former was R. Wor. Bro. H. E. Baron Ampthill, D. G. M. of Madras, and the latter R. W. Bro. H. E Lord Kitchener of Khartoum, D. G. M. of the Punjab. Lord Ampthill was elected honorary member of the Lodge on 11th July, and we still have the honour of bearing his Lordship's name on our rolls. Lord Kitchener is a member of the Lodge.

For the first time after many years the Brethren attended Divine service on the Sunday beginning Masonic week, 11th September, and the custom has now become an annual one and will always be associated in our minds with Wor. Bro. Leigh who orginated it. The subscription after the service is usually given to the Mayo Orphanage, a local institution for orphan girls.

1905. 29th May.—A circular was read from D. G. L. inviting Lodges to consider measures to be taken for the alleviation of the many sad cases of loss and injury suffered by our Masonic Brethren in the Dharamsala earthquake of the 4th April 1905. The Wor Master proposed the grant of Rs. 100 from St. John's Box and Rs. 150 from Lodge funds (increased on an amendment to Rs 200) towards the funds being collected by D. G. L., and a further sum of Rs. 185 was promised on the spot by the Brethren present at the meeting. The total amount sent to D. G. L. in answer to their appeal was Rs. 695-14.

A question arose as to whether a Past Master of a foreign constitution could carry his rank with him in a Lodge under the English constitution, and on referring the point to D. G. L., we were supplied with a copy of their Circular No. 8 of 1st June 1894, containing a ruling by G. L. " that the W. M. or P. M. of a Lodge under the Scotch constitution is not at liberty to occupy the Master's chair in a Lodge under the English constitution, or to confer degrees in such a Lodge." D. G. L. added that this also applied to a Master or P. M. under the Irish constitution.

10th July.—A vote of thanks was recorded to "Brother Faletti for his generosity in presenting the Lodge with crockery and cutlery."

I have been asked to say something with reference to our Lodge Summons. The present practice of inserting a copy of the Summons in our Minute Book is of comparatively recent date it is therefore not possible to say what form our first printed Summons took. In the early days the W. M. called his meetings when he liked and when he had business to transact and the Summons calling the Meeting was sent round by peon book. The earliest Summons we can trace today is one for April 1873 which is here reproduced.

The simple Summons was the one in use down to 1891 when the typically Masonic style shown in Plate 2 was introduced. It was replaced—very regretably I think—in 1893 by a badly printed reproduction of the earlier type until in 1905 a form, from which our present Summons has gradually evolved, came into use.

13th August.—The W. M., in announcing Wor. Bro. Leigh's death, said, "I need not here dilate upon the details of his public career, or yet of his private life. Let it suffice to say that he was as honoured in the one as he was loved in the other. It is more to his Masonic career that I would commend the attention of this Lodge. I do not think I am betraying his confidence—for indeed most of you are already aware of it – when I say that the late Wor. Bro. Leigh owed much in his youth to the masonic fraternity and throughout his own masonic career he never allowed himself to forget it, by striving to repay what he considered to be a life-long debt to the order. Of how he paid it back a hundredfold may be learned in part from a perusal of the pages of the past 30 years of the history of Freemasonry in the Punjab, and perhaps more particularly of the minutes of this Lodge. It can but be an imperfect record of the manifold acts of kindness and secret benevolence. When his right hand was used in the cause of charity and his left hand knew it not, often too, when he could but ill afford it, must ever remain hidden from our ken ; but we know he will find his deeds recorded by the pencil of the Almighty Architect to whom he has now gone to render his last account." A stone is to be erected in the Simla cemetery to his memory at the expense of Lodge Himalayan Brotherhood, the R, A. Chapter "Dalhousie" and Chapter "Rose Croix" combined.

1907. In this year, Wor. Bro. Longridge was instrumental in effecting a reciprocation between us and Lodge "Humility with Fortitude" No. 229. E. C. Calcutta. By this arrangement a brother of either lodge had the privilege of becoming a temporary member of the other during his stay in Simla or Calcutta, as the case may be, without proposal or balloting and without payment of the usual joining fees.

12th August.—The Lodge unanimously approved of the proposal of the W. M. that the Masters, Past Masters, and officers of the "Kitchener" Lodge be appointed honorary members of Lodge "Himalayan Brotherhood," and the W. M. announced at the following meeting on 9th September that the "Kitchener" Lodge had paid us a similar compliment.

At this meeting, the following resolution was recorded :—

"This Lodge having been informed that certain Brethren had obtained a charter under the Scottish constitution for a new Lodge and are about to be duly formed, express their good wishes for the welfare of the new Lodge." The Lodge "Elysium" was duly founded shortly after.

1908. On the 20th January a letter was addressed to the Hony. Secy. P. M. I. that rule 22 (d) of the rules of the P. M. I. as at present constituted, should be expunged on the ground "that such a clause constitutes the P. M. I. in practice nothing more nor less than an insurance society," and the views of the Secretary were invited on the point.

The Secretary, P. M. I., replied in letter No. 60, dated 20th February 1908 as follows:—

"The Trustees of the P. M. I. have carefully considered the suggestion contained in your letter of the 20th January, namely, that Rule 22 (d) should be annulled.

"The rule in question provides in effect, that "no child shall be eligible as a candidate for admission to the foundation unless the father shall have   *   *   *   contributed a sum at least equal to Rs. 12 per annum, to the P. M. I., for the period during which he was a subscribing member of a Lodge; provided that for any sufficient reason this condition may be waived".

"The Trustees understand you to represent that this rule is regarded by your Lodge as open to objection on the ground that it introduces into the dispensation of masonic charity in the Punjab an element of insurance, contrary to the principles of the Craft which inculcate open-heartedness towards all poor and distressed masons.

"In the sense that Freemasonry is not operative but speculative the Trustees are not disposed to deny that something like an element of insurance may be discerned in the spirit of Rule 22 (d). But it is a nominal, not a material element.

"The essence of all insurances, whether secular or symbolic, is that men make present provision for future needs. In the case of ordinary insurance societies such provision is monetary and adquate, that is to say there is a scientifically calculated relation between the amount of the fees to be paid in and the amount of the benefits to be drawn out.

"In the case of the P. M. I. it cannot be said that there is any sort of commercial ratio between the minimum qualifying contribution, which is a total annual sum of Rs. 12 (vide rule 22 (b) in conjunction with rule 22 (d) and the maximum obtainable benefits which may comprehend the maintenance of as many as four or even six young children up to the age of 18 years at a cost per child of Rs. 300 per annum or an aggregate expenditure of from Rs. 10,000 to Rs. 20,000.

"Obviously no insurance company in the world would offer such terms or could long remain solvent if it did. But there is undoubtedly a moral relation between the two sides of this compact. In the sense of Holy Writ "Remember now they Creator in the days of thy youth while the evil days come not" every candidate for our order is taught by one of the most impressive of all masonic ceremonies that the distinguishing characteristic of a Freemason's heart is charity, and if notwithstanding this experience, a mason refrains from supporting, even to the humble extent of Re 1 a month, the only masonic charitable institution in the Punjab, the Trustees cannot think that his claims upon the benevolence of the P.M.I. ought to be treated as equal with the claims of Masons who have been regular and perhaps generous contributors.

"It will be observed that there is no question of altogether excluding a non-subscriber from the benefits of the P.M.I. The object of rule 22 (d) is merely to secure that masons who have done their duty to the fund shall not in their day of distress have their claims to relief imperilled by competition with masons who have not. In practice the attitude of the fund towards non-subscribers has always been as considerate as the available resources permit. That the resources are not more ample is due to the lamentable fact that very many masons in the Puujab who could well afford to help this extremely deserving charity steadily refuse to open their purse strings".

The above reply was considered by both ourselves and the "Kitchener" Lodge, with whom we were in perfect accord, and on the 26th May we sent the following rejoinder : —

"With reference to the correspondence ending with your lette No. 60, dated 20th February 1908, regarding Rule No. 22 (d) of the Rules of the P.M.I., we are directed to communicate to you the following extracts from the minutes of the Regular meeting of the "Kitchener" Lodge No. 2998-E.C. held on Monday the 2nd March 1908:—

The Lodge having considered the reply of the Trustees of the P.M.I. to the representation made conjointly with Lodge "Himalayan Brotherhood" No. 459-E.C. regarding the deletion of clause (d) of rule 22 of the Rules of the P. M. I., were unanimous in deprecating the continuance of the rule as it now stands The Lodge are not convinced by the arguments used by the Trustees in support of the rule and still remain of opinion that the rule and these arguments are not consistent with the principles on which our order is founded. It was therefore, unanimously resolved that the Trustees be requested to circulate to all Lodges in the Punjab and to all other subscribers to the Institution, being Freemasons, the whole of the correspondence *in extenso* (including this letter) which has passed between the Trustees and this Lodge on this subject, with a view to obtaining a vote from the whole masonic fraternity of the Punjab as to whether this rule should be allowed to stand or be expunged.

"The above resolution and the draft of this letter were read and discussed at two separate regular meetings of Lodge Himalayan Brotherhood No. 459-E.C., and a majority of that lodge agreed to the adoption of the above resolution.

"We are further directed to remark that the gist of the arguments used by you in the above quoted letters appears to be contained in the following clause: —

'The object of Rule 22 (d) is merely to secure that masons, who have done their duty to the fund, should not in their day of distress have their claim to relief imperilled by competition with masons who have not.'

"With reference to this statement it seems to us that, according to the views of the Trustees, a Brother, who paid the minimum of Rs. 12 per annum to the P. M. I. but remained in arrears with respect to lodge dues, would have a greater claim than one who paid his lodge dues regularly but was unable to increase his masonic liabilities.

"We cannot admit the principle that he who, from his abundance should have subscribed to the funds of the P. M. I. should have any more secure right to the advantages of the Institution than he who, in his poverty, has been unable to do so. To our minds the claim of the latter upon the beneficence of the fraternity is infinitely more worthy of attention than that of the former.

"To our minds, in the best interests of Freemasonry, that any impression should be allowed to get abroad of our charity being purchasable by the payment of any series of small or large subscriptions, or that such payment should establish any prescriptive right or claim in competition with others to our benevolence, is most undesirable.

"The sheet anchor of Freemasonry is Charity and the distribution of our charity should be uninfluenced by any other consideration than the necessities of each case.

"We are further of opinion that all cases duly nominated by the lodges or individuals entitled to make a nomination, whether the father was a subscriber or not should be submitted with full particulars and voting papers by the Trustees to the whole body of entitled voters for election, and that their decision should be final.

"The responsibility of the Trustees would thus be much reduced and would be confined to deciding annually as to how many individuals it would be possible, from the funds available, to give assistance.

"It might be urged against this suggestion that such a practice would lead to canvassing for votes. We are of opinion that such canvassing would not be an unmixed evil. We believe that it would lead to a decided stirring-up of general interest in the institution, which would in our opinion, result in nothing but good."

The Secretary to the P. M. I. replied in letter No. 153 of 20th June 1908 that his letter of 20th February 1908 was merely intended to express the views of the Trustees present at the meeting at which our letter of 20th January 1908 was considered, and that the Trustees had no power to alter the regulations which could only be effected in the manner laid down in the rules. He then added "In this connection the Trustees would point out that the regulations have been recently revised by a committee appointed by the governing board whose report. will be submitted to a meeting of the board to be held on 23rd instant In view, however, of the resoluations of Lodges "Kitchener" and "Himalayan Brotherhood" the Trustees propose to ask the board to postpone consideration of the amended regulations so as to enable your lodge to put forward the proposal contained in your letter."

In the revised regulations, referred to above, the clause we had originally objected to is contained in para. 18 which is quoted below in full—

"18. All children of deceased Freemasons, who are left wholly destitute or whose relations or friends (if any) are unable wholly to maintain and educate them, or whose income from Government or other Funds, or property is insufficient wholly to maintain and educate them; and the children of Freemasons who are themselves in indigent circumstances, and wholly or partially unable to maintain and educate their children, shall be eligible as candidates for admission to the Foundation, without distinction of race or religion. Provided that no child shall be eligible as candidate for admission to the foundation unless the father shall have—

(a) Attained to the degree of Master Mason.

(b) Paid not less than one year's subscription to a Craft lodge within the Punjab Masonic District;

(c) Continued during residence in the District, to be a subscribing member of a Craft Lodge within the Punjab Masonic District, or in the case of a Serving Brother, or other member exempt from subscription under the By-laws of his Lodge, regularly contributed to the Fund of Benevolence;

(d) Contributed a sum at least equal to Rs. 12 per annum to the P. M. I. for the period during which he has been a subscribing member of such Lodge;

Provided further that the Trustees may, for any sufficient reason to be declared by them in writing and subject to the confirmation of the Board, declare any child of a Mason who has not complied with the requirements of sub-clauses (c) and (d) (or either of them) of this clause, eligible as a candidate for admission to the Foundation."

In reviewing these revised regulations the "Kitchener" Lodge‘ among other recommendations, suggested that the whole of the provisos to rule 18 which commenced the second para. of the rule beginning "provided that no child, &c.", to the end of the article, be expunged, and although this went somewhat beyond our original proposal we concurred.

It unfortunately happened, however, that when this amendment was finally put to the vote at a meeting of the governing board of the P. M. I. on the 16th January 1909 it was lost because it was not supported by a majority of two-thirds of those *actually present* at the meeting as required by rule.

Matters therefore remain *in statu quo* for the present. It is interesting to note that these very restrictions were objected to by this Lodge twenty years ago when Wor. Bro. English in a letter of protest on other points in the P. M. I. rules, which had just then been revised, wrote in this connection as follows :—

"The provisions in regulation—imposing certain conditions as essential to eligibility of children for the benefits of the institution, are considered to be unmasonic; admitting that between two brethren whose claims are otherwise equal, consideration should be paid to any marked difference in progress in, and zeal for, the tenets of the Craft, it nevertheless appears to this Lodge to be contrary to the spirit of the Order that the children of Entered Apprentices and Fellowcraftsmen should be expressly debarred, and that they (together with the children of masons of all degrees who die before the completion of three years* subscription to a lodge in the Province) should be absolutely excluded from the benefits of the Institution." (Letter dated 23rd August 1889).

*Now one year.
E.O.W.

24th August.—At the inspection of the Lodge this year the Inspecting Officer, Colonel Pease, D. G. S. W. made the following remarks in the course of his address in Lodge—"that he was happy to say after a careful examination of the books, and records, that everything was in perfect order and that the Lodge had made good progress since its last inspection nearly four years ago. The number of members had increased notwithstanding a large number of resignations, and the financial position of the Lodge today was excellent and on a sound basis."

There is nothing further of importance to record up to the close of the year 1908 to which date my labours have extended and these extracts may now be appropriately concluded with a few remarks about the Tyler.

The office of Tyler is not one sought after and in our long history there are frequent allusions to the difficulty of finding a suitable person willing to fill the appointment. With few exceptions the office was an annual one, but in 1895 we were fortunate in our selection of Bro. Arthur Morriss who served us faithfully as Tyler without a break till the early part of 1906 when he left Simla. The Lodge's appreciation of his services is recorded in the minutes of 14th May 1906 when it was also decided to present him with a Tyler's jewel, the first presentation of the kind ever made in our Lodge. Poor Morris did not wear his jewel long, for I think, he died in the winter of 1907-08.

Our Tyler now is Bro. B. E. French who was almost unanimously elected in May 1907, and it is a curious coincidence that our history of over 70 years should begin and end with the name of French—father and son.

C. J. French was our first initiate and was proposed as a candidate on the night this Lodge was founded; he died in 1885, six years before his son was initiated in our Lodge.

In continuing the Record of the Lodge from the end of 1908 up to which time the late Wor. Bro. Wilsey brought his "Extracts from the Minutes", one is struck with the even and almost uneventful progress of the Lodge. During the period we are about to consider seventeen Brethren have in succession ruled the Lodge, but such has been the loyal and faithful support which has been accorded to each that the Minutes show little but proof of sound and steady Masonic work at all times conducted with that Peace, Love, and Harmony which is now so characteristic and traditional. The Lodge has steadily maintained its membership, and thanks to the care and conscientious zeal of our Masters, the Accounts have never been a cause of real anxiety.

1910. The first item to note is a proposal to hold a Combined Installation Banquet of our Lodge with Lodge "Kitchener". This idea, which would have been productive of much fraternal fellowship between the two Lodges was not discussed as the latter Lodge was not prepared to consider it. The death of our most Gracious Majesty King Edward VIIth, our King Emperor and Defender of the Craft is reported, and the Lodge was placed in mourning for six months.

At the July meeting of this year it was passed unanimously that the Lodge which had for many years past been holding two Regular Meetings per month should now hold only one, and at the October Meeting it was resolved that "as the W. M., I. P. M., both Wardens and many of the P. Ms. would be absent from Simla that the Lodge should close from December to February inclusive."

1911. D. G. L. Circular asking for support in the suggestion that 8 annas per quarter be levied on each member in the District, in order to form a Building Fund for the new District Grand Lodge Hall in Lahore, was discussed. On the proposition of Wor. Bro. Lloyd it was decided to express our inability to support the levy owing to our heavy liabilities in connection with our own Temple. Wor. Bro. Faletti vainly tried to point out what was obviously the duty of the Lodge by an amendment that "as the senior Lodge in the District, it should be our duty to cheerfully accept the proposal and set a good example to the other Lodges,"

Wor. Bro. Lloyd's proposition was carried, but the need for a more suitable home for Punjab Masonry was so pressing that we had to fall in line with the other Lodges in the District in supporting what is now a quarterly levy of 0-8-0 to the Building Fund.

Bro. Col. E.W. Maconchy assumed the office of Master this year, and at his first meeting in July addressed the Lodge in terms of justifiable severity on the matter of outstanding dues. With reference to certain offenders he informed the Lodge that letters had been sent saying "they are formally summoned to appear in Lodge at the regular meeting in August to show cause why they should not be excluded under para 210 of the Constitution. They will also be told that *part payment* of their dues will not be accepted, as this is simply an evasion which constantly goes on, they must pay in full and give me an assurance of regular payment in future or resign, the alternative being Exclusion.".

On the recommendation of the Permanent Committee, the Coupon-System of payment for Bar refreshments was tried for a year. It proved such a failure, however, that it was very soon discontinued and will not be tried again I imagine.

1912. At the January meeting "The Antient Charges were read in an impressive manner by the Wor. Master" (Wor Bro. R. Watson Acting Master). The model Tripod and Perfect Ashlar for use on the S. W's. Pedestal, presented by Wor. Bro. Maconchy, were received and suitably acknowleged.

1913. At the July meeting Wor. Bro. Capt. W. Alves was unanimously elected an Honorary Member "in consideration of his Masonic services and long association with Lodge Himalayan Brother-hood ".

Gauntlets for the W. M. and Wardens were for the first time purchased.

1914. A meeting which deserves to be recorded as showing in a remarkable manner the Universality of Masonry was that held on June 14th, when Wor. Bro. R. E. Holland, W. M. initiated into Freemasonry H. H. The Maharaja of Patiala, and afterwards raised to the Degree of M. M. Bro. Ivan Chen, Chinese Plenipotentiary.

In August a Petition is brought before the Lodge for the founding of another Craft Lodge in Simla. The Petition which was signed by the following 23 brethren, many of whom were members of our Lodge, was brought forward in the interests of the Indian Masonic Community, and was approved of and signed in open Lodge by the Master and his Wardens.

Wr. Bro. E.O.W. Wilsey (W.M.)	Bro. H.H. The Maharaja of Patiala.
„ E. W. Baker (S.W.)	„ Perushottan Sinha.
„ Radha Kishan.	„ E. S. Baillie.
„ W. F. Stowell.	„ R. T. Waugh.
„ John Tinson	„ H. R. Phelps.
„ W. T. McCarthy.	„ W. Cotton.
„ F. von Goldstein.	„ C. B. Maiden.
„ H. Barsby.	„ P. C. Mukkerjee.
Bro. Ram Ratan Puri (J.W.)	„ I. D. Puri.
„ D. H. M. Framjee.	„ Ramji Das.
„ G. K. Roy.	„ B. E. Stephens.

Bro. G. W. B. Widger.

It resulted in the formation of Lodge "Prospect" No. 3742-E.C., which was consecrated on May 5th 1915 and which, by providing an outlet for the keen Masonic aspirations of our Indian Brethren in Simla, has filled a long felt want.

The immediate affect of the Great War is seen by an Appeal from the St. John's Ambulance Association for a donation to their War Funds to which a sum of Rs. 500 was cheerfully given.

At the October Meeting of this year, a proposal was made that the Lodge by placed in recess for the Winter Months. This was no doubt considered a retrograde step and the proposal was dropped.

1915. At the November Meeting, a Petition for the formation of a Craft Lodge in Patiala and signed by the following brethren was presented to the Lodge for Recommendation :—

H. H. The Maharaja of Patiala (W M.)	F. von Goldstein.
	R. H, Crump, I.C.S.
H. H. The Maharaj Rana of Dholpur (S.W.)	Gen. Gurnam Singh.
	Raja Ranbir Singh.
H. H. The Maharaja of Jind.	Kanvar Shamsher Bahadur Singh.
D. Johnston.	Kalifa Hamid Hussain.
Surg.-Gen. Sir Pardy Lukis.	Sardar Bhagwan Singh
John Tinson.	Major K. M. Mistri.
C. H. Gwynn.	Sardar Shamsher Singh.

Col. C. H. James.

Lt.-Col. A. C. Elliot (J.W.)

Radha Krishna.

Aziz-ud-din Ahmed.

R. E. Holland I.C.S.

C. J. Prior.

O. C. Sullivan.

A. W. Dyer.

Tika Raghu Nath Singh.

W, A. Higgins.

Dinshaw Framji.

G. Russell.

Dr. Behari Lal Dingra.

Sardar Tara Charan.

C. W. Bowles.

Sardar Gobindra Singh

Sardar Gokal Chand.

Kour Chitter Singh.

Sardar Sachit Singh.

Capt. Kishan Singh.

J. M. Des Roches.

H. Barsby.

A. E. Tansey.

C. Imrie.

Juggat Nath Seth.

The Petition was approved of and signed in open Lodge by the Worshipful Master (Wor. Bro. C. J. Prior) and Wardens, and shortly afterwards on April 15th 1916, Lodge "Phulkian" was consecrated, Wor. Bro. H. H. The Maharaja of Patiala being the first Master.

1916. A third Petition was this year presented, this time for the formation of another Craft Lodge in Delhi to which Petition the recommendation of the Lodge was also accorded, and the Worshipful Master in the Chair (Wor. Bro. R. Watson) and the Wardens duly signed it in open Lodge.

The Petition was signed by the following Wor. Brethren and Brethren, the majority of whom will be recognised as members of our Lodge.

Wor. Bro. H. F. Cleveland (W.M)

" " R. Heard.

" " L. P. More.

" " John Tinson.

" " C. J. Knowles.

" " E. W. Baker.

" " R. A. Needham.

" " S. M. Rice.

" " H. Barsby.

" " P. Sinha.

Bro. H. G. Russell (S.W)

" F. K. Graves (J.W)

" B. E. French.

" R. R. Puri.

" B. R. Moberly.

" D. H. M. Framjee.

" P. C. Mukherjee.

" C. W. F. Melville.

" A. I. Sleigh.

The Petition of the Brethren being granted by Grand Lodge, Lodge "Raisina" No. 3819 E. C. was consecrated on January 9th 1918, under the Hiram of Wor. Bro. Col. H. F. Cleveland as First Master.

Thus our Lodge continues, as it did so signally in the early days of it's life, to encourage the extention of the benefits of the Craft of Masonry in the Punjab.

At the October meeting of this year, the melancholy news of the death of Wor. Bro. Lt. Col. J. A. Longridge while on Active Service in France reached us. The Minutes record that "The Worshipful Master gave a brief sketch of the Masonic services of the late Wor. Bro. Col. J. A. Longridge, and brought specially to notice the Charity with which his name would ever be affectionately associated, viz., The Simla Masonic Hospital-Bed Fund, which he was instrumental in founding and in which he took the very greatest interest".

1917. An Appeal from the Indian Branch, Joint War Committee of the Order of St. John of Jerusalem and the British Red Cross Committee, was immediately met by the vote of Rs 500/-.

Notwithstanding the calls on the Charity on all consequental on the Great War, it is worthy of note that Wor. Bro. L. P. More, our P. M. I. Steward during this year, made a record Collection on behalf of this Charity of Rs. 3750/- Rs. 2250/4 being devoted to the Children's Foundation and Rs 1499/12 to the Widows' Foundation.

Masonry in the Punjab, and this Lodge in particular, suffered a great loss in the death of Wor. Bro. Genl. Sir Pardy Lukis. In announcing the death to the Lodge at the November meeting, the Worshipful Master, Wor. Bro. C. J. Knowles said:—

> "He was amongst us for many years and was twice our Master. He never forgot and was always proud to acknowledge the fact that this was his Mother Lodge, and in it was laid the foundations of that distinguished Masonic career, the close of which it is our painful duty to record. Beloved and respected by all who knew him, by his untimely death the Lodge loses a true friend and genial companion, and the Brotherhood in general a perfect Mason and a wise counsellor".

Wor. Bro. Lukis, who was at the time of his death D. D. G. Master and S. G. Deacon of England, was indeed "a Pillar in Freemasonry" and was buried with full Masonic honours, numbers of his brethren paying their last sad tribute of respect to departed merit

1919. In this year and the next was seen the effect of the great wave of Masonic activity which was apparent in all parts of the English Constitution, no fewer than 20 meetings being held in 1919 and 20 in 1920.

Wor. Bro. G. Reeves-Brown was installed in June, and at this meeting it was proposed and seconded that in consideration of the great services rendered to the Lodge by Wor. Bro. Wilsey, who had that evening laid done the pen of the Secretaryship of the Lodge after having occupied that office since 1908, and had earned the gratitude of the Lodge for his arduous work in compiling the Lodge History, should be donated a gift of Rs. 2000- either in plate or purse!. Wor. Bro. Wilsey immediately proposed that this proposition be postponed to some future meeting, when the proposal being brought up again he thanked the Lodge for the kind thoughts that had influenced such a proposal, and asked to be allowed to keep the typewriter which he had used for so long.

In July was held a Meeting quite unique in the annals of our Lodge, when a Summons was issued for "an Emergent Meeting at Freemasons Hall, Simla, on Sunday the 27th July 1919 at 12-30 p.m. for the purpose of a Solemn Masonic Thanksgiving on the Conclusion of Peace". Conformable to the Summons, a combined Masonic Service was held with special officers appointed for this Special Occasion. Worshipful Bethren of all Lodges working in Simla accepted office for this Meeting, thereby proving the unity and friendly feeling which is prevalent in this Masonic centre. The List of Officers was as follows:—

Wor. Bro. G. Reeves-Brown	...	Worshipful Master.
,, ,, H. I. Macdonald W. M. Lodge "Elysium"	...	I. P. Master.
,, ,, A. I. Sleigh W. M. "Lodge "Kitchener"	...	Senior Warden.
,, ,, S. V. Haldipur W. M. Lodge "Prospect"	...	Junior Warden.
,, ,, R. Watson	...	Chaplain.
,, ,, J. W. Walker	...	Secretary.
,, ,, J. Tinson	...	Director of Ceremonies.
,, ,, A. Ambrose	...	Assistant Director of Ceremonies.
,, ,, Col. B. R. Moberly	...	Senior Deacon.
,, ,, E. O. Wilsey	...	Junior Deacon.
,, ,, E. B. Higgs		Organist.
,, ,, W. T. McCarthy	...	Inner Guard.
,, ,, Col. R. Heard	...	Steward.
,, ,, Col. R. A. Needham	...	Steward.
,, ,, E. W. Baker	...	Tyler.

The Service was well attended, and the Collection made thereat in aid of The Lord Roberts Homes for Disabled Soldiers and Sailors amounted to Rs. 759-.

It may be noted here that the Charity of the Brethren was again evinced at the Masonic Service in September held this year under our Lodge, when the Collection, which for many years past has been given to

the Mayo Orphanage, amounted to the record total of Rs. 1740-15-3.
At the October meeting following, it was proposed that 250 copies of the
Sermon preached by Wor. Bro. The Revd. A. P. G. Maunsel at this
Divine Service be printed for the brethren, 150 for this Lodge and 100
for Lodge "Elysium".

This year we must note the advent of the Irish Constitution into
Simla, for on St. John's Day in December 1919, "The Donoughmore
Lodge" No. 458 on the Registry of the Grand Lodge of Ireland was
consecrated. The following List of the Founders show that the great
majority were English Masons and members of our Lodge. Lodge
"Donoughmore" working in the closest fraternal amity with its Sister
Constitutions in Simla, has established itself on a firm basis and is now
being well and vigorously worked.

Bro. Major G. C. Fenton R. E. W. M.

Wor. Bro. Col. R. Heard I.M.S. S.W. Wor. Bro. John Tinson J.W.

„	„ ˙ C. H. Gwynn.		„ „	A. J. Lamb.
„	„ H. Barsby.		„ „	Lt. Col. J. C. de K
„	„ R. T. Clarke.			Bruce Kingsmill.
„	„ Arthur Parry.		„ „	C. V. Jefford.
„	„ H. L. O. Garrett.		„ „	G. A. Scales.
„	„ G. A. Ball.		„ „	D. C. Edgar.
„	„ C. V. Smyth.		„ „	W. P. Todhunter.
„	„ Maj. G. I. Davys.		„ „	G. FitzGerald.
„	„ B. A. Bevan Petman.		„ „	S. A. Nunn.
„	„ Lt. A. F. Humphreys.		„ „	G. W. B. Widger.
„	„ H. I. Macdonald.		„ „	C. C. Perry.
„	„ G. Reeves-Brown.		„ „	E. Pay.
„	„ A. E. Higgins.		„ „	W. H. Carruthers.
„	„ W. T. McCarthy.			

1920. At the April meeting 1920, our New Warrant or Warrant
of Confirmation for which a petition had been submitted arrived, and
Wor. Bro. R. Watson after a short review of the history of the Lodge
formally handed it over to the safe-keeping of the Worshipful Master.

At this meeting the P. C.'s recommendation that the Lodge Regalia,
which showed signs of being past all renovation, be replaced by a new set
was accepted, and also that a Secretary's Jewel be presented to Wor.
Bro. J. W. Walker who had taken over the office of Secretary from
Wor. Bro. Wilsey, and who was about to leave Simla "as a memento
of his connection with this Lodge and a token of regard and esteem".

1920.—June 14th Bro. Capt. P.H. Marshall was duly installed as Wor. Master, his first business being that of presenting the Immediate Past Master, Wor. Bro. G. Reeves-Brown, with a Past Master Collar and Jewel which had been presented by ten of his initiates. "as a memeto of their Initiation into Freemasonry at his hands during the year of his Mastership".

Wor. Bro. Marshall's year was one of great activity no fewer than 20 meetings being held and 48 Degrees conferred during his year of Office.

In January, Wor. Bro. Wilsey who had again accepted the Office of Secretary, had again to resign this office and in return for his past services to the Lodge it was carried unanimously that he be asked to accept a Life Membership of the Lodge which he accepted "with grateful thanks". We were, however, again debarred from honoring this old stalwart, this time by D. G. Lodge which informed us, as we should have known, that Life Members were not recognised by the English Constitution, and our resolution made in January had to be regretfully cancelled.

1921.—Wor. Bro. W.G. Dollman took over charge of the Lodge as Master, and on behalf of the members received a donation of an engraved poignard presented by Wor. Bro. G. Reeves-Brown "as a token of his affection for the Lodge".

1922.—At the August Meeting of this year, the Lodge was able to express the appreciation of the past services of Bro. B.E. French by asking him to accept election as a Honorary Member. Bro. French, who was the son of our first initiate so prominent in the first few years of the Lodge life, has like his father always been a keen and true Freemason.

For years he had filled the office of Tyler, had frequently taken on the duties of Acting Secretary, and had always given of his best to the Lodge to which he is so attached, and from a letter received as I write we know how much he still, though unable to bo with uo in Lodge, holds the welfare and prestige of the Lodge very dear to him. The motion to elect him an Honorary Member was carried with acclamation.

Wor. Bro. Dollman presented the Lodge with a Silver Square and Compass as a token of his regard for the Lodge.

After 44 years active Masonic work, Wor. Bro R. Watson, our Senior Past Master, received from our M. W. The Grand Master the high honour of Past Asst. Grand Dir. of Ceremonies of the Grand Lodge of England.

Initiated in 1882, Wor. Bro. Watson has throughout his Masonic career devoted himself to his Mother Lodge with unswerving zeal. With his unrivaled Masonic knowledge and experience, he has been a tower of strength for many years to succeeding Masters, and the news of his elevation to Grand Lodge Rank was received with acclamation by the Lodge recognising it as a well-earned and merited reward.

1923.—The Permanent Committee this year took cognisance of the Appeal in aid of the Masonic Memorial Fund which had reached us from our Grand Master, and recommended that the Lodge endeavour to subscibe 100 guineas to be spread over 5 years. The state of the Lodge finances, combined with the Rent and Donation charges, plus such items as District Grand Lodge dues, etc., have made this proposal almost impossible, and faced with what was a hopeless task, the Wor. Brother who had accepted the Stewardship for this Fund reports little success.

The Lodge put forward a proposal to the District Grand Lodge with reference to the representation of this District among the list of Hall Stone Lodges – – a proposal which aimed at the nomination of the four senior Lodges as Hall Stone Lodges, and the combined resources of the various Lodges in the District being pooled to this end——but it received no support from Headquarters.

In June this year, Bro. Felix von Goldstein was installed as Master. As the eldest son of Wor. Bro. Felix von Goldstein, our Worshipful Master in 1874, he helps to link the Lodge up with our Brethren of former times and, like his father, he has been from his initiation full of energy and zeal, not only in the Craft, but in it's appended Degrees.

At the September meeting three Rulings were recorded which have importance.

1. In the case of a Seconder of a candidate having resigned the Lodge before the ballot is taken, it is necessary for a new proposal Form to be made out with a new Seconder.

2. A duly Installed Master under either of the Constitutions (i.e. Scotch or Irish) shall, if not otherwise disqualified, be entitled to be present at a Board of Installed Masters, and to form one of the quorum; but not to preside or instal a Master, unless requested to do so by the Board. Nor can a visiting Master or Past Master of another Constitution preside in the Lodge he is visiting. This will not interfere with the right of the Master of a Lodge to invite a visiting Master or Past Master of the three Constitutions to perform any ceremony without assuming the Chair.

3. A Ruling from Grand Lodge with reference to the secrecy of the Ballot. "The object of the ballot, as I understand it, is to protect the voter. The secret is his secret, and he cannot be compelled, and

should not even be asked, to say how he voted. But I think and submit to you that a voter is entitled to state voluntarily how he voted, at all events if he does so for the purpose of testing the correctness of a declaration of the result of the ballot. I know of no law or rule of conduct to prevent his doing so. Indeed I do not see how the propriety of such a declaration is to be tested unless he is at liberty to do so".

Wor. Bro. Goldstein, who had taken over the Lodge finances in rather a low ebb, forcibly brought to notice the condition of Lodge funds and the large list of outstandings that were due. Probably over-enthusiasm in the cause of Charity during the past few years had something to do with our poor financial condition, but by observing rigid economy the Lodge was again placed on a fairly sound basis.

1924. - At the Meeting in May, the news of the death of Wor. Bro. Wilsey was conveyed to the Lodge. Initiated in 1898 our late Wor. Bro. Wilsey had during the past 26 years earned the gratitude of the Lodge – his Mother Lodge. Elected Master in 1903, Bro. Wilsey accepted the Office of Secretary in 1908 which office he filled almost to the time of his death.

His wonderful Masonic knowledge was probably unrivalled, 'and was at all times willingly and loyally placed at the disposal of the Worshipful Master. He was early marked out for advancement in District Grand Lodge rank, and was P.D.J. Grand Warden at the time of his death.

He died at the age of 76 full of zeal and enthusiasm for the Craft he loved so well. On the proposal of our next Master, Wor. Bro. H. Brown, a fund was started to provide for the erection of a suitable Tomb stone in memory of our departed brother "to which all Masonic Bodies in Simla be asked to subscribe". The Stone erected by the Fraternity of Simla is a small proof of the affection and esteem which the late Bro. Wilsey enjoyed.

A pleasing duty was performed when at the Sept. meeting, the W.M, Wor. Bro. Harry Brown presented to Wor. Bro R. Watson on behalf of the Lodge a Jewel of the office of Ass. Grand Director of Ceremonies suitably engraved. After referring to the past services of Wor. Bro. Watson to the Craft in general and to this Lodge in particular, he asked him to accept the Jewel "as a token of esteem and deep affection of the members and appreciation of the high honour which had been conferred" on him by the Grand Master.

The activities of the Lodge Steward for the P.M.I. this year resulted in a report that he had been able to make Bros. Junior Warden, Secretary and Inner Guard, Life Governors of the Institution, these with Worshipful Master, Senior Warden and Treasurer making six of the Regular Officers of the Lodge with this qualification.

In this year an important proposal was put forward by Wor. Bro. G. Reeves-Brown which, after having been strongly recommended by the Permanent Committee, was accepted by the Lodge. It was to the effect that the Honorarium of Rs. 45 which had for some years past been paid monthly to the Secretary should cease, and the office become a strictly Honorary one.

In making his proposal Wor. Bro. Reeves-Brown explained the reasons underlying it. Firstly, it was made to place the Lodge finances on a sounder basis, and secondly, to bring the office of Secretary, which for years had, by reason of its high salary, become something akin to that of a Serving Brother's office, back into it's proper position in the rungs of the Lodge offices as a high and important one ranking next to that of the Wardens.

There seemed no reason why Lodge Himalayan Brotherhood with it's keen members should be called upon to pay so highly for the advantage of having a capable Secretary, and the proposal, being put, was carried.

Additional force was added to the necessity for this proposition by the realization of the fact that the old Lodge was not, as in the old days, tilling the soil of the Simla Masonic field alone, but that the advent of four other Craft Lodges on the land, all of which were vigorously plough-ing the ground in all directions. could not but have a retarding effect on the material prosperity of the Lodge calling for retrenchment in all possible directions. Bro. H. Cheetham was our first Honorary Secretary to be followed by Bro. E. Adhemar with the same capable and efficient service.

1925.—At the June meeting of this year Wor. Bro. John Tinson was inducted into the Eastern Chair as Master. Wor Bro. Tinson became our Master already grey in the service of Masonry.

Initiated in 1894 in Lodge "Temperance and Benevolence," Calcutta, Wor. Bro. Tinson has during the past 32 years lived a very active Masonic life. Advanced in "The Chapestone Lodge" of Mark Masters, exalted in Chapter "Holy Zion", and perfected in Chapter "Sandeman", he has always been an ardent supporter of these and other appended degrees in all of which he has earned high Provincial rank. His activi-ties as Founder of seven Lodges and Chapters, and his work in the Punjab District has earned for him the rank of P. D. G. J. Warden and P. D. G. P. "J", and he is one of the few Masons in the East who has been admitted to the 31st Degree.

At his installation meeting Wor. Bro. Tinson was able to report to the Lodge the following appointments to District Grand Lodge Rank of members of the Lodge :—

To be Deputy D. Grand Master, Wor. Bro. R. Watson.

Past District Senior Grand Warden, Wor. Bro. Capt. P. H. Marshall.

Past District Junior Warden, Wor. Bro. John Faletti.

District Grand Standard Bearer, Wor. Bro. Felix von Goldstein.

when it was proposed by Wor. Bro. Faletti that the Lodge mark their high appreciation of the high District Rank attained by Wor. Bro. Watson, by asking him to sit for his photograph, an enlargement of which to be hung in our hall.

At a Permanent Committee Meeting held on August 13th, an important proposal was brought forward by Wor. Bro. Harry Brown and subsequently accepted by the Lodge—"That a valuation of Lodge property be made and the same be correctly recorded. An annual depreciation of 10% to be written off and credited to a new Property Fund to be opened".

In 1915 a similar proposition had been made by the Worshipful Master (Wor Bro. C. J. Prior) who had said that he "drew attention to the fact that although 10% depreciation was written off annually from the assesed value of the Lodge property, the amounts so written off were not set aside, as he thought they should be, for the eventual replacement of property". He then suggested the formation of a Property Fund by the immediate transferring of Rs. 200 from the General Fund. After some discussion, however, "and no formal proposal being made, the matter was dropped".

The effect of this rather short-sighted policy was seen when the Lodge ·in 1921 had to pay over Rs. 1000 from General Funds for the very necessary purchase of a new set of Regalia, a payment which seriously affected the Lodge finances. The Property Fund has now been opened and should in a few years be sufficient to meet any demands.

At the last Permanent Committee, Wor. Bro. Reeves-Brown proposed that in the interests of our Absent Brethren, a yearly Account of the Lodge's work be prepared and printed and issued to all members. It was felt that the sentimental ties which bind an Absent Brother to his Lodge sometimes perhaps were very thin, and it was with the intention of strengthening those ties by the issue of a short account of the activities of the Lodge thus keeping our brethren, not in Simla, in touch with all that happened in their Lodge during the year under review, that the Lodge readily approved of the proposal.

1926. In June Wor. Bro. Tinson installed Bro. G.R. Parker as his successor in the Chair. It is a happy coincidence that the last fact which I have to record is one which so intimately connects this year 1927 with the first year of our Lodge life, for at the April meeting 1927, Wor. Bro. Reeves-Brown presented to the Lodge on behalf of Bro. B. E. French and his family, the Grand Lodge Certificate af his father Bro. C.J. French our first Initiate. Thus does this old Brother live with us today as he did so prominently in the year 1838. His Certificate, the first ever issued "in the Himalaya Mountains", is now framed and will ever link us up with our brethren of pre-Mutiny days, and with this fact recorded my task is completed.

Brethren, the re-editing of the earlier History of our Lodge and the completion of our history down to 1927 has not been an easy task, but if a reading of my effort has for its readers but a small proportion of the pleasurable interest, the compilation has had for me, I shall feel rewarded. We are members of a fine old lodge. It is a Lodge which has in the past done sterling work for Masonry in this conntry, and with the prestige and reputation it has earned and by the love and loyalty it calls for and receives from all who are connected with it, it will continue to occupy with pride the position of The Premier Lodge in the Punjab.

III. The Warrant.

Although the Lodge was founded in May 1838, the Warrant is dated London, 26th March 1839, and was probably not received till late that year. It is curious to note that the receipt of such an important document is nowhere recorded. When the Lodge reopened in 1849, it did so under a fresh Dispensation and in this document itself the officers were authorised "to act as such until a fresh Warrant shall be obtained". No Warrant, however, was ever received. At all events there is no record of the receipt of a new Warrant and the only one we have, and under which we work today, is the warrant of 26th March 1839 now almost undecipherable from damp and other causes, though fortunately the name of the Master, and the date, are quite clear. A copy of the Warrant, or so much of it as can be deciphered, is given below.

L. Augustus,......................

G. M.

To all and every our Right Worshipful and Loving Brethren, We, Prince Augustus Frederick of Brunswick............Duke of Sussex ....Earl of Inverness, Baron of Arklow, Knight of the................. ....Puissant Order of the Garter, K. T. etc.

Grand Master.

Of the Most Antient and Honourable Fraternity of Free and Accepted Masons of England

SEND GREETING.

KNOW YE... ....the sanction of the United Grand Lodge of England............................at the humble petition of our.. right..McDonald, William.................. ....James Brian Clarke............................ John T. Chisholm, J. Taylor and Jacob Hoff............ ......Do hereby Constitute.............................Free and Accepted Masons under the title ....HIMALAYAN BROTHERHOOD.................. the said Lodge to meet at Simla..................and third Wednesday in every month.. .... and raise Freemasons according... ....craft in all Ages... ....and further.. .... trust and confidence reposed in ....do appoint...................... the...............Master shall be.. and according to the laws of............thereby be fully invested......with Barker McDonald to..............................by the said Brethren are or ....have been ....said Lodge do observe perform.........and orders contained in

the Book of Constitutions.   And We do.........you to make
such By-laws for the Government of your Lodge as shall be............
....................Grand Lodge or transmitted by.............Master
members appear proper and necessary..
or by our Deputy Grand Master...........and we do......... ....
of the Craft a copy whereof you are................ ...And We do require
you to cause all............in procedure in your Lodge to be entered
in a book to be kept for the purpose. And you are in no wise to
omit to send to...............The Right Honourable Lord Henry John
Spencer Churchill, our Deputy Grand Master or to the Deputy Grand
Master for the time being, a list of the Members of your Lodge and
the names and designations of all the new initiated.........and Brethren
who shall...............and money payable thereon. It being our Will
and Instruction that this our WARRANT of CONSTITUTION
shall continue in force so long as... ....will conform to the laws
and Regulations of... ....
our Grand Lodge
And....... ....the said Robert Barker......... ......of these present

GIVEN under our Hand and the Seal of the Grand Lodge
at London this 26th day of March A.L. 5839; A.D. 1839.

By Command,
WILLIAM H. WHITE, G.S.

On the 6th July 1860, it was decided "that a duplicate of our
Warrant, in consequence of the dilapidated state of the original, be
applied for and permission at the same time be obtained to retain the
original." If any action was taken on this resolution the result was
probably that Grand Lodge refused to issue a new warrant as we know
from a reply on record from Grand Lodge to a similar application made
in August 1899 that a duplicate Warrant is never issued, "but in the
case of the document becoming illegible or lost, what is termed a Warrant
of Confirmation is issued on the application of the Master and Wardens
and at least four other members of the Lodge." (G.L. letter 28th August
1899.)

It is recorded in 1887 that our Warrant was "renovated" and
reframed by Wor. Bro. Colonel Sanford but it would I think be advisable to act on the suggestion of Grand Lodge and obtain a "Warrant
of Confirmation."

1919.—The Permanent Committee presided over by Bro. G,
Reeves-Brown. S.W. took the question of the Warrant in hand this
year. It was now almost indecipherable and in shreds and it was
recommended "that a Confirmation Warrant be applied for and that
the old Charter be framed and hung in a suitable place".

This recommendation being passed by the Lodge, action was taken
and at the meeting held on 12th April 1920 our preent Warrant of
Confirmation was received and handed over by Wor. Bro. R. Watson
Senior P.M. to the safe keeping of the Worshipful Master, Wor. Bro.
G. Reeves-Brown.

A copy of this Warrant of Confirmation is here recorded.

ARTHUR G. M.

To all and every our Right Worshipful, Worshipful and Loving Brethren

WE

ARTHUR WILLIAM PATRICK ALBERT

Duke of Connaught and Strathearn Knight of the Most Noble Order of the Garter
etc., etc., etc., etc.

GRAND MASTER

OF THE MOST ANCIENT AND HONOURABLE FRATERNITY OF FREE
AND ACCEPTED MASONS OF ENGLAND

SEND GREETING

WHEREAS it appears by the Records of the Grand Lodge that a warrant of Constitution bearing date the 26th March 1839 was granted to certain brethren therein named authorising them to open and hold a Lodge of Free and Accepted Masons at Simla Punjab, India and which was then registered in the Books of the Grand Lodge as No. 673.

AND WHEREAS by the general alteration in the numbers in the year 1863 it became and is now registered in the Books of the Grand Lodge as No. 459 under the Title or Denomination of

No. 459. THE HIMALAYAN BBOTHERHOOD LODGE

AND WHEREAS the Brethren composing the said Lodge have by their Memorial represented to us that their Warrant has been destroyed by damp and they have prayed us to grant them a Warrant of Confirmation in lieu thereof NOW KNOW YE that we being satisfied of the reasonableness of the said request, and from the confidence reposed in the Brethren, do hereby grant this our WARRANT of CONFIRMATION unto our Right Trusty and well Beloved Brethren Gerald Reeves-Brown, Percy Harold Marshall, Bertram James Robertson, Richard Watson, John Tinson, Edward Owen Willasey Wilsey and James William Walker composing the said Lodge authorising and empowering them and their successors to continue to assemble and hold a Lodge of Free and Accepted Masons at the Freemasons Hall, Simla, Punjab, India on the second Monday of every month and to make, pass and raise Freemasons according to the Ancient Custom of the Craft in all ages and Nations throughout the known World. AND further at their said petition and of the great trust and confidence reposed in every of the above named Brethren WE DO APPOINT the said Gerald Reeves-Brown to be MASTER, the said Percy Harold Marshall to be the SENIOR WARDEN and the said Bertram James Robertson to be the JUNIOR WARDEN for opening and holding the said Lodge and until such time as another Master shall be required elected and installed, strictly charging that every member who shall be elected to preside over the said Lodge and who must previously have duly served as Warden in a Warranted Lodge shall be installed in ancient form and according to the Laws of the Grand Lodge, that he may thereby be fully invested with the dignities and powers of his Office. And we do require you, the said Gerald Reeves-Brown, to take special care that all and every the said Brethren are or have been regularly made Masons and that you and they and all other the Members of the said Lodge do observe, perform and keep the Laws, Rules and Orders contained in the Book of Constitutions and all others which may from time to time be made by our Grand Lodge or transmitted by us or our Successors, Grand Masters or by our Deputy Grand Master for the time being. And we do enjoin you to make such By-Laws for the government of your Lodge as shall, to the majority of the Members appear proper and necessary, the same not being contrary to or inconsistent with the General Laws and Regulations of the Craft, a copy whereof you are to transmit to us. And we do require you to cause all such By Laws Regulations and also an account of the proceedings in your Lodge to be entered in a Book to be kept for that purpose. And you are in no wise to omit to send us or our Successors, Grand Masters or to OUR DEPUTY GRAND MASTER for the time being, at least once in every year, a List of the Members of your Lodge as shall, and descriptions of all Masons initiated therein, and Brethren who shall have joined the same, with the fees and moneys payable thereon It being our will and intention that this our WARRANT OF CONFIRMATION shall continue in force so long only as you shall conform to the Laws and Regulations of our Grand Lodge.

GIVEN UNDER OUR HAND AND THE SEAL OF THE GRAND LODGE AT LONDON THIS 6th OCTOBER A. L. 5919 A. D, 1919

BY COMMAND OF HIS ROYAL HIGHNESS THE M. W. GRAND MASTER.

P. COLVILLE SMITH G. S. _____ J. F. HALSEY D. G. M.

IV.   The Temple and Building Fund.

1843.   Our records make no mention of a Temple of any kind before 1843.   The Lodge used to meet wherever room could be found in hired buildings, but on the 28th July 1843, Bro. Charde made a free gift to the Lodge of a piece of ground on which to build a Temple and the work of clearing the site was put in hand at once. The available Lodge funds (some Rs. 200) were used to meet the present expenses, and a circular was sent to every Lodge in the Bengal Presidency and to Masons in Simla inviting subscriptions.   By the 21st September the ground was nearly ready, and on the afternoon of Tuesday the 26th idem, the Brethren after opening Lodge in the 3rd Degree, marched in procession to the site and laid the foundation stone "in due form" of our first Temple, the "Hut" which we have heard referred to and which an imaginative artist portrayed on our Banner some years after all trace of it had disappeared.

1844.   On the 21st June 1844, it was reported that the *walls* and out-offices were completed but that work was at a stand still for want of funds.   It was than decided to make another appeal to Lodges and individuals, and on a paper being circulated in Lodge that evening a sum of Rs. 412 was subscribed by the ten Brethren present. The roofing, which was estimated to cost about Rs 700 was then put in hand, but evidently the work did not progress, for a report made to
1845   Lodge on the 20th June 1845, exactly a year later, shows that the building was still unfinished and it was estimated that another Rs. 500 would be required to complete it.   Appeals were again made for money and apparently the Temple was finished by the end of the year, as at the last meeting a resolution was passed that the available funds of the Lodge be used for the purchase of furniture and fittings of the new Lodge rooms.   Our first Temple then took over two years to build but cost us only about Rs. 3,000.

1846.   The new building was occupied in 1846 and some altera- tions were immediately made in it so that the rooms could be used for Divine service until the new Church (the present Christ Church) was completed.   Our Temple alas ! soon began to show signs of decay which does not say much for the builders.   On the 11th September 1846, a sum of Rs. 100 was given to the Chaplain "for the present temporary roof of the Masonic Lodge in addition to what the repairs of the same may require", and at the last meeting this year (14th October) the "dilapidated state" of the Lodge is referred to and it was left to the Brethren remaining in Simla for the winter to have the place properly repaired.

1847. Evidently nothing was done because at the first meeting next year a committee was appointed to report on the state of the building. This report was not submitted to the Lodge before the 18th August, and like most other matters brought up at that meeting was "ordered to lie over."

1849. When Lodge met again, two years later (8th August 1849) the Worshipful Master stated that the Lodge rooms had been found to be in a "frightfully dilapidated state", and repairs being immediately necessary to prevent the building from falling down, Bro. Charde had undertaken the work at his own expense "the assets of the Lodge, so far as can be ascertained, being only Rs. 0-15-10"! Presumably these repairs were carried out, but matters were not improved much because on the 17th October 1849, it was decided to put a pent roof over the rooms as soon as possible and a sum of Rs. 1,000 was borrowed from the bank for the purpose.

1855. The "Hut" however, almost utterly collapsed a few years later, and on the 5th January 1855 a committee recommended "that in consequence of the ruinous state of the Lodge building it be pulled down and measures taken for its being rebuilt." A building committee was thereupon formed and authorised to proceed with the work, the cost being limited to Rs. 2,500. At the first meeting of the Lodge in 1855 it was decided to rent "Melrose" (present Volunteer Club) for the month of April at Rs. 15 per mensem, so apparently the second Temple "on the site where the original formerly stood" must have been expected to be finished by May, but as a matter of fact it was not ready till much later and was probably not occupied till 1856. In September 1855 it was decided to invest the property in Trustees and to empower them to obtain a loan of Rs. 4,000 from the bank "for the purpose of defraying the liabilities incurred in its re-erection." The orginal estimate therefore was considerably exceeded.

1856. The old Account Books show us how deeply indebted the Lodge was in these critical days to Chapter "Dalhouse" which had started working in 1850.

During the years 1856 to 1860 the Chapter transferred to Lodge Funds upwards of Rs 2500- and for some years afterwards the Lodge accounts show the inclusion of Chapter Fees, and fees for the Degrees of "Ark and Mark" and Super-Excellent frequently. It is apparently correct to say that had it not been for old Chapter "Dalhousie" our Lodge would have found it almost im-

G. R. B. 1927.

possible to keep going. This knowledge cannot but increase the love and loyalty to this old Chapter of all it's members, and should be an inducement for all members of the Lodge to show their appreciation today by taking this Degree in the Chapter at the earliest opportunity.

1858. When the new rooms were ready, the Permanent Committee recommended that they be made available for evening parties at a rental of Rs. 50 a night. Whether the Lodge rooms were much used for such purposes is not known, but a party of some sort was held in the rooms early in 1858, because on the 19th July of that year, a letter was read from the P. D. G. M. commenting on the impropriety of this proceeding. The Lodge replied, on the advice of some of the Brethren who said that they had actually attended balls in England held in Lodge rooms, "that there appeared to be no objection to the appropriation of the hall for the purposes of instruction or innocent recreation", but P. G. L. reiterated their opinion that the custom was improper, in a letter read to the Lodge on the 10th September 1858.

1863. On the 24th June 1863, the Lodge rooms were asked for by some Brethren for a ball and the Worshipful Master agreed remarking "that the use of the Lodge rooms for such purposes was not unusual". The ruling of the P. G. L. of 1858 was clearly overlooked.

1866   In the Minutes three years later (7th August 1866) is recorded a strong objection to the use of the Lodge room for purposes of gaiety.

1869. 3rd May.—There was quite a long discussion on the propriety of renting the banqueting room to the Presbyterians for Sunday services, and it was decided to let them have the use of the room on the understanding that they would have "one collection for wear and tear of the Lodge property during the season". Later on, however, the room was rented for Rs. 50 per mensem. How long it was used for this purpose cannot be stated.

1870. In 1870 the Lodge was found to be so badly in debt that it was decided to sell the Lodge estate, and this was effected by the end of the year for the sum of Rs. 3,000, the furniture being expected to fetch another Rs. 500. The Lodge was finally vacated on 15th October 1870, about 14 years after the rebuilding, and our unfortunate Temple, which must have cost us one way and another something over Rs. 10,000 excluding the value of the site, had to be sacrificed to save us from extinction owing to gross mismanagement and want of supervision over our funds.

1871. The Lodge met in the "Assembly Rooms" where the municipal market now stands, on re-opening on 5th June 1871. The next meeting was held in the "United Bank" premises, now, I think, the "Alliance Bank", and the room was evidently hot and stuffy, for at the first meeting it is carefully recorded that one Bro. "asked the W. M. whether it was not possible for the Lodge to the worked in a properly ventilated room as be had found it very opressive during the last two hours, in addition to which the whole of his underclothing was completely saturated with perspiration". The Brethren perspired in this room, however, for only a few more meetings, as on the 7th August the Lodge was held in "Benmore" and continued to meet there till the present Town Hall was built.

1873. It is recorded in the minutes of 1st September 1873 that Bro. Goldstein "freely offered to make the Lodge a present of a building site on the consideration that a Lodge and no other building be erected upon it. The W. M. thanked Bro. Goldstein for his handsome offer and arranged to meet him on the ground that the boundaries might be pointed out". At the meeting of 3rd November following, it was decided "that Rs. 300 be taken from Lodge Funds and deposited at interest as a nucleus of a building fund". Here the matter ended for some time, but it is satisfactory to note that the Brethren had already realised the desirability of again having a Temple of their own.

1875. On the 19th July 1875, it was decided "that an additional sum of Rs. 200 be placed in deposit for the future benefit to the Lodge." On the 18th October following, Rs. 500 was placed to the credit of the building fund and the W. M. who was probably also P. Z. of the R. A. Chapter "Dalhousie" stated that "owing to the flourishing state of the funds of Chapter "Dalhousie", the Chapter would be able to place Rs. 500 to credit of the building fund".

1877. Two years later, on 16th April 1877, it was decided unanimously "that a committee should be formed to take into consideration the question as to the best means of providing a permanent building wherein the Lodge might hold its meetings". Nothing, however, appears to have been done at this time, as on 1878 the 15th July 1878 the subject came before the Lodge again when another committee was nominated "to give a report at the next regular meeting of the Lodge of the conclusions they had arrival at as to the best course to be pursued for obtaining the desired object". At this next meeting on 2nd September 1878, the following is the record of the discussion which took place. The Worshipful Master stated * * "and there seemed no prospect of the obtainment of a special Lodge building, he would propose that the Lodge accept the offer made by Wor. Bro. Goldstein placing his concert room at their disposal for meetings * * On the Worshipful Master's proposition being seconded by Wor. Bro. W.C. Willson, Wor. Bro. Ottley pointed out that at the last regular meeting it had been accepted that under the by-laws the subject was one which must first be considered by the Permanent Committee * * * * The Wor. Bro. suggested that the Lodge was bound to abide by its by-laws. Wor. Bro. Willson having suggested that this was an emergent case not provided for by the by-laws, the decision of the

Lodge was taken on the point and the majority present assenting to that view, the motion of the Worshipful Master was put and carried." Consequent on this decision Wor. Bro. Willson, who was P. Z. of R. A. Chapter "Dalhousie", at a subsequent meeting of the Lodge asked for the refund of a sum of Rs. 400 given by the Chapter to the building fund in 1875. There was considerable opposition to this request which was spoken of as a proposal "for diverting money from the Lodge building fund" but the Lodge had ultimately to give in, and a sum of Rs. 400 plus Rs. 90 interest accrued since 1875, was paid back to the Chapter on 1st June 1879 leaving, it is recorded, a balance of Rs. 1,270 to credit of the building fund.

1881. Apparently matters remained in *statue quo* till 1881 when Bro. Colonel Sanford at the meeting of 17th October "addressed the Lodge at some length on the advisability of increasing the building fund by every possible means, and proposed that the following amounts should be paid by the Lodge toward attaining this end, *viz*:—

"Rs. 2 from every joining fee.

„ 4 „ „ Initiation fee.

„ 3 „ „ Passing fee.

„ 5 „ „ Raising fee."

This proposal was carried unanimously.

1882. Next year, on 17th April, the Lodge considered an important communication from the Deputy Commissioner of Simla "regarding the lease by the Lodge, and other Masonic bodies in Simla, of rooms in the contemplated "Kursaal." The letter clearly gave the Brethren great offence and "after some discussion as to the terms of the lease and the tone of the letter, it was decided that the Lodge be called off for a short space to allow of a reply being drafted by Wor. Bro. Phelps and Bro. Colonel Sanford." On resuming labour, Bro Col. Sanford proposed—"That a reply be sent to the Deputy Commissioner as President of the Municipal Committee stating that Lodge "Himalayan Brotherhood" can only answer for itself as one of the Masonic bodies meeting at Simla, and that as far as it is concerned it is perfectly well housed at present. That it has no wish to be specially considered in the new public buildings about to be erected. That this Lodge is quite unable to entertain any proposal to take a lease of accommodation in those buildings at a rental of Rs. 1,200 per annum for 21 years. That no action on the part of the D.G.M. could bind this Lodge, or any other Lodge, to any such conditions, or to any conditions at all, as to their place of meeting and that this Lodge declines to be guided in any such matter by the action of the United Service Institution or any other institution whatever. That this Lodge regrets that the information upon which the proposal of the President of the Municipal Committee appears to have been based should have been furnished without due consideration of the regulation (possibly "requirements" was meant) and true interests of Freemasonry." Immediately after the adoption of this reply, Wor. Bro, Goldstein after "adverting to some of the uncalled for remarks contained in the letter from Major Nisbett, President Municipal Committee, stated that some years ago he had offered the plot of ground below "Benmore" to the Lodge for the purpose of building a Masonic Hall, and he had now much pleasure in renewing that offer and whenever the Lodge had sufficient funds to commence a building the said plot should be at its disposal free of charge." I am told that we were unable to accept this very generous offer because the Municipal Committee would not at that time allow any building on the site,

1883. 23rd April.—"Bro. Watson reported that in accordance with instructions given at the last regular meeting, he had ascertained from the Alliance Bank that the sum to the credit of the building fund amounts to Rs. 1,270 and that it was invested in the 6 per cent. deposits. That the Manager had informed the Secretary some time ago that the bank had decided to close their 6 per cent. deposits and had asked for instructions regarding reinvesting, but as yet had received no reply. They remarked the amount was payable immediately or at 2 month's notice according to usual bank terms with interest to 31st December last amounting to Rs. 265-14-0. Wor. Bro. Freeman instructed Bro. Watson to withdraw the sum under the most advantageous terms and place it in the Simla Bank at 6 per cent". Clearly then the resolution of the Lodge of 17th October 1881 was never acted on for Rs. 1,270 was the credit of the fund on 1st June 1879. At the meeting of 10th September 1883, however, it was decided "that the sum due to the building fund be paid to that account," what amount this was is not stated. On 1884 the 14th April next year it was decided on Wor. Bro. Sanford's motion that a sum of Rs. 400 be transferred to the building fund from the general fund.

1885. As regards the offer of rooms in the Town Hall the matter was taken up again and settled by a committee composed of Wor. Bros. Carson, Donaghey, Irwin and Scott and Bros. W. Smith and Watson, and at the meeting of 8th June 1885 it was decided to lease the rooms in the Town Hall for 5 years at a rental of Rs. 600 per annum. Some misunderstanding must, however, have arisen after this, for on the 14th September Wor. Bro. Carson, who was now the Master, brought up the subject again "explaining how the case stood viz, "Benmore" was not available from the beginning of next season and the accommodation offered by the Municipality in the Town Hall under construction was not sufficient, while the arrangement of the rooms it was proposed to allot was most inconvenient. The question of providing proper accommodation from the beginning of next season was therefore of a most pressing natuie. * * * He said that at a meeting of the Permanent Committee held on 13th September it was resolved to purchase if possible a house situated in a central position, and to apply to D. G. L. for a grant of funds and that negotiations were accordingly going on regarding two houses understood to be for sale * * * " After some little discussion it was proposed and approved that the matter be left entirely in the hands of the W. M. and the Permanent Committee to settle, and the W. M. then stated "that he intended to call an emergent meeting of the Lodge on which occasion he expected to be able to lay before it the result of his enquiries regarding the houses referred to above and any further information that may be elicited from the Municipal Committee regarding the accommodation for Masonic purposes in the Town Hall." As a matter of fact, no emergent meeting was called but at the next regular meeting on 12th October the W. M. laid before the Lodge the correspondence between himself and the Municipality who evidently had made some modification in the terms of their original offer, for the W. M. now suggested "as there was no other proposal of any kind before the Lodge, while the accommodation offered by the Municipality in the Town Hall for Masonic purposes seemed suitable it should be accepted." This was put to the vote and agreed to unanimously and the Lodge held its first meeting in the Town

1886

Hall on the 21st June next year, the Installation night. The meeting was very largely attended and we had numerous visitors. The ceremony of consecration "was performed in due form, and with the solemnity of procedure proper on such occasions, by Wor. Bro. Carson assisted by Bro. the Revd. Dr. H. M. Robinson and Bro. Revd. A. H. Hildesley, the D. G. Chaplain." Bro. Hodder acted as organist on this occasion. Before moving to the Town Hall our first three meetings this year were held in Wor. Bro. Carson's house "Belmont".

1890. 30th June. It was decided to transfer a sum of Rs. 100 from the general to the building fund and that the balance of the latter account " be placed in the Bank in a separate fixed deposit accout for 12 months and renewed periodically. On 12th October 1891 a further sum of Rs. 200 was transferred to this account and a similar amount was credited on 6th June 1892. On the 12th September this year in the course of his address the R. W. the D. G. M. (Parker) said "the only point in which he desired to see improvement was the accomodation of the Lodge. He pointed out the necessity for the Simla Lodge above all others having spacious accommodation. He hoped the Brethren would see about raising a building fund in the shape of debentures or otherwise and promised assistance from D. G. L. funds. He also said he would like to see the Lodge more like a club where members could meet every evening, read the papers and have light refreshments; this would do away with the necessity for expensive entertainments". On the 10th October 1892 the handsome sum of Rs. 500 was credited to the building fund from the general fund, but at the meeting of 13th November 1893 it was decided on Wor. Bro. Carson's proposal "that the building fund be abolished and that any monies not already transferred to the fixed deposit account of that fund should be transferred to the Lodge general account, but that the amount now in the Bank as a fixed deposit of the building fund remain there as a special account and no payments made therefrom without the special vote of the Lodge."

The building fund was, however, revived on a motion by Wor. Bro. Leigh in 1903 and from that time till it was finally closed in 1907, the monthly dues included a certain amount in aid of the building fund.

1895. Another change of Lodge rooms was mooted this year. On the 12th August Bro. Walmsley gave notice that at the next regular meeting he would propose "that owing to increase in membership and the small accommodation afforded by the present Lodge rooms more commodious quarters should be sought for," but at the next meeting it was decided that the question "be held over for the present," and the subject was not again referred to till 1897.

1897. On the 12th July this year, Bro. Faletti asked that some active steps be taken to carry out the scheme for the proposed new Masonic building. He remarked that for several years the scheme had been talked of and subscriptions promised, but up to the present as far as he knew nothing practical had been done, and he felt sure he was only expressing the wishes of the majority of the Brethren in making the proposition he did. He understood that at the Installation banquet some generous donor had promised Rs. 1,000   *   *
* He therefore proposed that the Worshipful Master be asked to nominate a committee to study the question and to report to the Lodge as soon as possible." At the next meeting of the Lodge a committee was accordingly formed, one of the members being Wor. Bro. Waston, but their deliberations and report if ever presented are nowhere mentioned. Judging from the records the matter must have been dropped for two years later, viz., on 10th July 1899, the W. M. Colonel Sandbach formed a small committee (Wor. Bro. Watson was again a member) "to enquire into and report to the Lodge on the practicability of acquiring a Lodge building of its own."

1900. The following para is taken from the Minutes of 12th March. "Wor. Bro. Major Shearer said that as he was the only Member of the committee for building a new Lodge present in Simla he could not officially, without his colleagues, lay any of the schemes before the Lodge, but he would briefly mention them and request that any

Brother who might be possessed of additional information would kindly send it to him so that he might lay it before the committee. Wor. Bro. Major W. P. Carson said he did not consider any of the schemes (5 in number) feasible."

1903. Three years later, on the 22nd May 1903 an emergent meeting was called to consider the question of purchasing "Belvedere" for a Masonic Temple. In placing the scheme before the Lodge Wor. Bro. Col. Sandbach said "that we had been for some considerable time trying to better our accommodation * * he detailed the efforts of the building committee which was appointed in 1899, to acquire fresh accommodation but without any result up to the present. The Wor. Bro. then went through the scheme, which had been placed in print in the hands of the members, stating that Mr. Ker (Manager, Alliance Band) was prepared to lend the Lodge the sum of R. 28,000 at 6 %, that Wor. Bro. Shearer, Bro. Cooper and himself had gone over the building and carefully considered its adaptability for Lodge purposes; that Bro. Cooper had undertaken to put up plans by September without charge and that he (Wor. Bro. Col. Sandbach) gave a personel guarantee that the whole of the Rs. 10,000 required to complete the sum needed to make the necessary alterations to the building would by this time next year either be paid into the Bank or promised. * * * He added that he felt that if we all put our shoulders to the wheel the scheme was a sound one and certain of succeeding. The Wor. Bro. then formally proposed that this Lodge should acquire the "Belvedere" estate for Rs. 30,000.

Wor. Bro. Alves seconded the proposal remarking "that he was sure no fairer scheme could be put to the Lodge * * He referred to the various sites considered, every one of which had failed to meet our requirements, that the repayment of the loan by annual sums of Rs. 500 seemed to him to be a minimum figure, he thought that we ought to be able to repay the debt at the rate of Rs. 1,500 per annum." A lengthy and rather hot discussion followed, the chief opponents to the scheme being Bros. Rudolf, Faletti, Rennick and Temple, principally on financial grounds and the undesirability of incurring such a large debt. "Finally Bro. Rennick proposed that the scheme be rejected in toto. Bro. Rennick's amendment was put to the vote. 15 members voted in support of it and as only 27 were present the original proposal was not put to the vote." The scheme was thus thrown out by a narrow majority of 3 and we lost, in my opinion, a most favourable opportunity of acquiring a building which would have been a credit to the masonic fraternity of Simla, and in many ways better suited to our requirements than the Temple built a few years later at a cost of something over Rs. 36,000, and which will probobly cost us considerably more yet to render it suitable to our wants. It is to be regretted that so many Brethren absented themselves from this most important meeting.

12th October. The Lodge approved of the Permanent Committee's recommendation "that the amount at present due by the Lodge to the building fund (the entire sum at credit of this fund was borrowed at 4% by the Lodge when it was in difficulties in 1900) be declared to be a building fund, and that this debt be liquidated by the payment from time to time of such sum as the general fund can afford." The fund was vested in the W. M. and the two Wardens, with one permanent trustee, Wor. Bro. J. B. D'Silva.

1906. In this year the question of a more suitable temple was once more mooted and after considerable enquiry and discussion it was decided to purchase the "Quarry" estate near the Church and build on the site a temple which should be the common property of the masonic fraternity of Simla. Work on the new building was commenced toward the close of the year and the Temple was ready for occupation by the end of 1907. The plans and designs were entirely the work of Wor. Bro. Capt. W. A. Stokes of the Royal Engineers to whom the masonic fraternity of Simla in general and this Lodge in particular are much indebted for his untiring energy in supervising the construction of the building. If the Temple is not all that could be desired, it is some satisfaction to know that after close on forty years we once more have a temple of our own and one which we hope will neither tumble to pieces nor be sold for debt like its two predecessors.

1907. At the meeting of the 12th December, in allusion to the approaching removal to the new Temple, the W. M. (Faletti) in a feeling speech reviewed the period of our tenure in the Town Hall. "Names which are prominent in Craft Masonry and to whom many thanks are due were mentioned, including Wor. Bro. Yeatman-Biggs, Prinsep, Carson, Collen, Burt, Sanford, Lukis, D'Silva, Miller, Watson, Patterson, Alves, Sandbach, Cullin, and others which will be found inscribed on the Lodge roll and in the Lodge minutes. Many who sought light in Freemasonry and found it in Lodge "Himalayan Brotherhood" could not leave the old Masonic Hall without some regrets. But let it be hoped that the success which attended us in the old meeting place may be more than doubled in the new Temple."

The 31st December was our last meeting in the Town Hall. The W. M. read Article 167 of the Book of Constitutions. The question of removal to the new Temple was then formally considered, and it was proposed by Wor. Bro. Watson and seconded by Bro. Fillingham that Lodge "Himalayan Brotherhood" be removed to the Masonic Temple, which was carried unanimously. Thus after 21 years we left the rooms in the Town Hall, and if we had feelings of regret at leaving a building which contained so many happy memories, they were tempered by the fact that we were going to a home of our own.

1908. The inaugural meeting of the new Temple was a regular meeting of Lodge "Himalayan Brotherhood" held on 13th January 1908, and, as was most appropriate, on this occasion the Lodge was opened by the designer and builder of the Temple, Wor. Bro. Captain Stokes, at the particular request of the W. M. Wor. Bro. Faletti. Wor. Bro. Stokes was specially elected an honorary member of the Lodge at this Meeting, and in honour of the occasion the Lodge gave a dinner at which a large number of the Brethren of the three Lodges in Simla were present.

Thus far, then, the task of providing ourselves with a suitable Home of our own was most successfully accomplished, and it was indeed a relief to become freed from the dismal accommodation and the inconveniences which we had suffered for twenty-two years. That long period had however been one of great advancement in Craft and Royal Arch Masonry as well as in other degrees but, as has been amply proved, good fortune guided us in determining our future in the manner indicated, as well as in other directions.

At the outset and owing mainly to the very modest scale of expenditure on which the original scheme had been based, difficulties had soon to be faced as will be seen from the following account of our Masonic Hall, for which I am indebted to Wor. Bro. R. Watson who has, for so many years, been Secretary to the Simla Masonic Fraternity. Being extracts from records beginning from the time of our purchase of the site and showing the improvements it has been found possible to introduce up to the present time, together with a rough but fairly accurate statement of the financial questions involved, the account makes us acquainted with the history of our Hall down to the present year 1927.

As has been shown in the preceding pages we became purchasers of what was known then as The Quarry estate, and the opportunity was indeed fortunate for central sites were becoming scarce and a convenient situation was the first essential in setting to work on building a Freemasons' Hall This property cost us in all Rs. 21,500, and up to July 1908 we had expended altogether Rs. 53,000; against which the sum of Rs. 16,000 had been collected as donations from Lodges and Brethren.

By May 1909 there had been further expenditure on the Building. Furniture had been provided, and an Electric Installation introduced, the latter having become possible by arrangement with the United Service Club who were the private possessors of a complete Power-station of their own years before the Municipal current became available to the Simla public. Up to the end of that year financial needs had been met by further voluntary contributions from Lodges and donations from Brethren: and Lodge Himalayan Brotherhood had made a gift of all the Lodge furniture it possessed, Wor. Bro. Faletti a quantity of crockery and glass, Wor. Bro. Sullivan the Hall clock, and so on.

In 1910 the position of the Trustees and the Committee was legalized, and the Masonic Fraternity became an established body and was duly registered under that designation by the authority of the Registrar of Joint Stock Companies at Lahore, and endowed with the privileges bestowed under the Indian Companies Act for the control of Benevolent or similar Associations. The considerable amount of work connected therewith as well as in the compilation and production of the Memorandum and Articles of Association, was most cordially undertaken, free of charge, by our very worthy and Worshipful Brother B. A. Bevan-Petman, Barrister-at-Law, to whom our most sincere thanks were accorded: and we trust that 'his kindliness in thus giving us the benefit of his invaluable advice and assistance will ever be remembered with high appreciation and gratitude.

In 1911, by mutual agreement between the Trustees and the Lodges and Chapters concerned, the system of voluntary contributions up to that time in use, was discontinued, and what has ever since been designated a Donation Assessment was introduced, with very satisfactory results. The amount thus payable annually was fixed at Rs. 2,000, based or a proportionate scale according to the gross yearly income of each Masonic body using the Hall: the amount to be paid in regularly in half-yearly moieties to credit of the Loan account at the Alliance Bank. This excellent system of assessment which had already been adopted in connection with annual Rents has worked admirably up to the present time, and the whole of the Lodges and Chapters have acted up to their original determination and have ever loyally met without any demur whatever the heavy liability thus voluntarily incurred, as a consequence of which our entire indebtedness has become a comparatively small matter, and will by the end of the year 1927 be completely discharged. It may be added here, that the yearly Rent Assessment is levied to cover current charges, including interest on the Loan, while the Donation Assessment has been entirely and solely used in the reduction of the Loan itself.

The New Masonic Temple, as it was originally named by its Architect and Builder, being constructed in ferro-concrete, i.e., a framework of steel perpendiculars, beams, rods etc., with concrete filling, was believed to be stronger and more durable than any other description of structure, while the cost was considered to be extremely moderate. On the whole the past twenty years have proved the correctness of these assumptions, and there has really been but little to complain of in respect of either.

The roof of the building was also constructed of light steel beams, overlaid with planking and covered with " Ruberoid ". This material proved to be most unsatisfactory, so much so that in after years despite much patching, painting, and other expenditure necessary to keep out rain and weather generally, it had to be replaced by iron sheets.

For the time being intolerable leaking had to stopped somehow, and the big job of providing eaves all around the building became urgently necessary, —which meant an immediate outlay of Rs. 1,100. At the same time it became apparent that a verandah along the entire length of the S.W. face of the Hall would have .to be put in hand, for during heavy weather, more especially monsoon weather, rain was driven actually through the walls of the two big rooms both upstairs and down: a truly woeful state of affairs! So the whole matter was thoroughly gone into by the Committee of Management, and in the end not only was the erection of the verandah decided upon, but the addition of accommodation, and incidental protection on the E., was also sanctioned. Up to this time the Bar had been in the dinner room,, —a dreadful arrangement, — and it was part of the new scheme to remove it to the end of the proposed verandah where also there would be a store-room and further improvements. Also to remove a most offensive drain from a neighbouring estate, to build certain retaining walls etc. All this programme of work meant heavy expenditure, but the Trustees were right in their anticipation of the approval and support of the Lodges and Brethren, which was very promptly and cheerfully accorded. The total cost of the improvements amouuted to about Rs. 10,000,—but it was, indeed, money well spent, for not only were our own pressing needs fully met, but provision was made in the way of better accommodation for the public use of the Hall. Indeed, it was soon to be proved that the outlay was sound and profitable, and we have since had every reason to be fully satisfied.

Up to the end of 1912 the total outlay amounted to Rs. 66,000,— there was further expenditure during the next two years including additional furniture, and improvement in the Electrical installation. However, by the close of 1914 the total amount of our indebtedness had been reduced to Rs. 25,500, while the total expenditure on Capital account stood at Rs. 70,000.

Between 1914 and 1918 an up-to-date improvement in the retiring room accommodation at the N.-W. end of the Hall was introduced: an Electric Heating Installation was provided for the Lodge Room and Robing-room, which has ever since proved to be a most efficient and convenient means of meeting our winter requirements.

By 1st January 1919 the balance Dr. on Loan Account stood at Rs. 20,000.

During this year the Hall was required by Army Head Quarters for the accommodation of Military Clerks at their mid-day meals. This afforded us a considerable and very acceptable addition to the average yearly income, as may be inferred from the fact that in 1919 the total receipts come to Rs. 3,260, the highest on record.

A scheme for the enlargement of the Hall was this year brought forward by Wor. Bro. Lt. Col. G. C. V. Fenton who thought that the existing accommodation was insufficient for Lodge requirements, while the cost of extension would in course of time come back to us in the way of increased receipts from the public. He produced plans and estimated the probable outlay at about Rs. 35,000. The Committee of Management after careful consideration of the project declared it to be impracticable for more than one reason and decided that it could not be entertained: so the proposal fell through, with an expression of thanks to the worthy Brother for all the trouble he had taken.

In 1920 the Hall was again requisitioned by the Military Authorities and ·a similar arrangement was made, as in the preceding year. Largely due to this, the income for 1920 from the hiring of the Hall to the public, came to over Rs. 3,000.

In 1921 the condition of the roof-covering became suddenly so very bad that the adoption of urgent measures became imperatively necessary. Accordingly the Committee of Management authorized its immediate replacement with corrugated galvanized-iron sheets, which was promptly carried out, and completed with great expenditure. It was unfortunate that, at that particular time, the price of iron was extremely high, involving a total expenditure of Rs. 4,000. But the entire main roofing was completely covered in, leaving only such portions on the N. as were comparatively unimportant, to be similarly treated at some future time.

By 1st January 1922 the balance on Loan Account had been reduced to Rs. !2,000

In 1923 came the failure of the Alliance Bank. We, however, lost nothing nor were we in any way inconvenienced by this most unfortunate occurrence, for the Liquidators permitted the transfer of the amount in Current Account to credit of the Loan Account, so that when they subsequently demanded the closing of the latter we were fully prepared, and the necessary transfer to Messrs Lloyds was easily effected Later on the balance had been sufficiently reduced to enable the Trustees to take advantage of the offer of the Simla Masonic Hospital-Bed Fund to lend us Rs. 6,000 then at their disposal. This was accordingly effected and the Loan Account at Lloyds was closed.

The lamentable failure of the Alliance Bank was very much regretted by the Trustees of The Masonic Fraternity, for they had for many years, since the origin of the Association in fact, greatly benefitted by the generous consideration of the Bank through that large-hearted gentleman the late Sir Arthur Ker, to whom we owe a large amount of gratitude.

We now arrive at the beginning of the end of this brief account of the efforts of the Committee of Management. With the close of 1924 the amount due on Loan Account was Rs. 6,000.

In 1925-26 a considerable amount of expenditure became necessary or was advisedly incurred on account of renewals, repairs, and improvements. The entire repainting and other triennial items, which had been deferred for a year or more, were made to fit in with alterations which had been contemplated for some considerable time past, and which have resulted in a satisfactory readjustment, and increase to, the general accommodation. Here, again, money has been well spent: more of our own necessities have been met, and the advisability of making the most of the floor-space in the main room on the ground floor has been recognized and accomplished, with a view to maintaining the popularity of the Hall in connection with public entertainments and other requirements. There is no doubt whatever that we shall, as hitherto, benefit by the forethought of the Committee of Management in this direction.

By the end of 1926 the balance on Loan Account had been reduced to Rs. 2,000, and the Chairman of Trustees at the Annual General Meeting held in May 1927 was enabled to announce that in all probability the Association would at the close of the year be entirely free from debt, and thus become the unencumbered possessors of a fine property while, last but not least, the•Lodges and Chapters would benefit by the extinction of the Donation Assessment, as such.

In conclusion the following figures may be found interesting and are therefore appended.

The total sum expended on Capital Account to the close of 1926 amounted to Rs. 82,884.

The total sum collected on Capital Account including the last of the annual Donation Assessments (for 1927) amount to Rs. 60,621-14-2, as shown in the statement below: which gives the total amount realized as Donations from Lodges and Chapters as well as the percentage of each:—

Statement of Donations realized from 1908 to 1927 inclusive.

	Rs.	A.	P.	Per cent.
Lodge Himalayan Brotherhood ...	14,471	2	0	28¾
Lodge Kitchener ...	11,550	4	0	23
Lodge Prospect ...	2,321	12	0	4½
Lodge Elysium ...	4,285	4	0	8½
Lodge Donoughmore ...	1,092	0	0	2¼
Carried over ...	33,720	6	0	

		Rs.	A.	P.	Per cent.
Brought forward	...	33,720	6	0	
R. A. Chapter Dalhousie	...	3,004	12	0	6
R. A. Chapter Simla	...	1,782	8	0	$3\frac{1}{2}$
R. A. Chapter Prospect	...	826	8	0	$1\frac{1}{2}$
R. A. Chapter The Scottish	...	1,461	12	0	3
Mark Lodge Pinnacle	...	1,935	4	0	4
Mark Lodge East and West	...	593	0	0	$1\frac{1}{4}$
R. Ark Mariner Lodge Sunshine	...	960	0	0	2
Himalaya Chapter Rose Croix	...	2,936	0	0	6
Himalaya Preceptory K. T.	...	2,136	8	0	$4\frac{1}{4}$
Blackham Conclave R. C. of C.	...	840	0	0	$1\frac{1}{2}$
					— Total 100
		50,196	10	0	

Add—from Brethren 9,097 6 7
from other
   sources 1,327 13 7
      10,425 4 2

   Total ... 60,621 14 2

The amount realized by Hire of Hall Public to date is Rs. 30,931.

R. W.
10th August 1927.

The Lodge Banner.

V. The By-Laws.

1841. The by-laws are nowhere mentioned before 1841. In this year on the motion of the W. M. the by-laws of Lodge "HOPE" dated Meerut, 1st October 1832 were adopted with some modifications, but no further action was evidently taken and the Lodge closed on 18th

1843.

November 1841, not to meet again till the season of 1843. On the 28th July of that year the by-laws were once more considered and finally approved on 1st September. They were, however, never submitted to, on sanctioned by, Provl. Grand Lodge, or Grand Lodge, as the W. M. thought this was unnecessary because the by-laws were really those of Lodge "Hope" which had already been approved. It is a pity that no copy of these ancient by-laws was preserved.

Evidently these same by-laws were adopted by the Lodge when it was re-established in 1849, as there is no mention of any others. On the

1851.

13th October 1851, in consequence of the Lodge constantly losing money by members leaving Simla without paying their dues, it was decided to correct the by-laws so that "every member shall on his departure from Simla, be considered to have resigned unless he shall signify to the contrary in writing to the Secretary or forfeit his rights by non-payment of dues."

1853. The earliest copy of the By-Laws that we have been able to trace are those dated 1853, and as but one copy is known to be in

G.R.B. 1927.

existance, these By-Laws have been incorporated as an Appendix to this book to place them on permanent record and as an item of great interest to future brethren.

1861. On the 15th August Mr. * * * proposed for initiation was balloted and blackballed, and he was again blackballed on the 9th September. It was in consequence proposed and resolved on 4th November that the by-laws be corrected so that no candidate for admission or initiation shall be eligible for a re-ballot under a period of 3 months.

1868. It was decided to ask D. G. L. to allow the lodge to work during the winter, but although this was approved the privilege, with occasional exceptions, was not taken advantage of and the lodge remained a "seasonal" one till many years later.

1871. 26th August. The Permannent Committee recommended that para. 8 of the by-laws be amended as follows: "Any member of this Lodge quitting Simla shall be held to have resigned unless he shall signify in writing to the Secretary his desire to be considered an absent member." This was not to apply to those who went annually to the plains on duty or for business. This rule is practically the same as the one it was found necessary to adopt in 1851.

1883 9th October. It was decided to have only one regular meeting in the month instead of two which was the practice apparently from the beginning of our career and in accordance with our Warrant.

1884. In the minutes of 11th August is recorded letter No. 513 of 8th idem from the D. G. Secretary notifying that the D. G. L. would only recognise membership of Lodge being terminated by resignation or exclusion, thus putting a stop to the practice in force for many years of striking a brother off the rolls when he left Simla.

1885. 4th November. It was decided "that should business before the Lodge require it there should be two meetings monthly." D. G. L. however refused to approve of a correction to the by-laws in these terms, and although they were addressed a second time on the subject the decision was adhered to, whereupon at the meeting on 10th May 1886 it was decided not to move further, as the proposal to have two meetings in the month was contingent on the discretion of the W. M. to hold the second meeting or not according to circumstances.

1888. 9th October. The W. M. (Carson) brought up the question of holding meetings in the winter "but as there appeared to be objections to regular meetings being held no action was taken." On the 11th May 1891 however Wor. Bro. Carson again raised the point and the proposal was then accepted by the lodge and approved by D. G. L. Our first regular meeting in the winter was held on 11th January 1892, and from this date the Lodge meets regularly throughout the year.

1889. In February D. G. L. asked for two copies of our by-laws corrected to date, and opportunity was then taken to thoroughly revise them as they had apparently been much neglected. This revision for one reason or another took over six years to complete, as the revised by-laws were not approved by G. L. till the 19th April 1895. It is not surprising therefore that at the meeting of 10th June 1895 it was resolved "that a vote of thanks be accorded to Messrs. Cotton and Morris for their kindness in having kept the type of the revised by-laws standing for so many years without extra charge."

1893. 13th November. It was decided "after lengthy discussion" on a motion by Wor. Bro. Carson that "the period of 13 months be fixed before a rejected candidate should be again proposed for. initiation."

1904. 14th November. A committee was appointed to entirely re-write and revise the by-laws which by this time "consisted of practically nothing else but corrections', and the revised by-laws were approved and issued towards the end of the following year. The only important point discussed on the revision before the draft by-laws were submitted to G. L. was the para. relating to St. John's Box. The para., framed by the committee, and which evidently followed the practice in force for many years read as follows: — "The Permanent Committee shall recommend the amount to be paid in each case of relief from St. John's box and submit the same to the W. M. who shall put it to the Lodge for confirmation. In urgent cases, however, the W. M. has power to order immediate relief to the extent of Rs. 50 to be given until it can be brought before the lodge."

In lieu of the above Bro. Arthur proposed and Wor Bro. Watson seconded that the para should read: — "That this fund is entirely at the disposal of the W. M. for distribution for such charitable purposes as may seem to him deserving." This important innovation was duly approved, and since this time the W. M. for the year has the sole control of St. John's box fund.

1907. 12th August. The Lodge approved the Permanent Committee's recommendation that from April to October two regular meetings be held monthly, viz., on the second and fourth Mondays of the month, and this amendment was duly approved by G. L.

1908. Early in this year the revision of the by-laws was again taken in hand, but this was practically only a reprint embodying the various corrections approved since 1905. The opportunity was taken, however, to simplify the wording of some of the rules and bring the book up to date consequent on the building of the new Temple. The only point of importance which may be noticed was a discussion as to the necessity for two meetings in the months of April to October as decided in 1907. D. G. L. had ruled that if the election of the W. M. took place at the first meeting in May, the installation must be held at the next regular meeting in that month and not at the first meeting in June as heretofore. The by-laws committee in consequence of this ruling recommended that the election take place at the *second* meeting in May, but when this suggestion came before the lodge on 27th July, it was proposed as an amendment "that the practice in force for many years of having only one regular meeting in the month be reverted to for the reason that the proposed correction would very undesirably curtail the period between election and installation, and that moreover as emergent meetings could be held at any time it seemed unnecessary to bind the lodge down to two regular meetings in the month when possibly there might at times be no work for a second meeting. "After some discussion Wor. Bro. Alves said that it was not obligatory to hold both regular meetings laid down in the by-laws, and that if the Worshipful Master saw fit any particular month to hold only one meeting, or indeed none, it was quite within his power to so decide." He therefore suggested that the date of election be allowed to stand, the rule following being altered to read that the installation is to take place at the "next regular meeting" which would be the first meeting in June, provided the second meeting in May was not held, a matter which the Worshipful Master could always arrange. This was accepted as satisfactorily settling the point, but Wor. Bro. Alves has turned out to be wrong in his interpretation of the

Constitutions, as G. L. has ruled that "the Worshipful Master is bound to summon the lodge for every regular meeting provided for by the by-laws." The lodge has in consequence of this ruling decided not to have two regular meetings in April and May.

1910. The amendments to our By-Laws which are to be noted are few. At the July meeting in 1910 the By-Law governing the Regular Meetings of the Lodge was amended on the proposal of Wor. Bro. Gilbert King to read "That the Regular Meetings of the Lodge he held in Freemasons Hall Simla on the second Monday in every month at such hour as the Worshipful Master may deem proper" In the early days of the Lodge, our Meetings had been held on any day and at any time the Lodge had business to contract. On occasions three meetings a week have not been uncommon, but the practice of two regular meetings a month became established and continued down to this year.

1913. A definite allocation to Refreshment Fund was made by amendment to by-law 22 "Dues" whereby the subscription is fixed at Rs. 4 plus Rs. 1 for Refreshments. This total subscription is exactly the same amount as was levied so far back as 1887, and it is as well to realize the necessity of considering whether in view of the much enhanced rate of expenses since this distant date, it is not time for the Lodge to face the fact of the inadequateness of the Refreshment Dues squarely, and instead of burking the question as has been repeatedly done in the past, agree to a substantial increase to meet our Steward's legitimate expenses.

1916. It being necessary to re-print the By-Laws, they were this year taken in hand for revision. Certain minor amendments were made and the By-Laws were approved at the August Meeting in 1917, and finally by Grand Lodge in April 1918 with the important amendment of the proposed By-Law "Exemption of Dues" whereby the Secretary only could be exempted from dues — the Lodge had in the By-Laws of 1908 exempted the Secretary, Treasurer, Organist, and Tyler !

Fees for Initiation were slightly raised and the Fees for the three Degrees were fixed at Rs. 75 Rs. 50 and Rs. 50 respectively. The 1926 By-Laws of 1918 are the ones in use today, but as I write the revision of these by-laws is under consideration by a Committee appointed in 1926, it being necessary to re-print.

VI. Accounts, Fees and Dues.

1838. On the 29th October 1838, the first statement of accounts was presented showing a balance of Rs. 275-6-0 in favour of the Lodge, and it was unanimously agreed that this "sum be reserved in deposit till next season."

1839. The accounts were presented again a year later (18th October 1839) which marked the close of the Lodge's first year of existence. On this date there was a balance in hand of Rs 188-12-8, and Rs. 230 were shown as due from members. This amount with "the list of debts" was made over to Wor. Bro. McDonald "to be disposed of as may be determined by the Lodge," and he was also authorised to receive the fees for one initiation and one passing that evening "in liquidation of the expenses incurred by this evening's meeting." The Lodge then proceeded to dispose of their assets (Rs. 418-12-8). They voted Rs. 200 in charity, and that "the surplus available funds of the Lodge, after having reserved Rs. 50 to be expended by Wor. Bro. Mc-Donald for Lodge furniture, and Rs. 20 on account of two Lodge guests at the ensuing Masonic dinner, be remitted to England on behalf of the Asylum for aged Masons." This account is not easy to follow, and unless Wor. Bro. McDonald was fortunate in recovering a good portion of the outstandings I am afraid the Asylum for aged Masons did not benefit much. The Lodge did not meet again for nearly two years, and the accounts were not presented until the meeting of 16th September 1841. It is then recorded that Rs. 147 were handed over to the Treasurer by Wor. Bro. McDonald, and this represented probably the balance in hand from sums collected in 1841, because the old account seems to have been quite disposed of at the final meeting in 1839.

1841

1843. It is not till 1843 that the accounts are again mentioned. When they were submitted on the opening of the Lodge that year, they showed a balance in hand of Rs. 240 and Rs. 254 outstanding. At the end of 1844 the cash in hand was Rs. 2-10-6 and the outstandings had risen to Rs.545-1-0, but by the end of 1845 matters had improved, the cash in hand being Rs. 718-3-8 and the outstanding Rs. 477. On the 17th June 1846 Bro. Charde, the Treasurer, asked to be placed on the absent list as he was leaving Simla. This was approved, and at the same time the Lodge decided to present Bro. Charde with a "Secretary's honorary jewel for the zeal and ability in the discharge of his duties as Treasurer and Secretary." Before the meeting Charde "expressed his earnest desire" that his accounts be examined, and the Permanent Committee with an additional member,

1844
1845

1846

were detailed for the **duty**, but evidently the committee never met. On the following 15th July another Treasurer was elected, but he only attended two meetings and next year, among other matters in a mess, were the accounts.

1847

Much interesting light is shed on our Lodge's affairs during the critical years of 1849-50 and onwards by an old Account Book which was found amongst a pile of rubbish and which evidently escaped Bro. Wilsey's notice. Wor. Bro. Curtis and Bro. Charde, his Secretary, started with energy to disentangle the Lodge from the hopeless mess into which it had fallen in the years 1846 and 47. At the first Committee Meeting held on October 17th 1849, Bro. Secretary's Accounts were examined and passed. He reported that outstanding dues and fees from 1846 and 7 amounted to Rs. 1966-8, of which only Rs 26 had been recovered while bills against the Lodge amounted to Rs. 467-10-2!.

A loan was obtained from the Simla Bank, and this, together with the proceeds of the vigorous working of the Lodge during the remaining months of 1849 and the year 1850, enabled the Lodge to gradually get on to it's feet once more. By the end of 1850, after paying Rs. 1461 for repairs to the Lodge, Rs. 633 for dues to Grand and Provincial Grand Lodge for previous years, and paying off all old liabilities the Treasurer was able to show only Rs. 200 odd due to the bank and outstandings well able to meet this ——a very creditable effort on the part of Bro. Charde. Of the outstandings still kept on the books from the years 1846 and 7, Rs. 1301 are considered "hopeful" and this sum includes Rs. 286-12-9 due from Bro. Chisholm, the W.M, of the years mentioned and Rs. 367-12-3 due from his Secretary Bro. Emerson !

The Accounts for 1850 include such items as:—

22 Toon Chairs ...	...	Rs.	60
For making Jewel for Deacon ...		,,	3-8
2 Black Velvet cushions	.	,,	5-5
Stool for kneeling and a ledge round pedistal. ...		Rs.	1.

1849. When the Lodge met again in 1840, the Worshipful Master mentioned that "assets of the Lodge so far as ascertainable were only Re. 0-15-10". The defaulters were numerous, especially among those who were on the roll at the close of 1847, and although they were repeatedly appealed to very few paid up, and large sums had to be ultimately written off

1853. By this year our funds had improved and the Lodge was able to place Rs. 500 in Fixed Deposit. This year we notice our first transaction with Messrs. Spencer, London when we bought "books and a set of Tracing Boards". These Tracing Boards were our second set the last having been bought just before the Lodge went into abeyance and were evidently not recovered, like much more of the Lodge property, when it re-opened. Spencers set are the Boards we still have with us to this day and they are therefore 73 years old. These were the days of Candles and candle sticks and the accounts show numbers of items for "Candles" which were apparantly by no means an inexpensive mode of illumination.

1854. The Accounts this year are of more than passing interest on account of the repeated entries for Fees paid for the Side Degrees worked by the Lodge at this time—The Ark and Mark Degree and the Super-Excellent Degree. The first entry is in October when Wor. Bro. Jeffery and Bro. Oakes paid for the "A. & M." Degree.

The fees for these Side Degrees were subsequently utilised by the Lodge to pay for the expenses of entertaining visitors, and an Account was opened in the Lodge Account Book which, in view of the fact that the "Ark and Mark" Degree, whatever it was, has long since vanished from Masonry and the Super Excellent Degree is today very seldom met with, deserves placing on permanent record.

The Account in question is given on the following page.

Brother T. Graham, Treasurer in A/C with Fund for General Purposes L.H.B. 673.

DR.

1856		Rs.	A.	P.
July 7th	To temporary loan from Lodge Funds	50	0	0
Nov. 24th	To Cash Bro. H. C. Smith S.E. Degree	24	0	0
1857				
Jan. 4th	To Cash Bro. F. H. Conolly S.E. Degree	24	0	0
	To Cash Bro. Tomkyns S. E. Degree	24	0	0
1858				
May 17th	To Cash Bro. W.M.H.T. Tapp	40	0	0
Nov. 6th	To Cash Bro. J. P. Caulfield A. & M. & S.E. Degree	40	0	0
	To amount transferred from Lodge Fund	81	9	0
	Total ...	283	9	0

CR.

1856		Rs.	A.	P.
July 16th	By Bro. Stewards Bill for Guests	17	12	0
Sept. 5th	By Ditto.	19	8	0
15th	By Ditto.	18	4	0
Oct. 21st	By Ditto.	29	12	0
Nov. 20th	By Ditto.	8	0	0
Nov. 24th	By Ditto.	8	0	0
Nov. 24th	By Bro. Stewards Bill S.E. Tiffin	21	4	0
1858				
Oct. 14th	By Bro. Stewards Bill for Guests	22	10	0
Nov. 18th	By Bill for Merino	5	10	0
23rd	By Bill for Saloo	6	10	0
1859				
March 1st	By Bro. Stewards Bill for Guests	42	12	0
	By Ditto.	83	6	0
	Total ...	283	9	0

1855. In October a loan of Rs. 4,000 was taken from the Bank, and in June the next year, the whole of the resources of the Lodge including this loan is transferred to Building Fund—Rs. 6,035-6-4 being available. It is now that Chapter "Dalhousie" plays a great part in the finances of the Lodge. During the next few years no less than upwards of Rs. 2,500 was transferred from the Chapter to the Lodge as the books show.

1857. September 12, by Bill for Bible, Rs. 32. This is the old Bible still in use today, and its age and the realization of the number of excellent Masons, both initiates and Masters, who have taken their Obs. on this old relic will ensure its retention for all times as our most cherished possession.

1864. The Lodge account Book shows us that from this year onwards the Refreshment accounts are allowed to get very much out of hand, and indeed there can be no doubt but that to the extravagence on this head was to a great extent due the load of debt that eveutually resulted in the forced sale of the Lodge Rooms and property in 1870.

It is interesting to note our Lodge's wine bills for these years, of which the following are a fair sample :—

	Rs.	a.	p.
July 4th—			
By Half dozen Brandy ...	18	0	0
Half dozen Sherry ...	18	0	0
Half dozen Port ...	18	0	0
Two dozen Soda Water ...	9	0	0
July 18th —			
By Half dozen Sherry ...	18	0	0
One dozen Soda Water ...	4	8	0
Six lbs. Candles ...	5	0	0
August 1st—			
By Half dozen Sherry ...	18	0	0
One dozen Beer ...	10	8	0
One dozen Soda Water ...	4	8	0

August 15th—

By Half dozen Sherry	...	18	0	0
One dozen Beer		10	8	0
Two dozen Soda Water		9	0	0

August 24th—

By 1 lb. 15 oz. Cheese	3	6	3
1 lb. Mustard	1	0	0
9 lb. Candles	6	12	0

Other items of interest are :—

Bro. Tim Graham's Donation Cup	...207	0	0

Bro. Graham was Treasurer at this time

May 1866, for Banner	64	0	0

———

1866. During the next few years, things did not apparently prosper financially, for at the meeting on 21st August 1866, the Worshipful Master mentions that the Permanent Committee had been directed to make a full report on the state of the Lodge, its indebtedness, etc., and to prepare a clear financial report. Wor. Bro. Hoff expressed his satisfaction at this resolution, and remarked that "for the past four years there had been no financial statement placed before the members, although it was obligatory on the officers of the Lodge to have this done." On the following 16th October "the proceedings of the Permanent Committee for the current year were read." It is not very clear whether this was the report ordered to be furnished, but I should think it was. The Worshipful Master remarked that although the financial report was not so complete as could be wished he hoped it could be accepted, and "that in spite of the difficulties and expenses entailed on the Lodge by the present banqueting arrangements, the Brethren were in a fair way of overcoming their financial difficulties." At the first meeting next year the

1867.   Worshipful Master said that on the first meeting of every month a progress report on the financial state of the Lodge would be presented, and it is noted that this "announcement was received with great satisfaction." I can find no record of the submission of such reports, but on the 5th August 1867, another committee report was presented showing receipts and expenditure "for the season 1866 and for the first quarter of 1867" and "these accounts showed that at the end of the year 1867 the debt of the Lodge would be reduced from Rs. 2,816 to Rs. 2,000 after writing off the sum of Rs. 215 as bad debts."

1868. With the minutes of the 8th June is recorded an analysis by Wor. Bro. Hoff of the pecuniary affairs of the Lodge, from which the following extracts are taken to show that matters had been drifting and things were decidedly going wrong : —

"The subscriptions to the Lodge due by members amounted at the end of the year (*i.e.*, 1867), after writing off Rs. 215, to Rs. 1,334. This amount is so very large that I am really incline to think it almost ridiculous placing it among the assets as I fear the greater part of it will have to be wiped off the list * * * The debt of the Simla Bank was not reduced at all last year, on the contrary it was increased, by a sum of more than Rs. 320, to Rs. 3,500. * * * The liabilities have been generally somewhat reduced but that has been effected by paying the "Upper India Commercial Association" nearly the whole of the amount due to that company. The said amount being exceedingly large it would I am sure be satisfactory to the Lodge to receive a written statement showing the details of this liability of Rs. 1,369 * * * The items I refer to are the Smyth Testimonial Fund and the Hoff Memorial Fund. So far as I am aware, no information has ever been afforded to the Lodge regarding the disposal of these Funds. * * * From motives of delicacy I refrain from making any suggestion respecting the Hoff Memorial Fund * * * it may have been very recently paid to D. G. L. but when I was in Calcutta the G. M. and the Grand Secretary were very impatient to receive it."

1870. There is no further mention of the accounts till the 18th May 1870 when the Permanent Committee went into them and made the following report :—

" The Committee, having before it the memo of debts due by the Lodge which are given as follows :—

	Rs.	A.	P.
Amount due to United Bank, Simla on 15th May 1870 ...	4,483	8	11
Other debts	40	8	0
Total ...	4,524	0	11

and supposing every debt to be paid up which the books show (*i.e.* sums due to the Lodge) the above amount would only be reduced to Rs. 3,439-4-3, is of opinion, after giving every matter mature and careful consideration, that owing to the very heavy liabilities the Lodge now has it is simply injudicious to continue in this state further and that only one alternative now remains *i.e.*, to sell the Lodge estate to enable the debts being cleared * * ." The committee recommended the writing off of a sum of no less that Rs. 512 due by members who had resigned or left Simla, while the average dues of 9 members of the Lodge still present were shown to be close on Rs. 110! One owed no less than Rs. 264 and another Rs. 225. Such a state of affairs was certainly no credit to the Lodge and shows clearly that the management was very slack indeed. This committee report was approved "after much debate" at the meeting of the 30th May, and the meeting of the 20th June it was decided to auction the Temple, which was ultimately effected for the sum of only Rs. 3,000 and the furniture &c, was expected to fetch another Rs. 500.

The accounts presented at the close of the season (10th October) showed the liabilities to be Rs. 2,934-4-0 and the assets Rs. 1,956-12-6 so that the Lodge started afresh with a debt of about Rs. 1,000, but 1871 apparently matters went well for, speaking in Lodge on 3rd July next year, the D. G. M. congratulated the Lodge on its being in a good state from a financial point of view, and at the meeting of 18th September the D. G. M. who was again in Lodge stated that "he was glad to find the Lodge was in such a flourishing condition, for whereas formerly the Lodge had been in debt there was now, he was gratified to learn, a fair balance at the Bank."

1873. The Lodge subscriptions this year were fixed at Rs. 3 plus Rs. 1 for refreshments. In July the rates were revised again and the dues were fixed at Rs. 3 plus Rs. 4 for refreshments, the absent members paying Rs. 2 per mensem "during the working season".

At the meeting of 1st September this year the accounts presented showed the assets to be Rs. 439-8-11 and the liabilities Rs. 103-12-0. St. John's box had a credit of Rs. 84-11-0.

1874. Early in 1874 the resolution of July 1873 was cancelled and the former arrangement reverted to *viz*, that the Lodge dues be Rs. 3 per mensem the charges "for refreshments being dealt with separately 1875 under the supervision of the Steward's committee." In 1875 the refreshments arrangement came up again on 17th May and it was resolved to have the "subject circulated with the summons for the next meeting in order to give the Brethren ample opportunity to consider the matter in all its bearings'. At the meeting of 7th June it was decided on the recommendation of the Permanent Committee "that a sum of Rs. 2 per month be subscribed and that a cold collation be provided every second meeting". Whether this was the outcome of the deliberations of the Brethren is not very certain, but the subject is not alluded to again for some time.

1880. On 21st June 1880 it was decided to raise the Lodge subscriptions to Rs. 7 per month "which would permit of suitable refreshments being provided for the Brethren and visitors."

1883. 10th September. The Lodge subscription was fixed at Rs. 2 plus Rs. 1 for St. John's Box "with regard to the Rs 4 for refreshments it was proposed (and agreed to) that the Rs. 4 be continued to be paid for the current year, and that a committee be appointed to consider the question of subscriptions for refreshments being paid by those partaking of the same. The matter came up again in 1884 May and June 1884 when it was definitely decided that the Lodge subscription be Rs. 3 per month, absent members Rs. 1-8-0 including Re 1 for St. John's Box, and that the refreshment fund be separated entirely from Lodge Funds. As stated in the notes of 9th June "the question of the refreshment fund was now for arrangement outside the Lodge" and the Worshipful Master asked Brother Campion to take the matter up remarking that he thought the subscription Rs. 4 per month would have to be continued Probably matters remained as they were for the subject is not again alluded to 1887 till 1887, when on 18th April the Worshipful Master brought up the unsatisfactory working of the refreshment arrangements the fund being largely in debt to the Lodge fund, and after some discussion it was decided "that the present practice of having the refreshment subscription optional be done away with and that the Lodge subscription be raised to Rs. 5 to include Rs. 2 for refreshments." It may be mentioned that at a subsequent meeting it is shown that a sum of no less than Rs. 585-1-6 "spent entirely in connection with the opening of the present Lodge" (i.e., the rooms in the Town Hall) was paid from Lodge funds. D.G.L., however, refused sanction to the correction of the by-laws consequent on the above decision as the D. G. M. was averse to the Lodge dues being mixed up with refreshment accounts, but the Lodge carried their point by the questionable expedient of omitting all reference to refreshments in the new by-laws, and recorded in the minutes that "it should be understood that as a rule not more than Rs. 2 should be taken out of the monthly subscriptions to provide for refreshments."

1893. 16th July.—It was decided that the monthly rate of subscription be reduced from Rs. 5 to Rs. 4 (excluding quarterages) for full subscribing members, absent members, wherever residing, to pay Rs. 0-8-0 per month excluding quarterages.

That this was an inopportune time for the change was pretty evident for the funds of the Lodge seem to have gradually gone down from about this time, due, I am afraid, to excessive expenditure on installation banquets and the ball, which were severe drains not only on the Masters but also on Lodge funds, as they seem to have been run on the most 1900 extravagant lines. By 1900 matters were in a bad way. The accounts submitted by the Permanent Committee on the 14th May that year showed that the Lodge was much in debt, owing almost entirely to the refreshment account, and Wor. Bro. Leigh thereupon proposed that the suggestion of the Permanent Committee that "the Treasurer be authorised to borrow from the building fund at 4 per cent interest the sum required to pay off the most pressing debts of the Lodge, be accepted" and this was agreed to. When the accounts were next presented on 10th December made up to the 31st October preceding they showed the Lodge practically clear of debt, but with a sum of Rs. 2651-0-4 due to the building fund. In consequence of this state of affairs the Permanent Committee recommended, and the Lodge agreed, that no donation be given this year from Lodge funds to the P. M. I which is the first and only occasion on record that the Lodge made no contribution to this great charity.

1902. 5th May.—The Lodge accepted the proposal of the Permanent Committee to increase the fees for joining, initiation, passing and raising, also that the subscription of full subscribing members be raised from Rs. 2 to Rs. 3 per month and that of absent members from Rs. 0-8-0 to Re. I per mensem, thus practically reverting to the rates decided on in 1887 which were Rs. 5 per month, this sum being "understood" to include Rs. 2 for refreshments.

1903. 10th August.—Wor. Bro. Leigh proposed that the Lodge should make payments in future at the rate of Rs. 250 per quarter towards liquidation of the sum due by it to the building fund (at this date amounting with interest to Rs. 2,954-14-1) and that the Lodge subscriptions be distributed as follows—to Lodge funds Rs. 3, to building fund Rs. I, to refreshment fund Rs. I. After some discussion Bro. Temple proposed as an amendment that the Lodge subscription be reduced to Rs. 4, Rs. 3 being for Lodge purposes proper and Rs. I for the building, and that the total cost of refreshments supplied at each Lodge meeting be charged in equal proportions to all members partaking thereof. This amendment was approved by a very large majority, and during the next few months, various suggestions were considered for running the refreshments on the lines proposed by Bro. Temple, but so far as light refreshments were concerned the system was found so troublesome and unsatisfactory that it was abandoned the following year on a motion by Bro. Faletti that in lieu of paying Rs. I to the building fund, we should pay 8 annas only to that fund and 8 annas towards light refreshments. (Minutes 10th October 1904.)

1904

1908. In the revision of the By-laws in 1908 all reference to the refreshment and building funds is omitted, but the subscription remains the same, Rs. 4. The following paragraph is however added:—

"The cost of light refreshments provided at regular or emergent meetings shall be met from Lodge funds.

"The Permanent Committee shall have the power to sanction the supply of suppers at any meeting, whenever they consider the same advisable and whenever the funds of the Lodge permit. The sum of Rs. 200 shall be paid from the Lodge funds towards the cost of Lodge guests at the annual installation banquet."

As regards our funds, matters steadily improved from 1900, thanks to the judicious management of a succession of careful Masters and Treasurers and the vigorous measures taken to keep down expenditure. The money borrowed from the building fund was speedily paid back, and when this fund was finally closed in October 1906, the handsome sum of Rs. 4,770 was transferred to the Trustees of the new Masonic Temple. By the close of the year 1908 our credit balance was Rs. 1,778-10-8 after giving a donation of Rs. 1,000 to the Masonic Temple, which must be considered a most satisfactory state of affairs.

From now on our Lodge, with all other Masonic Bodies in Simla, has had to face the cost of our New Masonic Hall, the total cost of which has run into the very high figure of approximately Rs. 80,000 and the burden of our share of this cost has sometimes been more than we could bear. The general scheme laid down by the strong Committee of the Association, a Committee which has always been such a great asset to the Fraternity, involved a levy of Rent, Charges for Lighting etc., and a yearly Donation estimated proportionate to the total income of the Lodge or Chapter. The proportion laid down has been a high one, and since 1908 our Lodge has had to find on an average Rs. 1000 per annum to meet these charges,.

These large sums coupled with District Grand and Grand Lodge dues which have run into a further yearly sum of Rs. 1000 (approx), have had the retarding effect on the Lodge finances.

Thanks, however, to the careful and watchful policy of each succeeding Master and their Permanent Committee, we have been able to meet these heavy liabilities and at the same time remember the claims of Charity to the full.

1912. That constant source of debate and discussion, the Refreshment Fund, again came to the fore, and a Coupon system of payment for refreshments which had been tried for a year and found to be defective having been abolished, it was accepted that " in addition to the present subscription each full subscribing member pays one rupee per mensem for Refreshments".

Our monthly Subscription was therefore raised to Rs. 5, one rupee of which was for refreshments and was to be managed by the Junior Warden. The supplying of Lodge refreshments for both Regular and

Emergent meetings on the small monthly subscription of Rs. 1 per Active member has been an almost impossible proposition, and with very few exceptions our Junior Wardens have had each year to call on the Lodge to pass payments from the General Fund to meet their Refreshment Bills.

Various propositions have been placed before the Lodge from time to time to place this question of Refreshments on a sounder footing, but all have either been shelved or burked in the past.

As I write, however, the question is down for debate in a very short while, when one hopes that the matter will be squarely faced and met with a realization that, what with high costs and our increased number of Visitors, it is no longer possible to do justice to this side of Lodge life— and an important side too – on the small sum at present devoted to it.

1919. During the years under review our Lodge's finances have seldom given cause for anxiety. During the years 1919, 1920 and 1921 the funds improved so much that we were able to completely renew our Regalia at a cost of over Rs. 1000, and place Rs. 1000 in fixed deposit.

Due perhaps to over enthusiasm in the cause of Charity and to some extent to that perennial source of anxiety--nonpayment of dues— our Funds became a matter of serious consideration, and in 1923 Wor. Bro. Goldstein **1923.** had to bring forcibly to the notice of the Lodge the depleted state of the General Fund. Thanks to the energy of the W. M. our Funds were coaxed back into a more presentable condition, and with our Charity being governed by the clause "without detriment etc" he was able to hand over to his successor a better financial statement.

1925. The proposal to abolish the payment of our Secretary in 1925 relieved the Lodge considerably, and today, notwithstanding the "counter attractions" offered by our friendly "rivals" the other Craft Lodges in Simla which have necessarily affected the recruitment of new members, our Lodge is in a sound condition in every way. Long may it so continue.

VII. Lodge of Instruction.

1839. The first reference to a Lodge of Instruction is in the minutes of 18th October 1839 when the Lodge voted "the establishment of a Lodge of Instruction in the Governor General's Camp on the approaching March." If any work was done it is nowhere recorded.

1862. A Lodge of Instruction is not again mentioned till 1862 when the following paragraph appears in the minutes of 6th October "Wor. Brother Wahab, officiating Master then proceeded to remark during the interval between calling the Brethren from labour to refreshment, that it was of much importance to have a Lodge of Instruction instituted ; that there was much to learn in the duties of the officers of a Lodge who, without such instruction, might often feel at a loss. The officiating Wor. Master then put a few questions on Masonic matters to Brother Henry, then in the Junior Warden's chair, and afterwards to Bro. Hamilton, the Senior Warden. Brother Hamilton declined to answer these questions stating that as Senior Warden of the Lodge he considered such examination, especially during the absence of the Master, unnecessary." A little unpleasantness probably followed, for it is recorded that "after a little discussion on the matter the Brethren were called from labour to refreshment and the Lodge was duly closed."

1866. On the 7th May the question was once more mooted but nothing was apparently done. Exactly a year later the Wor. Master at the first meeting said "that on nights when no regular degree work was done a Lodge of Instruction would be held." Nobody, however, seems to have had any idea of what was required and speaking again on the 10th June the Wor. Master said that "he himself had not had the advantage of graduating in a Lodge of Instruction, and that he had found it difficult to obtain any precise information on the subject * * * * * he had therefore found it necessary to strike out a plan for himself." All that was done however was on *one* occasion to raise the Lodge to the 2nd and 3rd Degrees "The Senior Warden acting as Master and the Junior Warden as the Senior Warden.".

1867

1884. The next mention of a Lodge of Instruction is in 1884 when the D.D.G.M. in his address to the Lodge on the 8th September pointed out the great necessity for holding Lodges of Instruction whenever practicable, but nothing was done on this suggestion.

1891. In 1891 however (13th April) the Wor. Master (Cullin) informed the Lodge "that a warrant had been obtained from D. G. L. for a Lodge of Instruction to be held during the winter. He proposed that this warrant be confirmed and that meetings of the Lodge of Instruction be held when convenient until the warrant is withdrawn by the Lodge." This was approved but whether it was ever acted upon there is nothing to show ; anyhow the warrant seems to have been quite overlooked (perhaps it was lost) because at the

1896

first meeting under Wor. Brother Watson on 13th July 1896 the formation of a Lodge of Instruction was again suggested and referred to the Permanent Committee for consideration, and in accordance with their recommendation a Lodge of Instruction was sanctioned at the regular meeting held on the 10th August. Again there is absolutely nothing to show that this sanction was ever acted upon ; certainly from the time I was initiated in June 1898 till quite recently I do not remember any such Lodge being in existence.

1907. The Lodge of Instruction was re-opened on 8th July 1907 under the Preceptorship of Wor. Bro. J. B. D'Silva the work of the

1908

year being devoted to Degree working. On reopening in 1908 Wor. Bro. Alves took over the Office of Preceptor and the Lodge worked twice a month, many of the various Sections of the Lectures being worked in addition to the Degrees.

1909. During the year 1909 Wor. Bro. Lloyd took over the Lodge, and under his Preceptorship membership rose to over 40 and much good work was done, a number of Addresses on Masonic subjects being added to the Ritual work of the Lodge.

1910. Wor. Bro. The Hon'ble Surgeon General C. P. Lukis next took over the Lodge as Preceptor although Wor. Bro. Lloyd was more often than not in the Chair., until the Lodge went into abeyance at the end of 1911.

In 1910 the funds of this Lodge of Instruction were such as to allow Rs. 100 to be donated to the Hall Building Fund.

1914. The Lodge was resucitated in May 1914 under the care of Wor. Bro. A. F. Humphreys, but it met but three times and again went into abeyance until again opened under the same Wor. Bro. as Preceptor on April 26th 1917.

1917. The Lodge put in an active years work meeting twice a month. At each Meeting this year a Lecture or Address together with Ritual work was a special feature, and much lasting good must have ensued.

1921. In April the Worshipful Master (Wor. Bro. Captain Marshall) introduced the question of re-opening the Lodge of Instruction, and after some discussion it was proposed that it be revived under the Preceptorship of this Wor. Brother. In September of the same year, however, the Secretary who had been appointed to take in hand the matter reported that owing to lack of membership the Lodge had not been able to start, and no further action appears to have been taken.

1926. During the past two or three years a number of Lectures on Masonic subjects have been from time to time delivered in our Lodge which have had the gradual effect of awakening a "desire for knowledge" on the part of our young members, and it is evident that the date is not far distant on which the Lodge of Instruction in some form or other will again take up it's duty of "employing and instructing our Brethren in Freemasonry".

VIII. The Banner.

1865. Our Banner is first mentioned in the minutes of 19th June 1865 when the "Senior Warden called the attention of the Worshipful Master to the state of the Banner of the Lodge. The number the Banner bore was no longer the distinguishing number of the Lodge and although the Lodge had been in existence for 11 years (sic) no device had yet been adopted. He suggested that something Masonic in character and appropriate to the locality should be selected to take the place of the present blank". G. R. B. 1927. A reference to the Lodge Accounts for 1866 shows that a new banner was purchased in May for Rs. 66.

1888. In 1888 a new Banner was purchased in Calcutta for Rs. 40! From a letter on record dated 19th August 1887 to D.G.L. 1891 it appears that the design of this banner differed slightly from the original, i.e., I suppose the Banner obtained in 1865 or 1866. The Banner of 1888 was replaced in 1891 by one presented by Bro. A. Grey.

1908. 24th August. It was proposed by Wor. Bro. Longridge "that as the old Banner could hardly be renovated and possessed the sentimental value attached to its antiquity it should be preserved as it is now and that as our funds could easily bear the expense, a new Banner be provided". This was approved and a handsome new Banner designed by Bro. Walter Smith, and carefully worked under Bro. Sullivan's personal supervision in Japan, was purchased at a cost Rs. 222 and is the one at present with us in Lodge. Wor. Bro. Longridge was, however, clearly unaware that our existing Banner was not so very old. We have no record to show what has become of any of the four previous banners.

IX. The Hospital Bed Fund.

1890. From the minutes of 11th August 1890, it would appear that a movement was set on foot by Wor. Bro. Cullin for the endowment of a bed in the Ripon Hospital, as in the notes of that date he asked the Brethren who had not already subscribed, to do so, but this most excellent idea must have then fallen through for want of sufficient support.

1906. Some years later, however, thanks to Wor. Bros. Captain Longridge and Major Heard, this Fund was actually established. On the 9th July 1906, the W. M. (Captain Longridge who had so ably acted as Secretary to the Masonic Ball committee in 1905) stated "that in view of the fact that a profit of some Rs. 500 had been made on last year's ball, which sum had been devoted by the ball committee to the formation of a nucleus of a fund for the eventual endowment of a masonic bed at the Walker Hospital, and that the profit of future balls would probably be devoted to the same object, it was desirable in order to provide for the present benefits of the scheme to annually raise a further sum of Rs. 500 exclusive of ball profits to meet current expenditure in order to enable all sums raised annually by ball profits to remain untouched and at interest for the object in view. He therefore proposed that Lodge "Himalayan Brotherhood" as the leading masonic body in Simla should make a donation of Rs. 200 to be handed over to the Trustees of the above mentioned scheme".

This fund is administered solely by the Worshipful Master and thanks to the exertions of successive Masters, profits from the annual ball and a handsome donation of Rs. 1,000 by District Grand Lodge in 1908, has now a credit balance of (roughly) Rs. 5,000.

1912. A proposal to divert this Fund to a Fund called "The Lady Franklin Fund" was made when the Permanent Committee recommended to the Lodge "that in accordance with a suggestion made last year and subject to the concurrence of the other Masonic Bodies in Simla, the amount standing to the credit of the Bed Fund be handed over to the administrator of the Franklin Fund on conditions set forth in a letter from the Director General I.M.S. that "all poor and distressed Masons shall be entitled to claim assistance from the Franklin Fund provided they are suitable cases for admission into Hospital". This proposal, which so entirely lost sight of the idea embodied in the original plan, was not accepted by the other Masonic bodies and was dropped.

1916. The Permanent Committee at the October Meeting this year thought "it would be greatly to the credit of Lodge H.B. to do everything in its power to hasten the founding of a free bed in the Walker Hospital, which would become a lasting memorial to the late

Wor. Bro. Lt. Col. Longridge whose name it would always bear". The Lodge was able to give donations with regularity during this and the following years and we have up to the time of writing subscribed over Rs. 2000.

1918. During the years 1918, 1919 and 1920 printed Appeals were issued by the Lodge under the signatures of Bros Wilsey and Walker as Secretaries, but it is to be regretted that the interest shown by the Sister Lodges in Simla was almost negligable.

From 1913 our Masonic Balls had ceased (owing to the Great War) and the welcome addition to the Fund which these annual events brought in was not received. The Fund, after deducting our annual payments to the Franklin Fund, amounted at the end of 1920 to the respectable total of Rs. 11,481-4-6 and then came the disastrous failure of the Alliance Bank which involved almost all Lodges and Chapters and the Bed Fund. With the Capital of the Fund thus cut down to a little over Rs. 6,000 and the sum said to be required for the endowment of our Masonic Bed having been very much enhanced, the prospects of ever realizing our ambitions seemed almost too remote.

1924. With the resusitation of the masonic Ball as an annual fixture and the prospects of the substantial profits accruing from this annual event, a Meeting was held in October 1924 when it was again proposed and carried that the original objects of the Fund be adhered to and further efforts be made to encourage the Fund.

It was resolved that with this object in view the management of the Simla Masonic Bed Fund be transferred to The Trustees of the Masonic Fraternity of Simla. This has been done and thus this Fund, which has been so intimately connected with our Lodge life since 1906, ceases to be in the hands of our Worshipful Master as sole Trustee but is now managed by the Trustees of the Masonic Fraternity of Simla. In the capable hands of Wor. Bro. R. Watson who has since it's inception had the interests of this Fund so much at heart, we may be assured that it will thrive and the original idea and motive will never be obscured.

1926. A Circular, being Notes from Minutes and Circulars in connection with this Fund was issued by the new Trustees and as it contains so much of interest to us bringing to the fore as it does, the good work of many of our members, it has been embodied in this History as an Appendix for permanent record.

In August of this year the Accounts of the Fund showed the sum of Rs. 9,924-6-6 to it's credit over and above the balance of over Rs. 6000 still due from the Alliance Bank.

X. The Library.

1843. A Library for the Lodge was considered so far back as 1843. On the 21st September of this year it was proposed to start a Library, but beyond the purchase of a few books the following year the scheme collapsed and the small sum which had been subscribed to start it was "borrowed" to help the building of the Temple in 1844. The

1853

Library is not again mentioned till 10 years later. At a Permanent Committee meeting on 1st July 1853, the starting of a Library was once more proposed but · without any practical result. On the 15th May next year, however, the following letter was read from Bro. Lord William Hay who was initiated

1854

passed and raised in the Lodge in 1853:— "I have the pleasure to send for presentation to the Simla Lodge five Volumes of books connected with masonry. When I first joined the fraternity I felt very much the want of a few books on masonic subjects, and I have no doubt many others become masons as I did with only a very ·vague idea of what masonry was. With a view to supplying the deficiency I have alluded to I wrote to London for the books which I have now the honour of presenting to you, and I hope that others will follow my example and thus establish a small Library of Masonic books for the use of our Simla Brethren".

1865

It is sad to record that at the meeting of 2nd June 1865 the Secretary brought to notice "that the only remnants of the gift which he now could get at consisted of three odd volumes".

1866. 7th May. "Bro. D'Cruz had recently made a most valuable contribution to the literature of the Craft in the shape of a work on the history of Freemasonry in Bengal, one copy of which had been presented to the Lodge. The work was of great interest and ably written."

1884. Many years later, on the 13th October 1884, it was decided to purchase an almirah in which all our masonic books should be kept, and the Secretary was instructed to ascertain what works were available, but here the matter apparently ended, and a library is not again

1892

alluded to till 1892. On the 14th March this year Wor. Bro. Cullin gave notice that at the next regular meeting he would bring forward a proposal to apply certain of the Lodge funds to the establishment of a library of masonic literature. The W.M. (McDermott) said this was a design he had himself long had in mind and would cordially support the proposal. Wor. Bro. Capt. Litster stated that in his time there was such a library small but select, and asked what had become of it. The W.M. replied "that it had evidently entirely disappeared as none but the very oldest members of the Lodge seemed to have any recollection of it." At the meeting of 6th June the Lodge voted Rs. 100 towards the establishment of a library, and on the 25th idem, Wor. Bro. Whymper P.D. G.M. presented the Lodge with a parcel of books to form the nucleus of a library, and also with a facsimile of the "Cooke, M.S.S." In acknowledging this handsome present the Lodge wrote. "If we gain the reputation of having a really good masonic library, it will be mainly due to the kind interest you have manifested in, and your valuable contributions to it" (letter dated 10th August 1892).

1901. The next reference we have to the Library is in 1901. On the 9th December "the Secretary announced the presentation of the following books to our Library:—

"From Bro. the Earl of Suffolk the History of Freemasonry in 7 Volumes.

"From Bro. A.G. Hammond Fendel's History of Freemasonry, 1 Volume, and Kenning's Cyclopedia of Freemasonry, 1 Volume.

"From Wor. Bro. C.P. Lukis The Freemasons' Liber Musicus, 1 Volume."

1902. On the 10th February following the Secretary notified that Bro. Arthur had presented the Lodge with a work entitled "The Origin and Antiquity of Freemasonry" by A. Churchward.

1903. By next year, thanks to the Secretary, Bro. Ruegg, the books we could find were placed in order and a catalogue was printed with a few rules for the issue of books Since 1906, we have had a regularly appointed Librarian, but I am afraid little interest is taken in the library.

1908. A small addition was made by Wor. Bro. J. A. Davison in this year but no mention is made as to what books were presented.

1914. The lack of resposible interest in the Library is again shown it being recorded that on the List of Books being checked several volumes were reported missing. It was decided that as there was always a difficulty in securing a good librarian, the Trustees of Freemasons Hall be asked to accept the Library as a gift to the Hall. This gift was, however, refused by the Trustees and the Permanent Committee then recommended the following remarkable proposal to the Lodge. " It has been ascertained that the Trustees of Freemasons Hall are not disposed to accept our Library even if the Brethren are prepared to present it to them. The only question therefore, to be considered is what means can be devised for it's proper care, as at present it is very much neglected for want of some one to look after it. The Committee suggests that, if a suitable brother can be found willing to accept the office of Librarian he be exempted from his dues ; that if no present member is willing to take the office it be offered to au outsider on condition that he becomes a member of the Lodge free of fees and dues for so long as he holds the office of Librarian. The Master of the Lodge for the time being, to have the power to cancel any Brother's appointment as Librarian should he be found wanting in his duties".

Needless to say this proposal was NOT carried.

1918. A Librarian was found, and in 1918 Permanent Committee had to consider a representation from him with regard to the poverty of and want of interest in the Lodge Library. They considered that it would be a more useful Library which could be gradually enlarged by periodical small contributions if the Trustees of Freemasons Hall be asked to accept it for the benefit of the Brethren in general "there is no reason why it should not in time become a valuable adjunct to a regular reading-room for the use of the Fraternity". Alas, ten years have now elapsed and the reading-room in still to be opened.

In September the Secretary notified the Lodge that the Trustees had formally accepted the Library and from this year, thanks to the never failing efficiency of the Secretary to the Trustees (Wor. Bro. R. Wason) the Library has been kept in good order and has occasionally been added to. As we write the beneficial effect of the number of Lectures and Addresses which have of late been delivered in our Lodge have resulted in a greater "desire for knowledge" and a greater activity for the interests of this Library is evident, amongst the brethren.

130

Our Charities.

From our earliest days the active principles of Beneficence and Charity have been practiced by our Lodge. Our present St. John's Box has been established from the Lodge's foundation in 1838 and the records of the early years show the practical way in which the just claims of the poor and distressed were met.

The Box has for many years past been in the hands and the prerogative of the Worshipful Master, the out-going Master handing over to his successor in the Chair the Fund and records.

In 1871 the Punjab Masonic Institute for Children was started, to be followed by the Foundation for poor and distressed Widows in 1913 and from the foundation of these Charities our Lodge has given them the fullest support.

During the past 20 years upwards of Rs. 20,000 has been afforded to Charity by the Lodge including donations to St. John's Box and to the above Institutions but excluding personal donations from members through the medium of our P. M. I. Steward.

In 1885 District Grand Lodge resolved to provide the following Jewels every year "for the encouragement of efforts for the collection of Funds for the benefit of the Punjab Masonic Institutions."

1. A Gold Jewel for the Steward who shall have collected the largest amount during the preceding year provided the amount be not less than Rs. 1200.

2. A Silver Jewel to the Steward, the amount collected by whom shall bear the highest proportion to the number of subscribing members of the Lodge appointing him, provided that the proportion be not less than Rs. 24 per member.

3. Three Bronze Jewels awarded as follows :—

   a. One to the Steward who shall have collected the second largest total, provided that the amount be not less than Rs. 1,000.
   b. One to the Steward whose total shall bear the second highest proportion to the number of subscribing members of his Lodge, if not less than Rs. 18 per member.
   c. One to the Principal Officer of the Masonic Body which shall have made the largest contribution of the funds of such Masonic Body to the Punjab Masonic Institution provided that the sum contributed be not less that Rs. 200.

The following list of Lodge successes since the time these Jewels were first awarded is one which the Lodge can well be proud of, showing as it does that the early tradition of the Lodge is fully maintained to this day.

List of Awards earned by the Lodge since Steward's Jewels were first instituted.

Year.	Jewel earned.	By whom earned.
1888	Gold ...	Worshipful Master.
1888	Silver ...	Bro. W. R. Cox.
1891	Silver ...	Capt. W. P. Carson.
1893	3rd Bronze ...	Worshipful Master.
1894	Gold ...	Wor. Bro. Col. A. G. Yeatman-Biggs.
1896	Gold ...	Wor. Bro. Maj. W. P. Carson.
1897	Bar to Bronze	Worshipful Master.
1898	Gold ...	Bro. Lt.-Col. G. E. Money.
1898	Bar to Bronze	Worshipful Master.
1899	Bronze ...	Wor. Bro. W. Alves.
1900	Gold ...	Wor. Bro. R. Watson.
1902	Gold ...	Bro. H. R. Arthur.
1903	Silver ...	Bro. Maj. A. W. Warden.
1904	Gold ...	Bro. W. Mackinnon, C.E.
1904	2nd Bronze ...	Worshipful Master.
1907	Bronze ...	Bro. R. E. Holland.
1908	Bronze ...	Bro. S. Treglown.
1911	Bronze ...	Bro. F. Von Goldstein.
1913	Gold ...	Bro. E. F. Lawson.
1914	Gold ...	Bro. H. G. Russell.
1915	Gold	Bro. F. Von Goldstein.
1917	Silver ...	Wor. Bro. Col. L. P. More.
1921	Gold ...	Bro. P. C. Kevan.
1921	3rd Bronze ...	Worshipful Master.
1923	Bronze ...	Bro. P. C. Kevan.
1924	Bronze ...	Wor. Bro. G. Reeves-Brown.

APPENDICES.

BYE-LAWS OF LODGE HIMALAYAN BROTHERHOOD, No. 673
WORKING UNDER THE CONSTITUTION OF THE GRAND
LODGE OF ENGLAND, AND HELD AT SIMLA, IN THE
HIMALAYAS, 1853.

DECLARATION. D.

It being necessary for the support and good government of all Societies to form certain rules and regulations for binding the Members thereof. We the undersigned Master, Wardens and Brethren of this Lodge, for the better promoting unity, order and harmony, and in conformity with the liberty given us by the Constitutions of Masonry, *(*Vide p. 59 para. 4,*)* do agree to the following; reserving to ourselves a power of alteration as the majority of us, or our successors, shall think fit:—

JAMES MACKENZIE, W. M.

C. E. DAVIDSON, S. W.

H. T. TAPP, J. W.

T. GRAHAM, *Treasurer.*

THOMAS WOOD, *Secretary.*

Simla Lodge Rooms,   1853

BYE-LAWS.

Chapter I.

Constitution, elections, qualifications.

1. This Lodge consists of Subscribing, Honorary, Absent, and Serving Members.

2. The Officers of this Lodge are, and shall be:—

A. MASTER,	TWO DEACONS,
TWO WARDENS.	A TREASURER,
A SECRETARY,	AN INNER GUARD &
A STEWARD,	A TYLER.

3. An Annual Election of Officers shall take place at the first regular night of Meeting after the 1st March of each year.

4. No brother can hold *any* office in the Lodge unless he be Master Mason.

Chapter II.

Regular and emergent meetings of the Lodge.

1. This Lodge shall hold its regular Meetings on the 1st and 3rd Mondays of every month at such hour as the Master may deem proper.

2. Every Member shall in all things pay implicit obedience and respect to the Master in the Chair, and should at any time a Brother so far forget himself, as to infringe this important rule, it shall be the duty of the Wardens to interpose and support the Master, in such manner as the exigency may require.

3. No Brother shall be permitted to speak unless he address himself to the Master standing, and while so speaking, he shall in no manner be interrupted, unless he make use of indecorous language, or wander into subjects unconnected with the question at issue; in either of which cases, the Master, or either of the Wardens may call him to order when the speaker shall immediately desist; but notwithstanding this, he may afterwards proceed, without interruption, unless he again deviate from order and decorum.

4. No discussion shall be permitted on any motion, unless the same be seconded; but when a proper motion has been made and seconded, it shall, on no account whatever, be overruled; nor shall any other matter or subject be entertained until the same has been impartially determined.

5.   A motion may be opposed either by dissenting from the same, or by proposing an amendment, which amendment may either be an alteration of the original motion, or a substitution of something else in its stead:—if an amendment be made and seconded, any Brother who may desire to address the Lodge either on the side of the original motion, or on that of the amendment, shall be impartially heard.

6.   When an amendment has been made and seconded, there cannot be an additional amendment proposed; the amendment must be first disposed of by being put to the vote; after which the original motion is to be submitted, when it shall be decided which of the two is carried.

7.   The votes are to be signed by each qualified member who assents holding up his right hand, which are to be counted, the *ayes* by the senior, and the *noes* by the junior Warden, and reported accordingly to the Master.

8.   Serving Brethern have no votes in the Lodge.

9.   All business whatever which does not exclusively appertain to higher degrees, shall be transacted in an Entered Apprentice's Lodge.

10.   No Member shall divulge the transactions of this Lodge to any but a Member of it, under pain of explusion.

11.   No Brother shall be permitted to quit the Lodge until it shall have been closed for the evening, without leave, asked and obtained from the Master.

12.   It is expedient that every Brother attend the Meetings of the Lodge: or in the event of inability so to do, that the same may be notified to the Secretary, previous to such Meeting.   If any Brother shall be absent from the regular Meetings of the Lodge for three nights in succession, without sufficient reason being assigned, the Secretary shall report the same at the Quarterly Meetings, when such Brother shall be admonished, or censured, at the discretion of the Lodge.

Chapter III.
General Quarterly Meetings.

In addition to the preceding Rules, for governing regular and emergent Meetings, which are equally applicable to Quarterly Meetings, the following which relate exclusively to the latter, have been established:—

After the Lodge shall have been duly opened, and all preliminary matters disposed of in the usual way.

1.   The Secretary shall submit a Report stating the names of Brethren who have been initiated and admitted, and of those who have ceased to be Members of the Lodge, the number of Subscribing, Absent,

Honorary and Serving Members, and such other matters and remarks in explanation, as he may be prepared to offer for the information of the Lodge.

2.   The Treasurer shall produce an abstract of his accounts with the Lodge, which shall be delivered to the Secretary for record.

3.   The Treasurer shall next lay before the Lodge a list of Members who have not paid up their fees or subscriptions for the current quarter, stating whether they have been written to, and offer any explanation he may be able to afford the Lodge.

4.   The Treasurer shall also present a list of such Members as, having been already reported as defaulters, *(Vide preceding paragraph)* at a previous Quarterly Meeting, now come under the operation of para. 4—Chapter VIII.   This list, unless good and sufficient cause be shown to the contrary, shall be handed to the Secretary, in order that their names be erased from the list of Members.

5.   The Brethren having disposed of all the regular Quarterly business, will proceed to study the good of Masonry, by discussing subjects specially reserved for Quarterly Meetings, at which a very full attendance of Members will always be expected.

6.   Ballots for the admission of Members or Candidates for initiation into the mysteries of Masonry, may take place at Quarterly as well as at regular Meetings; but initiations cannot be held except in particular and very urgent cases.

Chapter IV.

The Permanent Committee.

1.   It being essential to the interests of the Craft that all matters of business to be brought under consideration of the Lodge should be previously investigated and understood, that the Lodge may be informed, and prepared to decide thereupon, a Committee shall be annually appointed by the Master, to consist of the Immediate Past Master, or in his absence one of the Wardens as Presiding Officer, and two ordinary members, with the assistance of the Treasurer and Secretary *ex-officio*.

2.   This Committee shall be convened as often as may be considered necessary, to take into consideration any matter referred to it by the Worshipful Master, by the Lodge, or by individual Members who may be desirous of obtaining its opinion or advice upon any matter previous to submitting it to the Lodge.

3.   That no alteration of, addition to, or abrogation of these Laws shall be made, unless proposed, seconded or carried in open Lodge, that on any such alteration, addition or abrogation being confirmed, the Secretary shall correct the Lodge-copy and shall send a Circular-copy of the same to all the Brethren Members, to enable them to correct their copies.

4. No motion involving matter of business or requiring reference or consideration shall be brought into discussion in the Lodge, (except in emergent cases,) unless it shall have been previously communicated to this Committee, which shall also be responsible that no paper be presented to the Lodge, with its sanction, containing any improper matter, or any offensive or indecorous language.

5. To this Committee shall also be submitted for examination the Treasurer's and all other accounts; and under its superintendence shall be made all transfers of Treasurer's, Secretary's, Steward's, or Tyler's accounts, books, papers, tools, jewels or other articles in their charge.

6. This Committee, when assembled, shall be governed by the Bye-Laws enacted for the Lodge, and the usages of the Craft during the time of business, and the Presiding Officer shall have power to summon before it any Member of the Lodge whose presence may be required.

Chapter V.

The Master, Wardens and Officers.

1. The office of Master being the summit of a Mason's laudable ambition, every Member should qualify himself for that high honor by learning how to perform the duties of a Warden: and the Wardens should always be competent to rule the Lodge and fill the Master's chair in his absence, should there be no Past Master present.

2. Regular attendance is commendable in all Masons, but absolutely necessary in the *Officers* of a Lodge, and no Junior Officer should be raised to a Senior Office unless he has faithfully and regularly performed the duties previously entrusted to him.

3. The Master is responsible to the Grand Lodge that the Treasurer and Secretary perform their duties correctly, and should therefore sign the minutes of the proceedings of every Meeting which shall be submitted to him in writing for that purpose, and himself and his Wardens should sign the Treasurer's accounts after they have been submitted for audit and found correct and satisfactory. The Steward's bills when approved by the Master, should be signed by him, as an authority for the Treasurer to discharge them.

4. The Treasurer shall, with the assistance of the Secretary, collect and receive all monies on account of the Lodge, of which he shall keep an account: he shall disburse no sums except by the Master's order or a vote of the Lodge, or by the authority of the Permanent Committee, and shall produce his books with an abstract of receipts and disbursements, and the names of all defaulters, at every Quarterly Meeting, as more particularly explained in Chapter III, paras. 2 and 4. He shall at the end of a year or on transferring his books to another, strike a balance and ob-

tain the signature of the Master and Wardens, in open Lodge, which shall be his release.

5. The Secretary is to issue summonses for all Meetings of the Lodge and its Committees; attend and take minutes of their Proceedings; receive all communications and lay them before the Lodge or its Committee; keep a full and correct list of the names of its Members and of all persons initiated or admitted therein, with the dates of their admission, initiation, passing, and raising; also of their ages, titles, professions, or trades; and generally perform such other business as has heretofore been done or may hereafter be ordered to be done by him.

6. The Steward shall have charge of the Lodge-rooms, furniture jewels &c., all which he shall keep in good order. He shall have charge of the refreshments, and obey the orders of the Master and his Wardens in all things, and especially in respect to the duties appertaining to his office.

7. The Tyler must be an expert Mason and a man of good repute; he shall receive such remuneration as the Lodge may direct. Nothing, save actual indisposition, can be a satisfactory excuse for the Tyler's absence, and which indisposition must, in due time, be intimated to the Master or Secretary. In the absence of the Tyler the Junior Master Mason shall Tyle the Lodge for that evening; which duty, should the absence of the Tyler require it, shall be performed by all the Members (Officers excepted) in rotation, unless a Member should be appointed by the Master as Acting Tyler, or voluntarily undertake the office.

Chapter VI.

Of proposing Members &c.

1. All Candidates for admission to this Lodge whether by joining or initiation, shall first be proposed and seconded by two Master Masons in open Lodge.

2. No person can be made a Mason in, or admitted a Member of this Lodge, if on the Ballot, two black balls appear against him.

3. No Member shall, on any account, disclose his own vote, or the vote of any other Member, should he happen to know it, under pain of expulsion.

4. Honorary Members pay neither admission-fees nor assessments, unless they should accept an office in the Lodge, in which case they become Subscribing Members.

5. That every joining as well as every newly Initiated Brother be furnished with a copy of these *Bye-Laws*, paying for the same.

Chapter VII.

Of visitors, &c.

1. No visitor shall be admitted into the body of this Lodge unless he produce a Grand Lodge Certificate, and is liable to work himself in; or, unless he is personally known to, is well vouched for, and is introduced by a Member who shall, before the opening of the Lodge, make known his name and designation to the Secretary, who shall record and report the same to the Master.

2. All Lodges being particularly bound to observe the same usages and customs, the Master and Wardens of this Lodge (or three Members deputed by the Master) shall visit other Lodges and a similar deputation from them be invited to visit this Lodge as often as shall be convenient, in order to preserve uniformity of work, and cultivate a good understanding among Free Masons.

Chapter VIII.

Contribution.

1. The following have been established as the rates of assessment to be paid monthly in advance:—

Subscribing Members	... Co.'s Rs.	3 0 0
Absent Members ...	,, ,,	1 0 0

2. St. John's Box devoted solely to charitable purposes, is supported by voluntary contributions from the Brethren at large, the Monthly Subscription of one rupee from absent Members, and one rupee per quarter *from* the Subscription of Subscribing Members.

3. The following are the Fees and Extra Charges made for admission, initiation, passing and raising:—

Joining.

	Rs.	as.	pie.
Admission or Entrance Fee as a Member,	12	0	0
Provincial Grand Lodge Registry Fee,	1	0	0
Ditto ditto Annual Subscription, ...	2	0	0
Quarterage to Fund of Benevolence.	1	0	0

Initiation.

Entered Apprentice or Initiation, ...	32	0	0
Steward's Fee, ...	2	0	0
Tyler's Fee, ...	2	0	0
Provincial Grand Lodge Registry Fee,	2	0	0
Ditto ditto Annual Subscription, ...	2	0	0
Grand Lodge of England Registry Fee,	6	0	0
Quarterage to Fund of Benevolence,			

Passing.

Fellow Craft on Passing,	...		20	0	0
Steward's Fee,	...	...	... 2	0	0
Tyler's Fee,	...	...	... 2	0	0

Raising.

Master Mason on being raised,	...	...	50	0	0
Steward's Fee,	...	...	... 2	0	0
Tyler's Fee,	...	...	... 2	0	0
Ditto ditto Certificate, ...	...	...	4	0	0

Absent Members.

Provincial Grand Lodge Annual Subscription,	...	2	0	0
Quarterage to Fund of Benevolence,	...	1	0	0

4. Any Member who shall neglect to pay up his Fees and Dues before each quarterly Meeting, shall be reported to the Lodge. Should the contributions of any Member remain unpaid for *two* quarters, he shall (unless good and sufficient cause to the contrary be shewn) be debarred all Masonic privileges, and cease to be considered a Member of the Lodge, and the same shall be notified to the Provincial Grand Lodge.

5. For the amount of the initiation and admission Fees of a Member, the proposer is answerable to the Lodge for passing, raising and all other regular Fees and Subscriptions for extra charges the Member alone is responsible.

6. No Member, who is one quarter in arrears of claimed Fees or Dues, can vote in the Lodge or propose a Member or a candidate, nor can he be passed or raised to any higher degree of Masonry, nor can any such application from him be read to the Lodge until the Treasurer has certified that no claims amounting to a quarter's dues exist against him.

7. When a Member of this Lodge is about to leave its limits, and wishes to be considered an *Absent* Member, he shall intimate the same to the Secretary *in writing* which shall exempt him from all payment, except his subscriptions as an absent Member until he notifies his return, or shall attend, or express, in writing to the Secretary, his desire again to attend, the Meetings of the Lodge.

8. Every Member of this Lodge on his departure from Simla shall be considered to have *resigned*, unless he shall signify to the contrary *in writing* to the Secretary.

Chapter IX.

Forms of Certificate, Application, &c.

No. 1.—*Form of Certificate.*

Lodge "Himalayan Brotherhood", No. 873.

CONSTITUTED AND HELD AT SIMLA, IN THE HIMALAYAS.

A. D. 185   A. L. 585

These are to certify that Brother... of..was, at the age of ....years, regularly and duly initiated into the mysteries of Free Masonry, in this Lodge on the........................... day of...................... that he was passed on the............................ day of................ ....and that he was raised on the.....................day of ....and having found him to be a worthy Brother, we recommend him as such to all Masons and Lodges, to be received after due examination.

To this certificate the said brother..................................has in our presence, signed his name, at full length, in the margin.

In testimony whereof we have subscribed our names, in open Lodge, this..............................day of the month of.............................. A.D. 185 , A.L. 585.

The Simla Masonic Hospital-Bed Fund.

Notes from Minutes and Circulars in connection with the Simla Masonic Hospital-Bed Fund : from its beginning in 1905 to the year 1925 ; by Wor. Bro. R. Watson.

The present year has been a notable one in the Simla Masonic Circle for the very considerable interest aroused in connection with the affairs of the Simla Masonic Hospital-Bed Fund which has, from force of circumstances no doubt, been lying idle for a considerable time, the last printed Statement having been issued in the year 1920, although in 1921 sums aggregating nearly Seven hundred Rupees were realized.

It is probably due to this fact that the Fraternity in Simla have been moved to reflect on the uncertainties inherent in a system of one-man control which has practically been the governing factor in the working of the Fund since its inception twenty years ago.

The last of the worthy brethren holding the position of Trustee to the Bed-Fund has undoubtedly been guided, and wisely guided, in falling in with the views of others who had been considering the advisability of handing over the future Management of the Fund to the Trustees of The Masonic Fraternity of Simla, a legally constituted body whose control of the affairs of that Association have been conspicuously successful, and through whom continuity of the satisfactory working of that Trust has been assured. As shown in another paragraph of these notes this consideration has been successfully developed.

It is not to be denied that much good work has been done in the past, and it is readily and universally acknowledged that while the Honorary Secretaryship was in the capable hands of the late Worshipful Brother E. O. Wilsey the handsome ▉bscriptions and donations realized were mainly due to to his exertions. This fact ▉s ever been gratefully borne in mind by the Masonic Brotherhood of Simla, and it is not likely to be forgotten while the Craft continues to flourish in this town.

It must at the same time be called to mind that the Brotherhood owes a deep debt of gratitude to those who first conceived the possibilities of such an Institution as a Masonic Hospital-Bed Fund, and foremost among these the name of Worshipful Bro. James Atkinson Longridge will ever be remembered with brotherly love and the highest esteem. At the first Meeting recorded in our Minute Book that worthy Brother made known his proposal to establish such a Fund and, in conjunction with Worshipful Brother Richard Heard, so well known so highly regarded by us all to the present day, and who was Wor. Brother Longridge's most willing and indeed very cordial adviser and helper in the development of the action proposed, the scheme immediately became a potential success, and the establishing of a Masonic Hospital-Bed Fund quite feasible.

Lieut-Colonel Longridge, a faithful subject of his King, a gallant Soldier, a true Friend, and a trusty Freemason, was killed in the Trenches in the early part of the Great War.

In the earlier days of the Simla Masonic Hospital-Bed Fund there were but seven Masonic bodies in Simla,—old Lodge Himalayan Brotherhood, Lodge Kitchener, Royal Arch Chapter Dalhousie, Mark Lodge Pinnacle, Ark-Mariner Lodge Sunshine, Himalaya Chapter Rose Croix, and Himalaya Preceptory of Knights Templars, and between these much assistance was afforded to the new scheme.

There is not, strange to say, any record of a Meeting of the so-called Committee of the Masonic Hospital-Bed Fund between the years 1907 and 1912 although during that period affairs appear to have progressed to a considerable extent, for at the Meeting held on the 4th of October 1912 it was announced that the credit balance of the Fund on that date amounted to over Rs. 6,000. At this Meeting Worshipful Brother Sir Pardey Lukis gave the Members present some interesting details connected with *The Lady Franklin Hospital-Bed Fund* with which we had become to some extent associated. He said :—

> "The object of the Fund is to pay either the whole or part of the Hospital bills of such patients as are unable to defray them from their own resources.........."

The Lady Franklin Fund had therefore almost indentically the same views that we have held in connection with our Masonic Hospital-Bed Fund and we have always been cordially invited to share in the benefits of the Fund upon certain Terms well known to many of us, and which are admitted to be most generous, varying as they have done with our changing fortune. It will be remembered that at one time the whole interest on capital was to be given : then, upon our own initiative, this amount was restricted : and that at a later period half of the reduced figure had been remitted in our favour owing to the disastrous failure of the Alliance Bank And, all through, the same advantages have been held out to us in respect of cases of sickness brought to our notice in which our help has been sought.

Before proceeding further let us call to mind the Terms above referred to.

These imply that while the support of the Simla Masonic Hospital-Bed Fund is accorded to it, the benefits of the Lady Franklin Fund will continue to be cordially extended to such cases as may lie within the scope of our own avowed intentions and that, as in the past, all necessitous cases recommended by us will at once be admitted.

It may be the opinion of some among us that we have on the whole paid more than our necessities have warranted, but that would be hardly a generous or indeed a reasonable view to entertain : for it has always been conceivable that circumstances of an exactly reversed nature might have occurred.

In this connection it should not be forgotten that we have at least given our support to a noble cause, eminently worthy of our support without consideration of possible benefits to ourselves,—and therefore that opportunities of exercising the basic principles of Freemasonry have been afforded to the Lodges and to the Brethren generally in this District. These ideals, supplemented by aid from Lodges and our own particular efforts in the cause of Relief and Charity, more convincingly and more frequently applied than in the past, will it is believed result in a greater measure of support and success to our present purposes and ultimate aims.

In connection with the original Constitution of the Simla Masonic Hospital-Bed Fund it may here be stated that at a Meeting held in October 1905 it was resolved that the intended benefits would be available at the Walker Hospital *for sick Masons, their Wives and Children, provided that such Masons were needy, and that for at least six months past they had been subscribing members of a Craft Lodge in Simla.* At a subsequent Meeting, held in August 1907, it was resolved *that the benefits of the Fund may be extended by the Committee to all Freemasons......whether subscribing to a Lodge or not.* It was further resolved *that the idea of some day endowing a Bed at the Walker Hospital be steadily kept in view.* In 1912 it was resolved *that the original objects of the Fund be adhered to :* that the aid of the Lady Franklin Fund be accepted and continued until The Masonic Fraternity of Simla were about to free themselves from debt and were *ready to take up the general question of endowing a Bed, or see thereafter any reasons to modify their present position.*

In 1921 (October) it was resolved *that an endeavour should be made to achieve the object with which the Fund was created............and that every effort should be made to increase the capital to the amount required.* But unfortunately there is no record in the Minute Book to show that any such commendable action ever took place. The cash accounts, however, detail receipts during that year from nine Lodges and two Brethren.

The next Meeting was, after a lapse of two years, held on the 14th September 1923 when there was a good representative gathering of Members, and Worshipful Brother General MacWatt representing the Lady Franklin Hospital-Bed Fund also kindly attended the Meeting. The Minute Book stated that the Chairman gave a brief history of the Masonic Hospital-Bed Fund, but there is no such entry in the book except those so often circulated by Worshipful Brother Wilsey and other Secretaries. The Chairman, (Wor. Brother Goldstein) also said he had convened that Meeting to consider the future of the Fund as owing to reasons given, any hope of obtaining a Bed in the Walker Hospital was now very remote, because :—

1.—The failure of the Alliance Bank reduced the Capital to Rs. 6,242-11-6.
2.—The price of a Bed in the Walker Hospital had been very considerably raised.
3.—Director General Indian Medical Service had appealed for the annual donation of Rs. 660 which could not now be met.

He them proposed *that the sum of Rs. 6,000, be lent to The Masonic Fraternity of Simla at 6% interest,* which was seconded and carried. The balance remaining in Capital account would thus be reduced to Rs. 242 and *he proposed that this sum should be utilized for augmenting a Masonic Aid Fund on the lines of the Government and the Trades Aid Fund, to which every Mason in Simla would be entitled to subscribe one rupee a month and grant relief to needy brethren.*

As might have been expected this proposition was opposed, and Bro. Abbott put an amendment seconded by Wor. Brother Howell-Jones to the effect that no arrangement be made to alter the constitution of the Simla Masonic Hospital-Bed Fund other than what might be necessary to legalize its position. However, the amendment was lost.

Wor. Brother Howell-Jones then proposed and Wor. Brother Walters seconded the motion that before proceeding any further the views of all Masonic bodies in Simla be obtained in connection with the original proposal. This was duly carried.

At the Meeting held on the 15th October 1924 it was explained that the main object before the Meeting was to arrive if possible at a definite conclusion as to the future management of the Simla Masonic Hospital-Bed Fund, the present capital of which stood at just over Rs. 7,000. *It was proposed, seconded and carried the original objects of the Fund be adhered to.*

It was further proposed that the management of the Simla Masonic Hospital-Bed Fund be transferred from the present Trustees (the Wor. Master of Lodge Himalayan Brotherhood) to the Trustees of The Masonic Fraternity of Simla. This was duly seconded by Wor. Brother General MacWatt, when an amendment was made that the proposed transfer be made, subject to the approval of Lodge Himalayan Brotherhood. The Minutes state that the amendment was carried, although there is no mention that it was seconded. The result of this discussion as recorded in the Minutes has since been challenged by the original proposer.

At this meeting it was resolved that for the year 1924 the sum of Rs. 300 be paid to the Lady Franklin Fund. And that in future years half the interest realized by us on Capital account up to a sum of Rs. 600 should similarly be paid to that Fund, until such time as the proposed Bed in the Walker Hospital or some similar Institution might be endowed.

So the transfer of the Management of the Simla Masonic Hospital-Bed Fund has been effected, practically with the full approval of all concerned, and the thanks of these are due to the last Trustee, Wor. Brother H. Brown, who has been one of the chief moving spirits in the matter.

Needless to state, the new management will do all in their power to introduce fresh life into the affairs of the Masonic Hospital-Bed Fund. They will endeavour, for one thing, to promote in all the Lodge and Chapters of the Punjab, and to re-kindle in the breast of every true Brother, a more lively sense of their duties and responsibilities as Freemasons and in the cause of Charity, than has recently been observable in connection with the Fund.

The Fund has experienced a dismal set back in the loss incurred by the failure of the Alliance Bank : but increased enthusiasm in the good cause will soon, we trust, warrant the optimistic view of our financial future which the Trustees confidently entertain.

We are promised by the Ball Committee of this year the profit on the Ball so successfully held last September, some seven hundred and fifty rupees. And we may also look forward with certainty to the fact that future entertainments of the same kind will furnish us with enhanced capital. The Liquidators of the late Alliance Bank have declared a further dividend for depositors, our share of which amounts, we believe, to about Rs. 800.

In conclusion it would be base ingratitude to omit, at this juncture, to express our very cordial thanks and obligations to our worthy Chairman, Worshipful Brother John Faletti, who has been so successful in his endeavours to direct our affairs. He has been one of the chief movers in connection with our Bed Fund. Let it not be forgotten that he was the original Treasurer at its inception in 1905-6 and that he, with his co-Trustees, is still at the Helm. It is well known to all that the success of The Masonic Fraternity of Simla has in no small measure been due to the capacity, sagacity, and cheerfulness with which he is so liberally endowed by nature. I must not forget to add that amidst the onrous duties of his daily life he has found time to go thoroughly through the accounts of the Bed Fund and that he has furnished a copy for record.

LIST OF OFFICERS.

List of Officers of Lodge "Himalayan Brotherhood" since its formation in 1838.

Office.	1838-39.	1839-40.	1840-41.	1841-42.	1842-43.	1843-44.	1844-45.
Master ...	R. B. McDonald	H. G. Gouland		J. T. Giels		J.G.W. Curtis	C. Cox.
Senior Warden..	W. S. Blackburn	G. Cox		P. W. Porter		J. T. Giels	W. Charde.
Junior ditto ..	D. O'B; Clarke	D. Seaton		W. Charde		T. Riddell	W. E. Carte.
Treasurer ...	J. W. Caplain C. J. French	C. J. French		Ditto		W. Charde	W. Charde. J. Christie.
Secretary ...	J. S. Chisholm C. J. French	C. J. French		Ditto		Ditto	Ditto.
Senior Deacon ..	—	J. H. Staines		G. Harriott		W. Master	R. Hill.
Junior ditto ..	—	H. W. Torrens		—		J. Christie	J. C. Curtis.
Inner Guard ...	—	J. Hy.		J. Christie		J. H. Staines	F. W. Ogilvie.
Tyler ...	—	J. Wood		—		—	—
Steward ...	—	—		—		—	G. E. Pool,

Lodge closed from October 1839 to August 1841.

Lodge closed from November 1841 to June 1843.

LIST OF OFFICERS &c.—(Continued.)

Office.	1845-46.	1846-47.	1847-48.	1848-49.	1849-50.	1850-51.	1851-52.
Master	J. B. Dodd	J. J. Marshall / J. S. Chisholm	There was no Installation and no officers were appointed this year.	Lodge closed from 18th August 1847 to 8th August 1849.	J. G. W. Curtis	J. Bracken	H. A. Ebden.
Senior Warden	J. S. Chisholm	P. Innes / J. W. Drummond			R. B. Wigstrom	E. D. Byng	H. B. Riddell. / E. J. Simpson.
Junior ditto	G. Bourchier	P. Petrovitz / H. B. Riddell			E. D. Byng	H. B. Riddell	G. E. Pool.
Treasurer	J. Christie	W. Charde / W.H. Emmerson			W. Charde	W. Charde	W. Charde. / T. Graham.
Secretary	Ditto	Ditto				W. Charde	W. Charde. / H. Tapp.
Senior Deacon	W. Charde	H. O. Gaynor / E. D. Hale			—	H. W. Bunbury	A. Pearson.
Junior ditto	C. E. Davison	E. C. Mullen / C. W. Russell			—	H. A. Ebden	T. Graham.
Inner Guard		H. Tapp			—	P. Goldney	—
Tyler	A. Jenkins	G. Dupuis			J. Walker	J. Walker	J. Walker.
Steward	G. E. Pool	....			—	—	—

LIST OF OFFICERS, &c.—(Continued.)

Office.	1852-53.	1853-54.	1854-55.	1855-56.	1856-57.	1857-58.	1858-59.
Master ..	J.A.D. Fergusson	J. Mackenzie	G. Jeffery	Lord W. Hay	J. Mackenzie		H. Tapp
Senior Warden..	E.C. Thorp	C.E. Davison	T. Graham	W.A. Hoghton	H. Tapp		S.R. Beechey
Junior ditto ..	E. Oakes	H. Tapp	Lord W. Hay	T. Wood	*D. Briggs* J.H. Maxwell		*F.D. Vivian,* A.B. Fenwick
Treasurer ..	T. Graham	T. Graham	T. Graham	T. Graham	T. Graham		T. Graham
Secretary ..	J. Walker	*Ditto* T. Wood	T. Wood	H. Tapp .	H. Tapp		T. Murray
Senior Deacon ..	J.F. Pogson	C.L.Montgomery	F. Perry	W.E. Ball	F.W. Drummond		J.P. Caulfield
Junior ditto ..	J.A. Guest	F.D. Vivian	J. Cockerell	B.J. White	E.J. White		H.M. Caulfield
Inner Guard ..	F.D. Vivian	W.A. Hoghton	A. Callander	S.R. Beechey	F.W. Vivian		Lord F. Hay
Tyler ..	J. Walker	J. Goulding	T. Fleming	R.J. Quinnell	C.W. de Russett		C.W. de Russett
Steward ..	—	—	—	—	F.D. Vivian		F.D. Vivian.

Lodge closed from November 1856 to March 1858.

LIST OF OFFICERS, &c.—(Continued.)

Office.	1859-60.	1860-61.	1861-62.	1862-63.	1863-64.	1864-65.	1865-66.
Master	*W.A. Hoghton* J.C. Curtis	T. Fleming	M. Clarke	T. Wood	T. Wood	T. Wood	J.H. Grant
Senior Warden	T. Fleming	F.D. Daly	G.N. Cheek	J.C. Hamilton	A.L.K. Quigley	W.H. Bishop	J.E. Cooke
Junior ditto	J.P. Caulfield	D.S. Henry	A.L.K. Quigley	J.G. Forbes	J. Craddock	C.H. Macleod	R. Dixon
Treasurer	T. Graham	T. Graham	T. Graham	T. Graham	T. Graham	T. Graham	T. Graham
Secretary	*T. Wood* F.D. Daly	F.D. Daly	F.D. Daly	W.R. Lewsey	C.H. Macleod	W.C. Willson	J.E. Cooke
Senior Deacon	E.G. Higgins	J.A.B. Campbell	A.R.P. Cecil	T. Cooke	T. Cooke	R. Dixon	W. Hill
Junior ditto	D.S. Henry	G.N. Cheek	W. Lemon	—	G.E. Campbell	G.H. Waller	A. Lyons
Organist	—	—	—	—	F.S. Cockburn	F.S. Cockburn	J. Elston
Inner Guard	C.W. de Russett	W. Lemon	R. Hill	—	W.H. Bishop	A. Lyons	W.C. Willson
Tyler	T. Murray	T. Murray	T. Cooke	R. Moorman	R. Moorman	R. Moorman	*R. Moorman* H. Gaunt
Steward	Ditto.	Ditto.	Ditto.	—	Ditto	Ditto	Ditto

LIST OF OFFICERS, &c.—*(Continued.)*

Office.	1866-67.	1867-68.	1868-69.	1869-70	1870-71.	1871-72	1872-73.
Master	J. E. Cooke	J. E. Cooke	T. M. Bleckley	T. G. Gardiner	W. E. Ball	H. R. Cooke	A. Litster.
Senior Warden	G. H. Waller	A. Lyons	H. R. Cooke	D. S. Henry	A. C. Cregeen	A. Litster	G. Hawksworth.
Junior ditto	W. Hill	H. R. Cooke	G. E. Campbell	C. H. Levinge	F. D. Daly	W. J. Haverty	J. I. Phelps.
Treasurer	T. Graham	T. Graham	C. H. Levinge	C. H. Levinge	C. H. Levinge	C. H. Levinge	B. L. Freeman.
Secretary	G. H. Waller	W. Newman	W. Newman	G. Hawksworth	G. Hawksworth	G. Hawksworth	P. J. Coyne.
Senior Deacon	W. C. Willson	*H. Smith* R. G. Macdonald	T. Bell	W. B. Davies	W. J. Haverty	J. I. Phelps	G. C. Caldecourt
Junior ditto	H. Smith	E. T. O'Connor	W. B. Davies	T. Jameson	J. I. Phelps	G. C. Caldecourt	W. Cotton.
Organist	J. Elston	J. Elston	J. Elston	J*. Elston		W. Mack	F. S. Cockburn.
Inner Guard	G. E. Campbell	J. A. S. Ellis	W. Yates	J. White	W. Cotton	F. W. deMonte	A. Jones.
Tyler	H. Gaunt	P. J. Coyne	P. J. Coyne	P. J. Coyne	P. J. Coyne	P. J. Coyne	F. von Goldstein.
Steward	Ditto.	—	—	W. J. Haverty	—	—	—

LIST OF OFFICERS, &c.—(*Continued.*)

Office.	1873-74.	1874-75.	1875-76.	1876-77.	1877-78.	1878-79.	1879-80.
Master ..	A. Litster	F. von Goldstein	A. Lister	J. Robertson	W. C. Willson	T. W. Rawlins	G. H. M. Batten
Senior Warden ..	P. J. Coyne	C. J. Marsden	G. C. Rivers	W. C. Willson	R. Burton	G. H. M. Batten	J. B. Hamilton.
Junior ditto ..	G. C. Caldecourt	T. Jameson	J. Robertson	J. Hopkins	W. L. Francis	J. L. Walker	C. C. Clavering
Treasurer ..	B. L. Freeman	A. Litster	T. Jameson	B. L. Freeman	B. L. Freeman	B. L. Freeman	W. C. Willson.
Secretary ..	G. Wallace	P. J. Coyne	P. J. Coyne	*B. L. Freeman* W. L. Francis	H. Elkington	B. L. Freeman	W. Anderson.
Senior Deacon ..	A. Jones	*B. Francis* *T. Morris* *G. C. Rivers*	T. E. G. Cooper	R. Burton	C. S. McRae	E. J. Topple	G. C. Caldecourt
Junior ditto ..	C. J. Marsden		E.S.P. Atkinson	A. Baker	C. C. Clavering	C. C. Clavering	W. M. Towelle.
Organist ..		W. McCarthy					
Inner Guard ..	B. Francis	E. W. Symes	R. Burton	C.S. McRae	W. Stephen	W. M. Towelle	J.B. Cowmeadow
Tyler ..	F. von Goldstein	A. L. K. Quigley	*A. L. K. Quigley* J. Flight F. von Goldstein	A.L.K. Quigley	W. Anderson	W. Anderson	C. S. McRae
Steward ..	—	—	—	C. Grinter	—	F. von Goldstein	—
P.M.I. Steward..					W. C. Willson	W. C. Willson	F. von Goldstein.

LIST OF OFFICERS, &c.—(Continued).

Office.	1880-81.	1881-82.	1882-83.	1883-84.	1884-85.	1885-86.	1886-87.
Master	J. I. Phelps	B. L. Freeman	G.E.L. Sanford	R. Wolseley	B. L. Freeman	W. P. Carson	H. P. Burt.
Senior Warden..	W. M. Towelle	G.E.L. Sanford	J. E. Myers	G. Townley	W. Smith	J. Burt	J. Burt.
Junior ditto ..	W. Ogden	G. Eyears	J. McDermott	E. v S. Cullin	R. Watsou	H. P. Burt	Mima Mall.
Treasurer ..	B. L. Freeman	W. Ogden	W. Ogden	R. Watson	R. Watson	R. Watsou	W. P. Carson.
Secretary ..	W. Anderson	C.J. Marckmann	*C.J. Marckmann* C. Mauley	G. Tauntou	J. Burt	Mima Mull	A. James.
Senior Deacon ..	J.B. Cowmeadow	J. McDermott	G. Townley	C. Mauley	C. F. Tufnell	A. James	E. Walmsley.
Junior ditto ..	C. H. Wickes	W. Singleton	C. H. Briggs	R. J. Polden	A. James	H. M. Framjee	C.F.S. Wright.
Inner Guard ..	A. M. Jacob	D. McGregor	C. Manley	Gokal Chaud	Mima Mnll	W. A. Wickham	J. Scott.
Tyler ..	R. von Goldstein	R. von Goldstein	R. von Goldstein	R. von Goldstein	R. von Goldstein	B. Simpson	B. Simpson.
Steward ..	—	—	—	—	—	—	W. P. Carson.
P.M.I. Steward	B. L. Freeman	G.E.L. Sanford	E. v S. Cullin	F. von Goldstein	F. von Goldstein	W. P. Carson	H. P. Burt.

Freemason's Hall Simla, 1926.

LIST OF OFFICERS, &c.—(*Continued.*)

Office.	1887-88.	1888-89.	1889-90.	1890-91.	1891-92.	1892-93.	1893-94.
Master ..	J. Burt	W. P. Carson	R. A. English	E. v S. Cullin	J. McDermott	E.H.H. Collen	H. Elkington.
Senior Warden..	R. A. English	Mima Mull	E.H.H. Collen	J. McDermott	R.G. Woodthorpe	W. G. Bowyer	W. G. Bowyer.
Junior ditto ..	A. James	C. R. Burn	E. Walmsley	*L. Dennehy* F. Leigh	H. Elkington	B. G. Wallis	F. G. Wigley.
Treasurer ..	W. R. Cox	W. R. Cox	W. J. Donaghey	W. J. Donaghey	W.J. Donaghey	*W. J. Donaghey* H. Elkington	R. C. Dockerill.
Secretary ..	E. Walmsley	E. Walmsley	A. Eaton	J. O. Power	J.E. Wilkinson	J. E. Wilkinson	E. Walmsley.
Senior Deacon..	C. F. S. Wright	F. Nowell	J. Smith	A Hale	W. H. Swales	F. G. Wigley	B. E. French.
Junior ditto ..	H. A. Beadon	J. Smith	G.T. Fillingham	W. Rochelle	C. T. Webster	J.H. Broughton	J. Bidwell.
Organist ..	—	—					L.E.A. Mausfield
Inner Guard ..	R. A. Pymm	B. Frame	J. Lennox	D. Carey	D. Carey	B. E. French	W. F. Stowell
Tyler ..	B. Simpson	B. Simpson	A. Hale	F. C. Hoff	E. Walmsley	E. Walmsley	*J. A. Williams.* J. W. Hale.
Steward ..	W. P. Carson	W. P. Carson	W. P. Carson	W. P. Carson	E. Walmsley	E. Walmsley	J. W. Hale.
P.M.I. Steward	W. R. Cox	E. Walmsley	H. A. Beadon	W. P. Carson	J. McDermott	W. P. Carson	J. McDermott.

LIST OF OFFICERS, &c.—(Continued),

Office.	1894-95.	1895-96.	1896-97.	1897-98.	1898-99.	1899-1900.	1900-01.
Master ...	R. Burton	Sir A. Miller	R. Watson ..	A. B. Patterson	W. Alves	A. E. Sandbach	G.H.C.Andersoon
Senior Warden..	Sir A. Miller	F. G. Wigley	G.H.C.Andersoon	H. Bower	G. E. Money	G.H.C.Andersoon	C. P. Lukis.
Junior ditto ..	B. E. French	W. Alves	A. E. Harris	H. J. Marcoolyn	W. F. Stowell	G. Curtis	H. R. Arthur.
Treasurer ...	W. P. Carson	W. P. Carson	W. P. Carson	W. P. Carson	G.H.C.Andersoon	W. Alves	W. P. Carson.
Secretary ...	E. Walmsley	H. C. Atkinson	F. J. Pilcher	F. N. Press	F. N. Press	J. Shearer	T. G. Sparkes.
Senior Deacon ..	W. Alves	W. F. Stowell	H. J. Marcoolyn	A. J. Craddock	G. Curtis	O. W. Cole	E E. Clarke.
Junior ditto ...	W. F. Stowell	G.H.C.Andersoon	C. A. Owen	T. G. Sparkes	J. Faletti	G. R. Crowe	E. O. Wilsey.
Organist ...	L.E.A. Mansfield	L.E.A. Mansfield	L.E.A. Mansfield	J. Webber	J. Webber	W. H. Jenn	W. H. Jenn.
Inner Guard ...	G.H.C.Andersoon	A. B. Wilson	T. G. Sparkes	J. Croke	O. W. Cole	J. K. E. Bowder	F. Binge.
Tyler ...	J. W. Hale	A. Morriss	A. Morriss	A. Morriss	A. Morriss	A. Morriss	A. Morriss.
Steward ...	J. W. Hale					H. Browne	
P.M. I. Steward	A. G. Yeatman-Biggs.	W. P. Carson	W. P. Carson	W. P. Carson	G. E. Money	W. Alves	R. Watson.

LIST OF OFFICERS, &c.—*Continued*.

Office.	1901-02.	1902-03.	1903-04.	1904-05.	1905-06.	1906-07.	1907-08.
Master	C. P. Lukis	J. B. D'Silva	E. O. Wilsey	F. Leigh	R. Heard	A. J. Longridge	J. Faletti.
Senior Warden	T. G. Sparkes	Earl of Suffolk	A. W. Warden	A. J. Ruegg	A. J. Longridge	J. Faletti	R. E. Holland.
Junior ditto	E. E. Clarke	E. O. Wilsey	F. Rennick	A. R. D'Silva	J. McGregor Cheers	R. E. Holland	G. T. Fillingham.
Chaplain	—	—	—	R. Watson	R. Watson	R. Watson	R. Watson.
Treasurer	W. P. Carson	H. R. Arthur	J. Faletti	J. Faletti	T. Taylor	F. G. Finch	R. T. Waugh.
Secretary	A. J. Ruegg	A. J. Ruegg	A. J. Ruegg	J. McGregor Cheers	S. E. Bird / F. W. Callaway	F. W. Callaway	H. L. Reynolds. / F. W. Callaway.
Dir. of Ceremonies	—	—	—	W. Alves	F. Leigh	J. B. D'Silva	J. B. D'Silva.
Senior Deacon	E. O. Wilsey	R. T. Rodgers	A. R. D'Silva	W. Mackinnon	W. Mackinnon	H. Pepper	E. W. Andrews.
Junior ditto	A. W. Warden	R. T. Tharle-Hughes	J. McGregor Cheers	B. Ingram	N. S. Harvey	E. W. Andrews	A. J. Westrap.
Organist	W. H. Jenn	T. W. Lloyd	T. W. Lloyd	T. W. Lloyd	T. W. Lloyd	T. W. Lloyd	G. Wilson,
Inner Guard	R. T. Rodgers	J. McGregor Cheers	B. Ingram	S. E. Bird	O. C. Sullivan	A. J. Westrap	S. Samuels.
Tyler	A. Morriss	A. Morriss	A. Morriss	A. Morriss { T. Taylor / W. Linford	A. Morriss { W. Linford / F. Wheeler	F. Wheeler / J. B. D'Silva / H. R. Arthur	B. E. French.
Steward							
P. M. I. Steward	W. P. Carson	H. R. Arthur	A. W. Warden	W. Mackinnon	J. Faletti	F. G. Finch	R. E. Holland.

LIST OF OFFICERS, &c.—(*Continued.*)

Office.	1908-09.	1909-10.	1910-11.	1911-12.	1912-13.	1913-14.	1914-15.
Master	T.W. Lloyd	A R. D'Silva	CP. Lokis	E.W.S.K. Maconchy	A H. McMahon	A.F. Humphreys	R E Holland
Senior Warden	E.W. Andrews	E.W.S.K. Maconchy	E.R. Abbott	R. Tharle-Hughes	A.F. Humphreys	C.J. Prior	E. Bertram Higgs
Junior ditto	W.H. Jenn	A.F. Humphreys	O.C. Sullivan	R.T. Waugh	S.E. Bird	C.J. Knowles	F. von Goldstein
Chaplain	R. Watson	R. Watson	R. Watson	R. Watson	R. Watson	J. Tinson	R. Watson
Treasurer	*R.T. Waugh* S. Treglown	S. Treglown	R.T. Waugh	C.J. Prior	C J. Prior	R.T. Waugh	W. Cotton.
Secretary	E.O. Wilsey	E.O. Wilsey	E.O. Wilsey	E.O. Wilsey	E.O. Wilsey	E.O. Wilsey	E.O. Wilsey
Asst. Secretary				—	R.T. Waugh	R.T. Waugh	R.T. Waugh till 1-10-14. W. Gilbert-King
Dir. of Ceremonies	J.B. D'Silva	J. Faletti	J. Faletti	J. Faletti	J. Faletti	J. Faletti	J. Mutimer
Senior Deacon	A.J. Westrap	G.Reeves-Brown	E.W. Hicks	S E. Bird	C.J. Knowles	E. Bertram Higgs	A.A. Phelps, till 1-1-15. G. Wilson till 1-5-15.
Junior ditto	E.M. Johnstone	Walter Smith	C.B. Daly	G.B. Sanford	F. W. Bagshawe	W.G. Dollman	P.C. Mukherjee
Organist	G. Wilson	P.H. Marshall G. Wilson	G. Wilson	G. Wilson	E. Bertram Higgs W.G. Dollman	G. Wilson	B.E. French
Inner Guard	G.Reeves-Brown	Gouri Kant Roy	F.I. Tellery	C.J. Knowles	W.G. Dollman	C.O.H. Teeling	B.E. French
Tyler	B E. French	B.E. French C.B. Daly	B.E. French	B. E. French	B.E. French	B.E. French	Ditto
Steward	J.A. Longridge	B.E. French H.R. Phelps	Ditto	Ditto	Ditto	Ditto	Ditto
P.M.I. Steward	S. Treglown		W. Gilbert-King	F. von Goldstein	G.Reeves-Brown	E.F. Lawson	H.G. Russell

LIST OF OFFICERS, &c.—(*Continued.*)

Office.	1915-16.	1916-17.	1917-18.	1918-19.	1919-20.	1920-21.	1921-22.
Master	C.J. Prior	E.Bertram Higgs	C.J. Knowles	H.F. Cleveland	G.Reeves-Brown	P. H. Marshall	W. G. Dollmas.
Senior Warden..	H.R. Phelps	C.J. Knowles	H.F. Cleveland	G.Reeves-Brown	P.H. Marshall	W. G. Dollman	B. J. Robertson.
Junior ditto	W.G. Dollman	P.C. Mukherjee	F.L. Milne	H. Hussey	B.J. Robertson	H. Brown	B. C. W. Otto.
Chaplain	R. Watson	R.E. Holland	H.R. Phelps	A.F. Humphreys	F.R. Evans	B. C. W. Otto	H. G. Russell.
Treasurer	W. Cotton	H. Brown	F..R Evans	A.N. Ross	E.R. Grant	C. J. Prior	C. E. Wills.
Secretary	E.O. Wilsey	E.O. Wilsey	E.O. Wilsey	E.O. Wilsey	J.W. Walker	E. O. Wilsey (till 1-11-1920) C. J. Knowles	W. E. Fursdon.
Dir. of Ceremonies	J. Tinson	L.P. More	A.F. Humphreys	J. Tinson	J. Tinson		H. Brown.
Senior Deacon ..	F.L. Milne	B.J. Robertson	H. Brown	F.R. Evans	B.C.W. Otto	A. E. Higgins	E. N. de Rhe Philipe.
Junior ditto	H.G. Russell	Beni Tewary	H. Hussey	B.C.W. Otto	E.N. de Rhe Philipe	C. J. Murray	G. R. Parker.
Organist	P.H. Marshall	P.H. Marshall	—	—	W. Hawes	G. Wilson	N. F. Turner.
Asst. Secretary..	—	—	—	—	—	—	—
Inner Guard	T.C. Maxwell	G.W.B. Widger	B.C.W. Otto	C.V. Jefford	G.R. Parker	F. W. Addinall	H. Bloodworth.
Steward	J. Mutimer	Ram Ratan Puri	E. Williamson	A.E. Higgins	A.E Higgins	F. R. Evans	A. E. Ellis.
Steward	F.J. Read	A.J. Hill	C.M.E. Warner	B J. Robertson	V.C. Millington	E. N. de Rhe Philipe	G. Daglish.
Steward	—	—	—	—	—	—	R. A. Maelzer.
Tyler & Steward	B.E. French	B.E. French	B.E. French	B.E. French	B.E. French	B. E. French	B. E. French.
P.M.I. Steward..	F. Goldstein	B.E. French	L.P. More	G.Reeves-Brown	H. Brown	F. W. Addinall	P. C. Kevan.

LIST OF OFFICERS, &c.—(Continued.)

Office.	1922-23.	1923-24.	1924-25.	1925-26.	1926-27.
Master	B. J Robertson	F. A. Goldstein	H. Brown	J. Tinson	G. R. Parker.
Senior Warden	F. A. Goldstein	R. Line	G. R. Parker	A. E. Higgins	J. W. B. Gardner.
Junior Warden	G. R. Parker	J. W. B. Gardner	F. R. Evans	C. E. Wills	H. E. Bloodworth.
Chaplain	A. E. Ellis	W. G. Dollman	C. E. Wills	H. E. Bloodworth	F. W. Addinall.
Treasurer	J. Sheppard	Sital Singh	Sital Singh	T. R. Sanderson	T. R. Sanderson.
Secretary	{ W. E. Fursdon / H. Brown }	J. Sheppard	J. Sheppard	H. J. Cheetham	E. S. Adhemar.
Dir. of Ceremonies	P. H. Marshall	A. W. Dyer	P. H. Marshall	H. G. Russell	H. Brown.
Senior Deacon	W. P. Todhunter	H. Whitelaw	H. E. Bloodworth	R. J. Shearcroft	R. J. Shearcroft.
Junior Deacon	{ H. E. Bloodworth / J W. B. Gardner }	R. J. Shearcroft	H. J. Cheetham	F. W. Addinall	E. H. Free.
Asst. Dir. of Ceremonies	R. Line	—	H. Whitelaw	J. W. B. Gardner	F. Newland.
Almoner			—	F. Newland	T. G. Fox.
Organist	H. J. Cheetham	H. J. Cheetham	—	W. J. Eades	W. J. Eades.
Asst. Secretary	—	—	—		
Inner Guard	R. J. Shearcroft	F. R. Evans	F. W. Addinall	K. D. H. Framjee	J. F. Masters.
Steward	H. Whitelaw	A. H. Berriff	E. H. Free	A. H. Berriff	A. H. Bradford.
Steward (Regalia)	P. E. D. Boyle	E. W. Brook	K. D. H. Framjee	E. S. Adhemar	C. H. Holliday.
Tyler	M. B. Ellison	M. B. Ellison	T. W. Veasey	T. W. Veasey	{ T. H. Jackson. / A. E. Higgins. }
P. M. I. Steward	P. C. Kevan	G. Reeves-Brown	T. R. Sanderson	J. F. Masters	F. Newland.

ROLL OF MEMBERS.

ROLL OF MEMBERS.

From 1838 to May 31st 1927.

I—Initiated.   J—Joined.   Rj.—Re-joined.

(Dates of Passing, Raising, Resignation etc. can be obtained from Bro. Secretary if required.

List I.

Members from May 1838 to close of 1839.

Names.		Profession or Occupation.	Date.
*Blackburn, W. S,	..	Supdt. Rev. Dept. N.-W.F.P.	J. 19-5-38.
Burnett, Robert, Lee	..	Military Officer, H.E.I.C. Service	I. 26-9-39.
*Caplain, J. W.	..	Merchant	J. 19-5-38.
Carr, George	..	Military Officer, H.E.I.C. Service	I. 6-9-39.
Carte, William Edward	..	Surgeon H.E.I.C. Service	I. 7-9-38.
Caulfield, James Gordon	..	Military Officer, H.E.I.C. Service	I. 21-6-39.
*Chisholm, John Seton	..	"Citizen of Calcutta"	J. 19-5-38.
Christie, James	..	Deputy Collector Loodeanah	I. 2-8-38.
*Clarke, D O'B	..	No record	J. 19-5-38.
Conlan, Richard Edward	..	Clerk	I. 7-9-38.
Conlan, Thomas	..	No record	J. 21-8-38.
Cox, George	..	No record	J. 3-5-39.
Cox, George Hamilton	..	Capt. Invalid Establishment	I. 21-8-38.
French, Charles John	..	Examiner of Accounts, N.W.P.	I. 31-5-38.
Gordon, Archibald Campbell	..	Surgeon, H. E. I. C. Service	I. 18-10-39.
Gouland, Henry Godfrey	..	Clerk	J. 8-6-39.
Hill, George Mytton	..	Military Officer, H. E. I. C. Service	I. 19-7-39.
Hoff, George Benjamin	..	Assistant Examiner of Accounts N.W.P.	I. 21-7-38.
Hoff, John C.	..	Clerk	J. 2-8-39.
*Hoff, John Jacob Lewis	..	No record	J. 19-5-38.
Horn, John	..	Clerk	J. 5-7-39.
*Lemon, J.	..	No record	J. 19-5-38.
Lindstedt, Charles William	..	Deputy Registrar Military Deptt.	I. 3-5-39.
*McDonald, R. Barker	.	No record	J. 19-5-38.
Michell, George Bruce	..	Military Officer, H.E.I.C. Service	I. 19-7-39.
Morris, Augustus Burke	..	Ditto	I. 20-9-39.
Seaton, Douglas	..	No. record	J. 3-5-39.
Sheetz, James	..	Sub-Medl. Department	I. 12-10-38.
Staines, James Henry	..	Clerk Lt. Governor's Office	J. 3-5-39.

* Founders.

Names.	Profession or Occupation.	Date.
Tapp, H. T.	Political Agent Subathu	J. 7-9-38.
Taylor, John	No record	
Thompson, George Powney	Civil Service	I. 21-6-39.
Torrens, Henry Whitelock	Deputy Secretary to Government of India, Secret. and Political Department.	J. 21-6-39.
Webb, Edward	No record	J. 3-5-39.
Wilson, William	Sergeant, G. G's Band	I. 5-7-39.
Wood, John	Sergeant, G. G's Band	J. 8-6-39.
Woodcock, William Henry	Military Officer H. E. I. C. Service	J. 21-6-39.

List II.

From 26th August 1841 to the 18th August 1847.

Names.	Profession or Occupation.	Date.
Anderson, George Gibson	Lieut., 15th B. I.	I. 8-9-45.
Anderson, J.	Surgeon to C.-in C.	J. 26-8-41.
Andrews, William Eyre	Captain, 44th B.I.	I. 8-9-45.
Atty, William Frederick Willis	Lieut., H.M's 31st Foot	I. 9-7-45.
Bagot, Alexander	Military Officer, H.E.I.C. Service.	J. 3-7-44.
Banks, J. S.	Captain, Assistant Secretary to Governor.	J. 15-7-46.
Barry, H.	Captain, H.E.I.C. Service, 71 N. Inf.	J. 17-6-46.
Barry, R. J.	Military Officer	J. 17-6-46. Rj. 19-5-47.
Basilico, Andrew	Lieut., 11th B.I	I. 2-9-46.
Batten, Joseph Gordon	Lieut., 37th B I.	I. 7-10-46.
Beatson, Albert Balcombe	Ensign, 11th B.I.	I. 18-8-45.
Beatson, Douglas Charles Twiny	Lieut., 14th B.I.	I. 19-9-45.
Beatson, W. F.	Brigadier, Nizam's Army	J. 1-7-46
Beecher, A.	No record	J. 26-8-41.
Bell, Adam	Surgeon, H.E.I.C., Service	J. 30-8-44.
Bellers, Robert Bridges	Lieut., H.M. Service 50th Regt.	I. 22-7-45.
Boileau, A.H.E.	Military Officer, H.E.I.C. Service.	J. 25-8-43.
Bourchier, George	Lieut., Artillery	J. 13-6-45.
Bovais, Edward Theadore	Clerk	I. 13-9-43.
Boys, William John Edward	Captain, 6th B.L. Cavy.	J. 24-6-45.
Brooke, R. P.	No record	
Burton, James Archer	Cornet, 3rd Lt. Dragoons	I. 6-8-45.
Campbell, Edward	Military Officer, H E.I.C. Service.	J. 16-9-41.
Caplain, J. W.	Merchant	Rj. 23-6-43.
Carrington, Arthur	Lieut., H.E I.C. Service	I. 8-7-43.
Carte, William Edward	Surgeon, H. E. I. C Service	Rj. 19-6-43.
Charde, William	Clerk Simla Bank	J. 26-8-41. Rj. 19-6-43.
Chisholm, John Seton	"Citizen of Calcutta "	Rj. 13-6-45.
Christie, Edward	Do	J. 27-8-45.
Christie, James	Deputy Collector, Loodeanah	Rj. 26-8-41.
Clarke, D.O'B	No record	Rj. 26-8-41.

Names.	Profession or Occupation	Date.
Colebrooke, Thomas Elliot ..	Captain 13th B. I. ..	I. 2-9-46.
Cox, George ..	No record ..	Rj. 21-6-44.
Cripps, John Mathew	Lieut. 26th L. Inf. ..	I. 27-8-45.
Curtis, James Charles ..	Military Officer, H. E. I. C. Service.	J. 6-9 44.
Curtis, James Gray William ..	Ditto ..	J. 23-6-43.
Daniel, C. E.	Clerk	I. 28-7-43.
Davison, Charles Edward	Merchant's Assistant	I. 2-8-44.
deMontmorency Raymond Elmeric.	Lieutenant, H. M's. 50th Foot	I. 21-6-45.
Dodd, John Beach ..	No record ..	J. 13-6-45.
Drummond, John William ..	Lieutenant, 70th B. I. ..	I. 19-9-45.
Dupuis, G. ..	No record ..	..
Ellice, G. W. ..	Ensign, H. E. I. C. ..	I. 14-10-46.
Elliot, A. J. H. ..	Military Officer, H. M. 9th Lancers, G. G's. Body Guard	I. 12-8-46.
Ellis, Henry Augustus Louis ..	Cornet, G. G's. Body Guard.	I. 7-10-46.
Emmerson, W. H. ..	Lieutenant, H. M's. 10th Foot	J. 3-6-46.
Erskine, J. C. ..	C. S., Commissioner, Umballa..	J. 23-6-43.
Faddy, S. Brougham ..	Military Officer ..	I. 19-8-46.
Farmer, Willam Roberts ..	Lieutenant. H. M's. 50th Foot	I. 17-6-46.
Fortescue, F. R. N. ..	Military Officer ..	I. 1-10 46.
Foster, George ..	Lieutenant, 16th B. I. ..	I. 3-6-46.
Frampton, Heathfield James ..	Lieutenant, H. M's. 50th Foot	I. 21-6-45.
Gaynor, H. O. ..	Lieutenant, H. M's. Service 39th Regt. ..	J. 3-6-46.
Geils, J. T. ..	Ditto ..	J. 26 8-41.
Goddard, Thomas ..	Captain, 44th B. I. ..	I. 3 9-45.
Goulnnd, Henry Godfrey ..	Clerk ..	Rj. 19-6-43.
Green, Theophilus ..	Lieutenant, 48th B. I. ..	I. 22-7-45.
Grindlay, Henry Robert ..	Lieutenant, 6th Lt. Cavly ..	I. 18-8-45.
Grisenthwaite, John Beaufoy ..	Clerk ..	I. 13-9-43.
Hale, Edward Dashwood ..	Lieutenant, Bengal Infy. ..	I. 3-6-46.
Hall, John Whittle Mackenzie ..	Lieutenant, 6th Lt. Cavly. ..	I. 22.8-45.
Harriott, G. ..	Captain, 16th Lancers ..	J. 26-8-41.
Hart, Henry ..	Lieutenant, H. M's., 31st Foot	I. 9-7-45.
Hewitt, W. H. ..	Colonel, 40th Regt. ..	J. 26-8-41.
Higgins, G. ..	Lieutenant, 3rd B. I. ..	I. 16 9-46.
Hill, Rowland ..	Military Officer, H. E. I. C. Service. ..	J. 25-8-43.
Hillier, G. E. ..	Captain, H. M's., Service ..	J. 19-5-47.
Hough, Harry Wainwright ..	Lieutenant, H. M's., 50th Foot	I. 21-6 45.
Innes, Percival Robert ..	Lieutenant, 1st Regt. Eu. Fus.	I. 17-6-46.
Innes, Peter ..	Major, H. E. I. C. Service ..	J. 6-8-45.
Jenkins, Alexander ..	Church clerk ..	I. 2-8-44.
Knatchbull, Reginald Edward ..	Military Officer, H.E,I.C. Service	J. 25-8-43.
Law, Robert ..	Lieutenant, H. M's., 31st Foot	I. 10-10-45.
Lawrence, John George ..	Lieutenant 24th B.I ..	I. 22-7-45.
Lindam, Charles ..	Lieutenant, H. M's., 10th Foot	J. 18-5-46.

Names.	Profession or Occupation.	Date.
Long, George Frederick	Captain, H. M's , 50th Foot	J. 6-8-45.
Lumley, J. R.	Military Officer, H.E.I.C. Service	J. 16-9-41.
Macready, George William	Surgeon, H. M's., 31st Foot	J. 9-7-45
Mactier, Anstruther	Lieutenant, 4th Lt. Cavly	I. 23-9-46.
Mainwaring, Norman William	Lieutenant, 73rd B.I.	I. 29-4-46.
Marshall, John Samuel	Lieutenant-Colonel, 54th B.I.	J. 18-5-46.
Master, Whalley	Military Officer, H.E.I.C. Service	J. 23-6-43.
Maxwell, Henry Hamilton	Lieutenant, H.E.I C. Service	I. 10-10-45.
McDonald, R. Barker	No record	Rj. 26-8-41.
McDonald, Peter	Tradesman	I. 2-9-41.
McGrath, F. V.	Captain, H.E.I.C. Service	J. 7-7-43.
Mouat, Charles Abney	Lieut. H. M's , Service, 50th Regt.	J. 19-9-45.
Mullen, Edward Cowell	Lieutenant, H. M's., 50th Foot.	I. 9-7-45.
Needham, Henry	Captain, H. M's., 50th Foot	I. 3-6-46.
Nightingale Manners Randolph	Military Officer	I. 2-9-46.
Ogilvie, William Falconer	Military Officer, H.E.I.C. Service	J. 30-8-44.
Owen, Arthur Walshman	Lieutenant, 11th B. I.	I. 18-8-45.
Pester, Hugh Lawrence	Lieutenant, 63rd B. I.	I. 8-9-45.
Petrovitz, Paul	Artist	J. 29-4-46.
Plaskett, Thomas Henry	Lieutenant, H.M's., 31st Foot	I. 6-8-45.
Pogson, John Frederick	Lieutenant, 47th B. I.	I. 26-6-46.
Poole, George Edward	Subordinate Medl. Dept.	I. 1-9-43.
Porter, F.W.	No record	J. 26-8-41.
Preyre, Louis Pierre	Clerk	I. 11-8-43.
Ramsay, Belcarres Dalrymple Wardlaw	Captain, 75th Regt.	I. 15-7-46.
Riddell, Henry Philip Archibald Buchanan	P. M. General	I. 3-6-46.
Riddell, T.	Captain, H.E.I.C. Service	J. 23-6-43.
Roberts, Henry S.	Clerk	I. 2-7-47.
Russell, Claud William	Lieutenant, 54th B. I.	I. 3-6-46.
Russell, James	Lieut. H M's , 50th Foot	I. 27-8-45.
Seaton, Douglas	No record	Rj. 26-8-41.
Siddons, George Richard	Bt Capt. Bengal Cavly.	I. 27-8-45.
Silver, John	Lieutenant, 2nd Eu. Regt	I. 12-8-46.
Stains, James Henry	Lt.-Governor's Office, Agra	Rj. 19-6-43.
Staples, Thomas	Lieutenant, 6th Lt. Cavly.	I. 22-8-45.
Talbot*	Military Officer	I. 19-8-46.
Tapp, Henry Thomas	House Agent	I. 18-8-45.
Tottenham, Francis Robert	Cornet, 7th Lt. Cavly.	I. 6-8-45.
Twycross. William Stephen	Lieutenant, 73rd B. I.	I. 25-5-46.
Valiant, T.	No record	..
Ventura	Ditto	..
Walmsley, Philip Map	Lieutenant, 16th B. I.	J. 18-5-46.
Wiley, Henry Williams	Lieutenant. H. M's., 50th Foot	I. 27-8-45.
Wollen, William Kelly	Military Officer, H.E.I C. Service	J. 25-8-43.
Wright, T. B.	Surgeon, Agency, Jeypore	J. 7-8-46.
Young, George Dobson	Captain, H. M's. Service	I. 22-7-45.

* Probably "John Talbot" Major Invailed Establt.

List III.

From 8th August 1849 to the end of May 1927.

Names.	Profession or Occupation.	Date.
Abbott, Evelyn Robins	I. C S.	I. 8-6-96.
Abdul Ahad	Sub-Overseer P.W.D.	J. 9-7-88.
		Rj. 10-9-17.
Acres, George	Military Clerk	I. 20-9-75.
Addinall, Frederick William	Military Clerk	I. 12-4-15.
Adhémar, Edgar Stanley	Mechanist Staff Sgt. R.A.S.C.	I. 10-3-24.
Alexander, Henry Victor	Mech.amst Sgt. Major R.A.S.C.	J. 14-5-23.
Alexander, Sidney Walter	Lt. 45th Mountain Battery	I. 13-1-19.
Allen, James George	Lt. I.M.L	J. 11-9-16.
Allnutt, George K.	Accountant P.W.D.	J. 5-5-73.
Alsop, Joseph Farrow	Chemist	I. 13-4-96
Alves, William	Conductor Comst. Department	J. 8-5-93.
Ampthill, Baron G.C S.I. Etc...	..	H. 11-7-04.
Anant, Prasad Dube	Clerk	I. 12-8-12.
		Rj. 8-10-23.
Anderson, John	Surgeon to H. E. the C.-in-C.	J. 15-5-50.
Anderson, George Henry Crawford	Merchant	I. 8-5-93.
Anderson, William	Military Clerk	I. 6-9-75.
Andrew, Arthur Miller	Military Clerk	J. 12-8-07.
Andrews, Ernest William	Military Clerk	J. 8-8-04.
Andrews, H. F.	No record	J. 18-5-63.
Andrews, Rev. Charles Freer	Clerk in Holy Orders	J. 11 7-04.
Anthony, Ernest Theodore	Accountant P. W. D.	I. 5-6-76.
		Rj. 10-8-85.
Arnold, Richard John	Clerk	I. 18-9-71.
Arthur, Harry Robert	Conductor, Ordnance Dept.	J. 11-4-98.
Ashworth, Robert Fredrick Weir	Military Clerk	I. 10-10-98.
Ashworth, William Hubert	Military Clerk	J. 10 2-19.
Atkinson, Albert	Sergeant R. A.	I. 9-8 97.
Atkinson, Edmund Stroud Paton	Survey Dept	J. 20-7-74.
Atkinson, Harry Crowther	Military Clerk	J. 12-11-94.
		Rj. 13-5-01.
		Rj. 12-3-06.
Auhinleck, John Claude	Lieutenant, Royal Artillery	I. 18-8-62.
Babonau, Thomas William	Clerk	J. 9-8-97.
Bacchus, George Henry	Lieut. 7th D. Gds.	J. 1-6-63.
Bacon, T. H.	No Record	J. 22-5-51.
Bagot, Alexander	Lieut. 15 B. I.	Rj. 8-8-49.
Bagshawe, Fredrick William	Major, I. A.	J. 12-6-11.
Bailey, George Edward	Manager, Messrs. Watts & Co.	I. 8-6-96.
Baillie, Edward Sterling	Asst. Surgeon S. M. D.	J. 14-6-97.
Baker, Alfred	Clerk	J. 6-9-75.
Baker, R.	School Master, Municipal Board School	J. 12-6-99.
Baker, Reginald Augustus Charles	Captain, I. A.	J. 10-5-20.
Ball, Arthur	Tailor	J. 11-7-98.
Ball, William Edward	Clerk	I. 16-5-53.
		Rj. 6-6-70.
		Rj. 3-6-72.
Barker, Alfred	Lieut. 66th B. I.	I. 17-10-50.
Barnes, James Fitz Ernest	Clerk	I. 13-8-00
Barrett, Edward	Electrical Engineer	J. 11-6-06.

H. Hony. Member.

Names.	Profession or Occupation.	Date.
Barratt, Lewis Victor ..	Military Clerk ..	I. 8-9-19.
Barsby, Harry ..	Engineer ..	J. 10-5-09.
		Rj. 12-8-12.
Bass, William Henry ..	Qr. Mr. Sergeant R. A. ..	I. 10-10-87.
Barstow, Robert William ..	Captain, H. M's. 63rd Regt. ..	I. 31-7-77.
Basudeo Singh ..	Taquildar ..	J. 8-9-13.
Batchelor, William Henry ..	Tailor's Cutter ..	I. 16-5-08.
Batten, George Henry Maxwell	I. C. S. ...	J. 2-8-75.
Battye, Fredric Drummond ..	Colonel, I. A. ..	J. 9-7-94.
Beadon, Harold Archibald ..	Asst. Secy. Simla Municipality	I. 12-7-86.
Beatson, Clare Lawrence ..	Assistant F. and P. Deptt. ..	I. 9-10-16.
		Rj. 10-5-20.
Beatson, John Walter ..	Clerk ..	J. 6.6-64.
Beatson, William ..	Law Agent ..	J. 5-8-67.
Beatty, Edmond Tyrrell ..	Military Chaplain	J 13-5-89.
Beckett, Henry Baron ..	I. C. S. ..	J. 13-4-96.
Beckett, John ..	Sergeant R. A. ..	I. 11-5-91.
Beechey, Stephen Richard ..	Artist (Painter) ..	I. 28-8-54.
Beer, William Peter ..	Warrant Officer, I. O. D. ..	J. 12-6-22.
Bell, James Richard Bruner ..	Consulting Engineer to Govt.	J. 8-10-94.
Bett, Joseph ..	Sanitary Engineer ..	I. 11-2-24.
Bell, William ..	Inspector of Army Schools ..	J. 12-9-98.
Belle, Theodore ..	Merchant's Clerk ..	J. 21-5-66.
		Rj. 6-6-70.
Beni Pershad Tewary ..	Clerk ..	J. 27-7-08.
Beresford, Lord William ..	Major, Military Secretary to H.	
	E. the Viceroy ..	I. 10-10-87.
Beresford—Barker, Harold ...	Capt. I A. R. O. ..	J. 15-6-21.
Berriff, Alfred ..	Merchant ..	J. 10-6-89.
		Rj. 8-6-96.
Berriff, Arthur Henry ..	Draper ..	I. 14-8-22.
Bharat Chandra Ghosh ..	Asst. Surgeon, S. M. D. ..	J. 13-6-98.
Bhupindar Singh Mahindar, H.		
H. the Maharaja Dhiraj of		
Patiala.		I. 18-6-14.
Bickell, James George ..	Chemist ..	I. 11-1-13.
Bidwell, James ..	Military Clerk ..	J. 14-9-91.
Bignell, Richard Augustus D'Oyly	Private Secretary to H. H. the	
	Maharaja of Kuch Behar ..	J. 9-10-88.
Binge, Fredrick William ..	Merchant's Assistant ..	I. 5-8-99.
		Rj. 12-7-09.
Birch, Edwin Thomas ..	Sergeant R. A. ..	I. 12-10-96.
		Rj. 9-11-03.
Birch, R. Graham ..	Lieut.-Colonel, Indian Army ..	J. 11-9-82.
Bird, Shearman Edward ..	Clerk ..	I. 23-6-02.
		Rj. 27-4-08.
Birdwood, Herbert Christopher		
Impey ..	Captain, R. E. ..	I. 11-7-92.
Bertie-Clay, Neville Sneyd ..	Major, R. A. ..	J. 15-10-02.
Bisheu Singh ..	Clerk ..	J. 11-11-07.
Bishop, William Henry ..	Ditto ..	J. 18-5-63.
		Rj. 21-7-68.
Bittles, George Henry ..	Conductor, Ordnance Dept. ..	I. 18-7-98.
Black, John B. ..	No record ..	I. 24-6-63.
Blades, William Scott ..	Merchant ..	J. 7-5-77.
Blake, Henry Thomas ..	Battery Q.M.S., R.A. ..	I. 30-4-06.
Bleckly,, Thomas McDougall ..	Surgeon, I.M.S. ..	J. 22-6-68.
Bliss, Frank ..	Chemist ..	I. 11-5-96.
Bloodworth, Harry Edwin ..	Military Clerk ..	I. 1-11-18.

Names.	Profession or Occupation.	Date.
Bodh Raj Saberwal ..	Civil Engineer ..	I. 22-8-11.
Blundell, T. L. ..	Surgeon, Dentist ..	I. 17-10-49.
Bosley, Cecil Alfred ..	Military Clerk ..	I. 22-6-18.
Boileau, Thomas Theophilus ..	Lieutenant H.E.I.C., Service ..	J. 16-5-53.
Bond, Francis George ..	Colonel R. E. ..	J. 14-5-06.
Bouwell, Edward Warren ..	Surgeon Dentist ..	J. 10-7-05.
Boulderson, Samuel ..	Lieutenant, 7th Hussars ..	J. 18-8-62.
Bowder, John Kelshaw Escot ..	Clerk ..	I. 11-7-87.
		Rj. 12-7-97.
Bower, Hamilton ..	Captain, I.A. ..	J. 11-6-94.
Bowles, Frederick Augustus ..	Brig.- Genl. I.G. of Artillery ..	J. 12-8-07.
Bowyer, Wentworth Grenville ..	Major R. E. ..	I. 11-5-91.
Boyd, John Greig ..	Flight Sgt. R.A.F. ..	J. 14-7-24.
Boyle, Percy Edwin Douglas ..	Military Clerk ..	I. 23-7-19.
		Rj. 11-8-24.
Bracken, John ..	Major H.E.IC. Service ..	J. 8-5-50.
Brackenbury, Richard Gunn ..	Lieut. H.M. S. ..	J. 20-6-52.
Bradford, Alexander Henry ..	Draper ..	I. 11-2-24.
Brake John ..	Military Surgeon ..	I. 6-7-63.
Bredin, Edgar Grantham ..	Military Clerk ..	I. 20-6-81.
		Rj. 10-6-89.
Breese, Charles Dempster ..	Wing Commander R.A.F. ..	I. 11-10-20.
Breething, William Joseph .	Capt. Indian Army .	I. 13-9-20.
Brewster, Frank .	Examiner of Questioned Docu-	
	ments (C.I.D.) ..	J. 14-10-18.
Bridge, Harry ..	Warrant Officer I.A.O.C. ..	J. 13-12-26.
Bridgeman, James ..	Staff Sgt. I.O.D. ..	J. 12-2-23.
Briggs, Charles Henry ..	Chemist ..	J. 17-4-82.
Briggs, David ..	Lieutenant H.E.I.C. Service ..	J. 16-4-55.
Briscoe, Stanley St. John ..	Banker's Clerk ..	J. 11-8-98.
Brook, Ernest William ..	Telegraphist ..	I. 12-2-23.
Brooks Harry ..	Military Clerk ..	J. 8-8-21.
Brooks, John Hatfield ..	Lieutenant, 1st L. C. ..	I. 5-6-50.
Broughton, James Hunt ..	Tailor ..	J. 11-5-91.
Brown, Gerald Reeves ..	Chemist ..	I. 7-6-07.
Brown, Harry ..	Military Clerk ..	J. 12-7-15.
Brown, Robert ..	Sub- Medical Department ..	I. 9-1-93.
Brown, Charles ..	D. S. Police ..	I. 19-9-70.
Brown, George Clement ..	Clerk ..	J. 7-6-0-5.
Brown, Thomas Henry de la Rue ..	Military Clerk ..	J. 9-10-93.
Brownlow Francis ...	Colonel, 72nd Highlanders ..	J. 87-6-78.
Bruce, Robert Robertson ..	Lieut. Bengal Artillery ..	I, 17-7-52.
Bruce-Kingsmill, Julian Cluade		
de Kenne ..	Lieut.-Colonel Royal Artillery ..	J. 12-8-18.
Buchner, Ernest ..	Band Master Viceroy's Band ..	I. 9-7-00.
		Rj. 12-6-11.
Bunbury, H. W. ..	Captain H. M's Service ..	J. 22-8-49.
Burn, Charles Rosden ..	Lieutenant 1st Dragoons ..	I. 10-10-87.
Burnham, Richard ..	Clerk ..	I. 21-8-71.
Burt, Henry Parsall ..	Civil Engineer ..	J. 11-5-85.
		Rj. 14-7-13.
Burt, John ..	Military Clerk ..	J. 12-5-84.
Burton, Francis Charles ..	Colonel, 2nd B. L. ..	J. 13-8-94.
Burton, Richard ..	Military Clerk ..	J. 19-4-75
		Rj. 13-7-85.
Bustard, Thomas Charles ..	Assistant Steiert & Co. ..	J. 14-5-06.
Butler, Edmond Arthur ..	Clerk ..	I. 20-8-55.
Butterfield, Herbert ..	Acctt. P.W.D. ..	J. 11-5-91.
Butterfield, William Rysdale ..	Acctt. M.W.D. ..	I. 17-10-87.

Names.	Profession or Occupation.	Date.
Byng, Edmund Disney	Lieutenant 1st En' B. Fus. A.D.C. to C.-in-C.	J. 8-8-49.
Bythell, W. J.	Major R E.	J. 12-11-00.
Caldecourt. George. Caldecott	Clerk	I. 4-6-66. Rj. 17-5-69. Rj. 5-4-75.
Callan, G.	Sergeant, R. A.	J. 9-7-00.
Callan, R. T.	Merchant	J. 4-5-63.
Callander, Alexander	Lieutenant H.E.I.C. Service	I. 3-10-53.
Callaway, Frederick Maynard	Assistant Finance Deptt.	I. 9-7-23.
Callaway, Frederick William	Military Clerk	J. 13-2-05.
Cameron, Hugo Roderick Angus	Ditto.	I. 8-1-94.
Campbell, Gilbert Edward	Nil	I. 4-5-63.
Campbell, John Algar Bullock	Merchant	I. 23-5-59.
Campbell, John Scarlet	Lieutenant, H.E.I.C. Service	I. 7-7-51.
Campbell, Leslie Stuart	Military Clerk	J. 12-9-98. Rj. 10-12-00. Rj. 12-10 08.
Campbell, Thomas	Engineer	J. 8-7-18.
Campbell William	Clerk	J. 19-4-75.
Campion, John M.	Civil Engineer	J. 14-5-83. Rj 14-10-95.
Cann, Mark	Brewery Manager	J. 26-7-09.
Cannock, William March Edwin	Flight Sergeant, Royal Air Force	I. 13-9-26.
Carey, Daniel	Battery Q.M.S., R.A.	I. 9-9-89.
Cargill, William MacGiluray	Civil Engineer	I. 13-4-08.
Carmichael, Andrew Blair	Sergeant, H.E., I.C. Service	I. 16-5-53.
Carrigan, Peter	Military clerk	J. 22-7-95.
Carson, William Paterson	Military clerk	J. 12-5-84. Rj. 9-4-88.
Carte, William Edward	Surgeon, I.M.S. Retired	Rj. 8-8-49.
Carter, R. H.	Lieutenant, H. Ms. 87, Foot	I. 4-9-52.
Caulfield, Henry Minson	Lieutenant, H.E.I.C. Service	I. 2-8-58.
Caulfield, John Palmer	Captain, H.E.I.C. Service	J. 19-10-58.
Cecil, Alfred Roger Park	Shop Assistant	I. 10-8-59. Rj. 20-5-61.
Chadwick, Harry	Sergeant, R. A,	I. 13-8-06.
Chalmer, John McKay	Clerk	I. 8-8-87.
Chalmer, Owen Ivan	Ensign, H.E.I.C. Service	I. 18-8-56.
Chandler, Herbert George William	Captain, I. A.	I. 1-5-07.
Channell, Stanley	Military Clerk	J. 12-1-20.
Chanter, Edward Jean	School Master	I. 13-9-86.
Chapman, Edward Henry	Military Clerk	J. 8-2 09.
Chappel. Herbert E.	Telegraph Engineer	J. 8-10-94.
Charanjit Singh, Ahluwalia	Of Kaparthala	I. 24-10-04.
Chard, Frank Henry	Military Clerk	I. 22-6-18.
Charde, William	Asst. Secretary, Simla Bank	Rj. 8-8-49.
Cheek, George Nicholas	Assistant Surgeon, Indian Army	I. 16-8 59.
Cheers, John	Military clerk	(Changed)
Cheetham, Henry Joseph	Warrant Officer, I. O, D.	I. 9-8-20.
Chester. Henry Dawkins Eardley Wilmot	Lieutenant, H. M's. Service	J. 20-6-59.
Chippendale, William Harold	Lieutenant, R. E.	J. 17-6-78.
Christensen, John	Clerk	J. 27-4-08.
Clark, W. Ronaldson	Major, I. M. S.	J. 8-1-00.
Clarke, Alexander	Chemist	I. 10-12-00.

Names.	Profession or Occupation.	Date.
Clarke, Ernest	Hotel Manager	I. 11-8-24.
Clarke, Edward Ernest	Draper	J. 14-8-09.
		Rj. 13-6-04.
Clarke, James Edward	Military clerk	J. 9-9-12.
Clarke, Lawrence Henry	School Master	I. 20-8-55.
Clarke, Melville	Captain, Indian Army	J. 1-10-60.
Clarke, Robert	I. C. S.	J. 11-5-96.
Clarke, William George	Deputy Superintendent of Police	I. 12-8-12.
Clarmont, Thomas	Clerk	J. 2-9-68.
Clavering, Carey Clarendon	Military clerk	J. 5-4-75.
		Rj. 1-5-82.
Clayton, George Henry	Asst. Secretary, Simla Municipality	I. 8-3-97.
Clerke, Louis Arthur Henry	Asst. Surgeon Sub M. D.	I. 12-2-00.
Cleveland, Henry Francis	Colonel, I. M. S.	J. 14-5-17.
Clifford, Robert Wigram	Lieutenant, 10th Lt. Cavalry	I. 4-9-52.
Coast, Michael W. Lade	Captain, H. M's. Service	J. 7-7-62.
Coates, Thomas Alfred	Assistant, Govt. of India	I. 9-8-26.
Cobbe, Alexander Hugh	Captain, H. M. S.	J. 20-6-53.
Cockburn, Francis Shaw	Professor of Music	I. 11-8-53.
		Rj. 4-5-63.
		Rj. 17-6-72.
Cockburn, Henry	Clerk	J. 4-5-63.
Cockerell, John	Lieutenant, H.E.I.C. Service	I. 7-11-53.
Coghill, Kendal Josiah William	Ditto	J. 18-8-56.
Cole, Edward	Sergeant Instructor, Simla Volunteers	J. 12-8-01,
		Rj. 12-3-06.
Cole, Owen Wynne	Clerk	J. 10-1-98.
Coleman, Peter Seth	Chemist	I. 14-9-03.
Collen, Arthur George Pomeroy	Assistant Commissioner, Uganda	1. 8-10-00.
Collen, Edwin Henry Ethelbert	Lieutenant, R. A.	I. 31-10-98.
Collen, Edwin Henry Hayter	Colonel, B. S. C.	J. 9-10-88.
Collyer, James	Jeweller	J. 15-6-21.
Colomb, Francis	Captain, I. A.	I. 11-3-95.
Condan, Thomas	Type Machine Expert	J. 13-6-04.
Connell, George Ernest	Assistant Army Headquarters	J. 13-2-22.
Conolly, Francis Henry	Lieutenant H.E.I.C. Service	I. 20-10-56.
Cooke, Henry Rex	Captain, R. A.	J. 11-9-99.
Cooke, William Ridge	Nil	J. 13-10-02.
Cooke, Hugh Rowland	Clerk	I. 27-5-66.
Cooke, John Edward	Ditto	I. 18-7-64.
Cooke, Thomas	Soldier, H. M's. Service	I. 8-10-60.
Cooke, Thomas Arthur	Colonel, H. M's. Service	J. 14-7-90.
Cookworthy, Colin	Lieutenant Bengal Artillery	J. 2-10-50.
Cooling, Charles Ernest	Lieut. I. A R. O.	J. 11-10-20.
Cooper, Ernest Milan	Chemists Asst.	I. 11-8-84.
		As serving.
Cooper, Harry	Major, A.D C., Viceroy	I. 22-9-88.
Cooper, Thomas Edward George	Engineer,	J. 18-5-74.
		Rj. 8-9-84.
		Rj. 14-11-98.
Cordell, Charles Alexander	Sub-Medical Department	J. 9-10-82.
Corfe, Ernest	Military clerk	I. 13-4-96.
Corstorphan, George	Accountant	J. 20-9-75.
		Rj. 10-9-83.
		Rj. 12-7-97.
Cotter, Preston Parr	Clerk	J. 8-3-09.
		Rj. 11-5-14.

Names.	Profession or Occupation.	Date.
Cotton, William	Merchant	I. 21-9-68.
Cotton, William	Chemist	J. 14-12-08.
Coutts, William Scott	Tailor	I. 1-7-72.
Cowan, Hugh Montgomery	I. C. S.	I. 28-9-07.
Cowell, J.	Photographer	J. 8-7-89.
Cowgill, Fred Fairbauk	Schoolmaster	J. 11-12-16.
Cowmeadow, James Bruce	Draper	I. 21-4-73.
		Rj. 5-5-79.
Cowmeadow, William Frederick Bruce	Draper	I. 11-1-15.
		Rj. 9-7-23.
Cox, Herbert Vaughan	Brigadier General, I. A.	J. 14-8-11.
Cox, Walter Radcliffe	Asst. Alliance Bank	I. 21-7-86.
Coyne, Patrick James	Clerk	I. 4-6-66.
Craddock, Arthur James	Architect	I. 14-11-92.
Craddock, James	Photographer	J. 18-8-62.
		Rj. 17-6-72.
Cragie, John Harry Smith	Colonel, H. M's. Service, Asst. A. G. Army Head-Quarters	J. 11-5-96.
Cragie, Patrick Niel	2nd Lieutenant I. S. C.	I. 20-12-99.
Crane, Alfred	Qr. M. Sgt. Pack Artillery	J. 8-6-25.
Crayden, Walter James	Clerk	I. 13-8-94.
Creagh, O'Moore	General, I. A. Commander-in-Chief in India	J. 11-10-09.
Cregeen, Archibald Crellan	Civil Engineer	J. 21-5-66.
Cripps, John Mathew	Lieutenant, 26th N. I.	J. 5-6-50.
Crofts, A. M.	Military Surgeon	I. 8-10-83.
Croke, John	Sergeant, U. L. (Groom to H. E. the Viceroy)	I. 9-10-93.
Croley, Frank William	Engineer	I. 14-7-02.
Cross, Frederick George Cashell	Military Clerk	J. 12-8-95.
Crouch, George Ernest	Army School Master	J. 14-5-17.
Crowe, George Ross	Asst. Surgeon Sub-Medl Dept.	J. 11-1-97.
Cullin, Edward Van Someren	Barrister-at-Law	J. 5-9-81.
Cumberland, R. F. W.	Military Officer	J. 7-8-52.
Cunnigham, Alexander	Major, H. E C. Service	I. 16-8-49.
Cuppage, Henry Croker	Lieutenant, 15 n. I.	I. 4-9-52.
Curtis, George	Military clerk	I. 11-11-95.
Curtis, James Charles	Captain, H. E. I. C. Service	Rj. 16-5-53.
		Rj. 4-7-59.
		Rj. 18-8-62.
Curtis, James Gray William	Military Officer, H. E. I. C. Service	Rj. 8-8-49.
Cutler, Alfred Usher	Hairdresser	J. 8-5-99.
		Rj. 10-6-01.
Daglish, George	Warrant Officer, I.U.L.	J. 12-4-20.
Daljeet Singh	Nil	J. 14-8-00.
Dallas, John Edwin	Asst. Secretary, P.W.D.	J. 11-8-90.
Daly, Anthony	Clerk	I. 24-6-61.
Daly, Charles Byrne	Military clerk	J. 10-8-08.
Daly, Francis Dermott	Agent, Simla Bank	I. 19-10-58.
		Rj. 6-6-70.
Daly, George Hickey	Sub-Medl. Dept.	J. 21-8-65.
Daly, William	Clerk	I. 8-10-60.
Daniell, Charles Astell	Lieutenant, H. E.I.C. Service	I. 5-9-53.
Dannenberg	Photographer	J. 11-6-61.
Darbari Lal Saihgal	Excise Deptt. Punjab	I. 14-7-13.
Davico, Andrea	Caterer	J. 12-8-07.

Names.	Profession or Occupation.	Date.
David, John	Lieut. I.A.	I. 11-4-21.
David, Percy Charles	Government clerk	I. 13-9-20.
Davie, James Couper	Manager, Kellner & Co., Simla	J. 14-5-06.
Davies, Alfred S.	Sub-Medl. Dept.	J. 4-8-73.
Davies, William Byers	Clerk	I. 10-9-66.
Davies, James John Herbert	Chemist	I. 18-7-98.
Davis, William Edwin	Clerk	I. 8-10-94.
Davis, Ronald Archibald	Military Clerk	I. 9-10-06.
Davison, Charles Edward	Merchant	Rj. 1850*
Davison, William Edward Septimus	Merchant	J. 7-7-51.
Davys, Gerald Irvine	Captain, I.M.S.	J. 11-11-07.
Dawson, John	Lieutenant H.E.I.C. Service	I. 1-5-54.
Dawson, Henry Charles	Sergeant Farrier, R.A.	I. 8-4-01.
Day, John George	Lieutenant R.E.	I. 31-7-77.
D'Cruz, Andrew	Clerk	J. 6-6-64.
DeBudé, F. R.	Lieutenant R.H.A.	I. 4-9-52.
DeFabeck, Frederick William Alexander	Surgeon Major I.M.S.	J. 21-5-77.
DeFrain, Ernest Edward	School Master	I. 7-12-91.
DeMonte, Frank William	Clerk	I. 15-7-67. Rj. 7-8-71.
Dennehy, Lachlan	Private Secretary to Maharajah Dholepur	I. 17-8-86.
de Rhé Philipe, Eue Neil	Clerk	I. 26-9-17.
deRozario, W.	Clerk	J. 13-7-96.
DeRussett, Charles William	No record	J. 19-5-56.
Desgratoulet, Louis Ernest	Agent	I. 4-5-63.
Devine, James Purvis	Nil	I. 12-10-91.
Dewar, Kenneth Purvis	Assistant Foreign Office	J. 11-8-19.
Dholpur, H. H. the Maharaj Rana of (see Udaibhan Singh.		
Dinshaw, Heerjeebhoy Muncherji Framjee	Merchant	I. 12-11-00.
Dinwoodie, John	Military Clerk	J. 11-6-06.
Dixon, Rowland	Clerk	I. 1-6-63.
Dobbin, George Miller	Captain, Indian Army	J. 3-10 59.
Dockerill, Robert Charles	Banker	I. 9-5-92.
Dollman, William George	Clerk	I. 10-5-09.
Donaghy, William John	Telegraph Dept.	J. 15-5-82.
Dorin, Henry Alexander	Lieutenant, H.E.I.C. Service	J. 3-9-55.
Dorton, Frank Stanislaus	P.W.D. Supervisor	I. 8-3-09.
Dorton, William	Clerk	I. 15-10-55.
Douglas, George	Military Clerk	I. 7-4-73.
Douglas, George Victor	Military Clerk	I. 11-2-18.
Douglas, Herbert Archibald	Major, I.A.	J. 14-7-13.
Daulat Ram	Superintendent of Post Offices	I. 13-10-90.
Doulat Singh, Maharaj	Military Secy. to H. H. the Maharajah of Jodhpur	J. 13-11-99.
Dowding, Henry Harris Hewitt	Captain, Essex Regt.	J. 14-1-01.
Dowler, Thomas	Clerk	I. 15-10-55.
Dowling, George	Clerk	J. 4-10-75.
Dracup, Richard Henry	Superintendent Railway Deptt.	I. 30-9-10.
Drake, Samuel	Retired Soldier	J. 12-7-15.
Drake, Thomas Oakley	Military Clerk	J. 9-6-90. Rj. 10-7-05.
Drake, William James	Registrar, P.W.D.	J. 12-8-12.
Drummond, Francis Walker	Captain, H.E.I.C. Service	J. 2-6-56.

* Without ballot in virtue of his exaltation to R. A. degree.

Names.	Profession or Occupation.	Date.
Drysdale, David	Military Clerk	J. 12-8-07.
D'Silva, Albert Robert	Clerk	I. 10-10-98.
D'Silva, George Thomas	Clerk	I. 10-10-98.
D'Silva, John Bower	Clerk	J. 12-9-98.
Duer, Charles	Major, I.M.S.	I. 10-4-11.
Duffin, Frederick	Ensign 70th Ben. Infantry	J. 18-6-51.
Duggan, William	Sergeant, R. A.	I. 14-9-85.
Dunbar, Charles	Clerk	I. 20-6-64.
Duncan, Andrew	Military Clerk	I. 26-10-08.
Dunn, Frederick John	Secretary, Army Canteen Board	J. 12-7-26.
Dunning, Harry Durden	Sergeant, 2-4th Dorset Regiment	I. 13-11-16.
Dunolly, Kenneth James Grant	Major, I. A.	I. 18-9-06.
Durham, William Robert	Major, I.M.D.	J. 12-6-22.
Dutt, R. C.	(See Raj Kumar Dutt.)	
Dwyer, Thomas	Chief Warder Military Prison Lucknow	J. 12-2-06.
Dyce, Frederick Lowis Stoll	Lieutenant, H. M's. Service	I. 21-7-62.
Dyer, Edward, John Reginald	Brewer	J. 11-3-07.
Dyer, John	Surveyor	I. 1-10-55.
Dyer, Augustus Wilhelm	Assistant Surgeon	J. 16-4-14.
Eades, William John	Military Clerk	J. 8-7-18. Rj. 12-1-25.
Eaton, Alfred	Military Clerk	J. 14-5-88.
Eaton, Albert	Draper's Asst.	J. 11-5-91.
Ebden, Henry Anderson	Civil Surgeon, Simla	J. 15-5-50.
Eckford, John James	Lieutenant, 6th Ben. Infantry	I. 22-5-51.
Edwards, Arthur	Military Clerk	J. 11-7-98. Rj. 12-11-06.
Edwards, Edmon Pinching	Band Master, 2nd Shrop. L.I.	J. 7-6-05.
Edwards, George Edward	Sergeant, R.A.	I. 30-4-06.
Edwards, William Henry	Military Clerk	I. 8-5-11. Rj. 8-8-21.
Elkington, Henry	Military Clerk	J. 1-5-76. Rj 13-4-91.
Elliott, G. H.	Soldier, H. M's. Army	J. 20-5-61.
Elliott*, John Bardoe Bowes	Military Officer	I. 4-5-63.
Ellis, Alfred Edward	Military Clerk	I. 25-5-18.
Ellis, John Alexander Simon	Clerk	I. 4-6-66.
Ellis, Stanley Oakley	Accountant, M.A.G's. Office	J. 11-8-19.
Ellison, Frank William	Sergeant, M.W.S.	I. 13-11-05.
Ellison, Maurice Brennan	Military Clerk	I. 10-11-19.
Elloy, Arthur Leonard	Assistant Surgeon	J. 8-6-25.
Elston, Joseph	Soldier	J. 14-8-65.
Elton, John Frederick	Captain, H. M's. Service	J. 21-7-62.
English, Robert Abraham	Dy. Ex., P. W. D.	J. 12-5-84. Rj, 13-6-87.
English, Thomas	Asst. Engineer, P.W.D.	J. 8-6-91.
Erskine, J. Cadwallader	Civil Service	Rj. 8-8-49.
Evans, Frederick Robert	Clerk	I. 10-7-16.
Evans, George Henry	Lieut.-Colonel Civil Veterinary Dept,	J. 12-9-13.
Eyears, George	Saddler	I. 1-7-78.
Fairhall, Richard	Inspector of Police	I. 17-10-13. Rj. 15-6-74.

* Name not traceable in Army List.

Names.	Profession or Occupation.	Date.
Falconer, Edwin Abraham ..	Asst. Secretary, Simla Munici-pality ..	J. 13-1-96.
Faletti, John ..	Hotel Manager ..	I. 14-5-94.
Farmer, John	Captain, Civil V. D. ..	J. 11-7-04.
Fateh, Din ..	Clerk ..	I. 29-8-04.
Faulconbridge, John Henry ..	Merchant	I. 11-4-04.
Fawcett, William James	Lieut.-Col. R.A.M.C. ..	J. 11-4-92.
Fazl Mahomed Khan ..	Curator, Eduction Dept. G. of I.	I. 10-2-13.
Fellows, F. W. ..	Lieutenant, H. M's. 96th Regt.	J. 17-9-51.
Fellows, Halford ..	Major, B. S. C. ..	J. 5-9-70
Fenwick, Alexander Brathwaite	Captain. H.E.I.C. Service ..	J. 20-6-53.
		Rj. 2-8-58.
Fenwick, George Roe ..	Clerk ..	J. 7-4-73.
Ferguson, James Alexander Duncan ..	Major, 6th L. C. ..	J. 12-5-52.
Fergusson, John Carlyle ..	I. C. S. ..	J. 8-4-07.
Fern, Thomas Jordon ..	Clerk ..	I. 14-9-85.
		Rj. 9-12-95.
Field, William Cadwell Faure ..	Major, I.S.C. ..	J. 9-5-98.
Fillingham, George Thomas ..	Assistant, Coutts & Co. ..	J. 1-5-82.
		Rj. 10-8-85.
		Rj. 10-9-88.
Finch, Frederick George ..	Military Clerk ..	J. 11-5-03.
		Rj. 9-3-08.
Fink, George Herbert ..	Surgeon-Major I.M.S. ..	J. 8-6-96.
Fitch, William Samuel ..	Military Clerk ..	J. 9-7-00.
		Rj. 13-4-03.
		Rj. 12-3-06.
Fitzgerald, Arthur ..	Captain, I.A. ..	J. 20-8-77.
Fitzgerald, Gerald ..	Military Clerk ..	J. 8-9-19.
Fitzgerald, Augustus Trelearen	Railway Engineer ..	I. 10-9-23.
Fitz Holmes, Percival Wilbert ..	Hotel Proprietor ..	I. 13-7-14.
Fitzsimons, Edward ..	Clerk ..	I. 21-7-62.
Fleming, Thomas ..	Clerk ..	I. 14-11-53.
Flight, John ..	Soldier ..	J. 6-9-75.
Force, Alfred ..	Tailor ..	J. 10-7-99.
Forbes, John Greenlaw ..	Lieutenant, Engineers ..	J. 7-7-62.
		Rj. 13-10-90.
Forster, Thomas Francis ..	Lieutenant, H.E.I.C. Service ..	I. 20-6-53.
Foster-Turner, Frederick Wentworth	Architect ..	J. 14-11-21.
Fox, Alfred Jacques Bourke ..	Clerk ..	I. 21-8-71.
Fox, John Godfrey ..	Military Clerk ..	I. 12-4-09.
Fox, Thomas George ..	Staff Sgt. I.A.O.C. ..	J. 12-4-26.
Frame, Robert ..	Sergeant, R.A. ..	J. 10-5-86.
Framjee,— ..	(See Heerjeebhboy ..	Muuchurjee).
Framjee, D. H. M.	(See Dinshaw H. ..	M. Framjee).
Framjee, K. D. H.	(See Keki D. ..	H. Framjee).
Francis, Charles Edward ..	Contractor ..	I. 13-8-83.
Francis, Benjamin ..	Merchant ..	J. 17-6-72.
Francis, Walter Lewellyn ..	Clerk ..	I. 6-9-75.
Franklin, Benjamin ..	Military Surgeon ..	J. 15-5-82.
Fraser, Samuel John ..	Sergeant, R.A. ..	J. 11-6-06.
Free, Edward Harry ..	Warrant Officer R.A. Force ..	J. 10-9-23.
Freeman, Benson Luke ..	Clerk ..	J. 19-6-71.
Freeman, Frederick P. William	Gentleman ..	I. 2-10-50.
French, Charles John ..	Nil ..	..

Names.	Profession or Occupation.	Date.
French, Bolivar Edwin ..	Clerk ..	I. 20-8-91.
		Rj. 10-5-97.
		Rj. 13-4-08.
French, Henry Lawrance ..	Registrar, Finance Dept. ..	I. 14-10-12.
Fry, Frederick Arthur ..	Sub-Conductor I.M.L. ..	J. 14-8-16.
Furnell, William Henry ..	Dentist ..	J. 4-8-56.
Fursdon, Walter Ewart ..	Military Clerk ..	I. 23-11-18.
Gabbett, H. W. ..	No record ..	J. 8-8-49.
Galbraith, William ..	Major General H.M's. Service..	J. 11-5-91.
Garde, William Capel ..	Ensign, H. M's. Service ..	I. 29-10-53.
Gardiner, Thomas George ..	Lieut.-Col. H M's. 1-3rd Foot..	J. 3-5-69.
Gardner, John William Bertrand	Military Clerk ..	I. 14-7-19.
Gardner, William H.C. ..	Army School Master ..	J. 10-6-89.
Garlick, George ..	Steward, U. S. Club ..	J. 10-4-99.
Garstin, William Thomas ..	Clerk ..	J. 20-8-51.
Gatesby, Thomas ..	Army School Master ..	J. 14-5-17.
Gaunt, Hugh ..	No record ..	I. 5-6-65.
Gausseu, William Augustus ..	Lieutenant, 14th Lt. Dgns. ..	J. 8-8-49.
George, Edward Claudius ..	Postal Dept. ..	I. 16-11-58.
Ghosh, B. C. ..	(See Bharat Chandra Ghosh)...	
Gibson, William Charles ..	Station Master E.I. Railway ..	J. 14-7-02.
Gifford, Noel Bingham ..	W. O. H. M's. Forces ..	J. 12-7-26.
Gilbert, Edmund Kerr Otho ..	Captain, H.E.I.C. Service ..	J. 4-8-56.
Gilbert, Edwin Osborne ..	Civil Engineer ..	I. 14-10-01.
Gilbert, George Brian ..	Overseer P.W.D. ..	I. 10-7-05.
Gilbert—King, William ..	Military Clerk ..	J. 9-10-06.
Gillan, Robert Woodburn ..	I. C. S. ..	J. 14-10-12.
Guibert, Joseph Fortune ..	Chief to H. E. the Viceroy ..	I. 10-10-87.
Girdlestone, C. G. ..	I. C. S. ..	J. 18-7-70.
Girling, Whitmore ..	Sub-Engineer P.W.D. ..	J. 21-5-77.
Glaysher, Charles Robert ..	Army Schoolmaster ..	I. 23-7-19.
Goad, Lockhart Boileau ..	Asst. D. S. P., N.W.P. ..	I. 9-9-01.
Goddard, Harry ..	Staff-Sgt. I.A.O.C. ..	J. 10-5-26.
Gokal Chand ..	Asst. Surgeon I.M.D. ..	I. 14-8-82.
Goldney, Philip ..	Military Officer, H.E.I.C. Service	J. 8-5-50.
Goldstein, Felix von ..	Musician ..	J. 8-6-68.
		Rj. 18-7-70.
Goldstein, Felix Adolph von ..	Engineer ..	J. 11-1-09.
		Rj. 13-10-19.
Goldstein, Robert von ..	Nil ..	I. 7-6-80.
		as serving Bro.
Goodenough, Herbert Lane ..	Lieutenant, I. A. ...	I. 16-9-89.
Goose ...	No record ...	
Gordon, William Robert Patrick	Asst. Examiner, P.W.D. ..	I. 14-9-85.
Gore, Albert Augustus ..	Surgeon Major-General, P.M.O. in India.	J. 12-8-95.
Gore, John ..	Captain, H.M's Service ..	J. 4-8-62.
Gorrie, Rev. L. Manifold ..	Chaplain ..	J. 10-1-27.
Gould, Basil John ..	I.C.S. ..	J. 12-6-11.
Gould, Jay ..	Major, I.M.S. ..	J. 10-7-11.
Goulding, John ..	Merchant's Clerk ..	I. 21-8-52.
Gouri, Kant Roy ..	Clerk ..	J. 11-6-00.
Graham, Timothy ..	Clerk ..	J. 30-10-50.
	Assistant Suptd., of Roads, Simla.	
Grant, Edmund Robert ..	Engineer ..	J. 10-2-19.
		Rj. 12-11-23.

Names.	Profession or Occupation.	Date.
Grant, John Hayes	Lieut. H.E.I.C. Service	J. 3-7-54.
		Rj. 19-5-56.
		Rj. 29-5-65.
Grantham, Peter	Assistant Controller of Textiles	J. 8-12-19.
Green, Charles, Robert Mortimer	Major, I.M.S.	J. 8-5-05.
Greene, John	Military Clerk	I. 11-8-19.
Greene, John Clinton	Lieutenant, R.A.	I. 11-9-65.
Greensmith, Joseph	Military Clerk	I. 11-3-18.
Grey, Arthur	Barrister-at-Law	J. 14-10-89.
Griffin, Robert	Saddler	J. 12-7-97.
Grindlay, Henry Robert	Major, H. M's. Service	J. 20-6-59.
Grinney, Philip	Sergeant, Viceroy's Band	I. 3-10-81.
Grinter, Charles Edward	Military Clerk	J. 3-5-75.
Grubb, John, James	Do.	J. 9-6-90.
Grüble, Ernst	Assistant, Bourne & Shepherd's	I. 1-6-06.
Grunwell, Hartley	Sgt., R.E.	I. 14-4-19.
Guest, Joseph Alfred	Merchant	J. 18-5-52.
Gunn, William	Captain, Army Vety. Dept.	J. 11-7-98.
Gurnam Singh	Confidential Secretary, Patiala State.	I. 17-7-14.
Hadow, Douglas Scott	Superintendent of Police	J. 8-12-19.
Haegert, Rudolph	Clerk	I. 12-7-86.
*Hale Alexander	Municipal Overseer	J. 13-6-87.
		Rj. 8-4-89.
		Rj. 9-6-90.
Hale, George Herbert	Lieut., H.E.I.C. Service	J. 18-8-56.
		Rj. 20-5-61.
Hale, James, William	Sergeant, R.A.	L. 9-9-89.
		Rj. 10-7-93.
		Rj. 14-9-03.
Halkett, James	Captain H.M.S.	J. 22-5-51.
Hamilton, Augustus William	Draper	J. 3-5-75.
Hamilton, James Charles	Lieut., H.E.I.C. Service	I. 16-6-53.
		Rj. 21-4-62.
Hamilton, John Butler	Surgeon Major, I.M.S.	J. 23-9-78.
Hamilton, The Hon'Ralph	Lieut., 3rd Hussars	J. 12-11-06.
Hamilton, Robert Thomas Francis.	Ensign, H.M's. Service	I. 18-7-53.
Hamlett, Robert Henry	Lieut. I A.R.O.	I. 12-8-20.
Hammett, Percy Arthur John	Military Clerk	I. 9-12-18.
Hammond, J.	Deputy Inspector General of Police, Punjab.	J. 13-8-00.
Harbord, The Hon'Walter	Lieut., H M's. Service	J. 23-5-59.
Harbour, Arthur Edwin	Mechanical Engineer	J. 27-6-10.
Hardaker, Richard	Lieut., Commissariat Deptt.	I. 10-6-89.
Harding, Charles Job	Overseer, P.W.D.	I. 15-5-54.
		Rj. 7-7-62.
		Rj. 4-8-68.
Hardinge, F.	Personal Int. to H.E. the C.-in-C.	J. 8-8-49.
Hardwicke, Cyril Edwin	Lieut., Tank Corps	L. 11-7-21.
Harrington, Frank	Photographer	J. 11-8-02.
Harrington, Herbert Baring	Telegraph Department	J. 11-7-59.
Harris, Albert Edward	Artist	J. 8-7-95.
Harris, Henry Truman	Manager, Messrs. Tellery & Co.	J. 10-6-95.
Harris, James Thomas	Lieut., H E.I.C. Service	I. 2-8-58.
Harris, Robert Robertson	Lieut. 67th B.I.	I. 22-8-49.
Harrison, Allan George	Banker	I. 13-9-97.

* As Serving Bro.

Names.		Profession or Occupation.		Date.
Harrison, Richard	..	Lieut., H.M's. Service	..	J. 4-7-59.
Harrop, Ernest	..	Sergt. 1st Battn. King's Liverpools.		I. 23-6-17.
Hartopp, Edward	..	Captain H.M's. Service	..	I. 2-8-75.
Harvey, Noble Spear	..	Assistant Surg. S.M.D.	..	J. 13-4-03
Harvey, Phillip	..	Lieut., Indian Army	..	I. 12-7-20.
Hassell, Alfred Charles	..	Jeweller	..	I. 14-7-24.
Haverty, William John	..	Military Clerk	..	I. 21-9-68.
Hawes, Walter	..	Army Schoolmaster	..	J. 8-4-18.
Hawkes, Frederick Welman	..	Captain, I.S.C.	..	J. 9-5-04.
Hawkins, John	..	Sergeant, R.A.	..	I. 25-6-06.
Hawksworth George	..	Accountant	..	I. 4-8-68.
Hay, J. M.	..	Surgeon to Lt. Gov. N. W. P. Agra.		J. 26-9-49.
Hay, Lord Frederick	..	I. C. S.	..	I. 19-7-58.
Hay, Lord William Montagu	..	I. C. S.	..	I. 17-10-53.
Healey, George Ernest	..	Permanent Way Inspector, K. S. State Railway.		J. 13-5-07
Heard, Richard	..	Major, I. M. S.	..	J. 13-2-05.
Heerjeebhoy Muncherjee Framjee	..	Merchant		I. 9-7-83. Rj. 11-7-87.
Henderson, Henry Bartley	..	I. C. S.	..	J. 19-10-58.
Henderson, John Acheson	..	A. D. C. to Viceroy	..	J. 9-7-88.
Henley, Arthur	..	Lieutenant, H. H. M's. Service		I. 23-5-59.
Henning, Carl Ferdinand	..	Clerk	..	J. 10-7-99.
Henry, Daniel Soloman	..	Merchant	..	I. 19-10-58.
Henry, William Daniel	..	Banker	..	J. 11-4-04.
Hentschell, Horman	..	Photographer	..	J. 10-6-95.
Herbert, Harry	..	Merchant	..	I. 1-5-54.
Hewett, John Prescott	..	Under Secretary to Govt, Home Dept.	..	I. 9-7-88. Rj. 8-6-91. Rj. 13-8 94. Rj. 7-6-05.
Hewett, Murray Selwood	..	Major Indian Army	..	J. 13-12-20.
Hewson, Francis Thomas	..	I. C. S.	..	I. 15-7-78.
Heysham, Thomas Bird	..	Clerk	..	I. 10-5-86. Rj. 10-4-11.
Hickey, Robert John Fayrer	..	Lieutenant 1st En. Ben. Fus.		J. 1-10-51.
Hickey, William Alex. George	..	Lieut. 32nd B. I.	..	I. 18-6-51.
Hickie, William Arthur	..	Army School Master	..	J. 9-7-88.
Hicks, Edward William	..	Military clerk	..	J. 10-9-06. Rj. 12-4-09.
Hicks, William	..	Warrant Officer	...	J. 9-6-02.
Hide ...	..	No record	..	..
Higgins, Alfred Edward	..	Military Clerk	..	J. 8-4-18.
Higgins, James Richard	..	Sub. Medl. Deptt.	..	J. 7-8-54.
Higgins, Edmund Gordon	..	Captain H. M's. Service	..	J. 4-7-59. Rj. 18-8-62.
Higgins, Percy Wardman	..	Military Clerk	..	I. 9-4-17.
Higgins, Walter Alfred	..	Superintendent, Motor Dept. Patiala State.	..	I. 17-7-14.
Higgs Ernest Bertram	...	Clerk	...	I. 14-10-07.
Hignell, Thomas Victor Paine	..	Out fitters' Manager	...	I. 13-7-25.
Hildesley, Revd. A. H.	...	Military Chaplain	..	..
Hill, Alfred John	..	Military Clerk	..	J. 12-7-09. Rj. 11-10-15.
Hill, George Edward	..	Captain, British Army	..	I. 11-10-20.
Hill, George Mytton	...	Captain, 17th B. I.	..	Rj. 3-7-50.

Names.	Profession or Occupation.	Date.
Hill, Harry Charles ...	I. G. of Forests ..	J. 12-8-95.
Hill, Henry Seymour ..	Captain, Bengal Army ..	J. 2-9-62.
Hill, Richard ...	Chemist ..	I. 10-8-59.
		Rj. 20-5-61
Hill, Rowland ...	Captain, 70th B. I. ..	Rj. 3-7-50.
Hill, William ...	Assistant, Messrs. Cooke & Kelvey.	J. 6-6-64.
		Rj. 6-6-81.
Hinde, Charles Thomas Edward	Colonel, Indian Army ...	I. 13-8-60.
		Rj. 16-9-62.
Hipkins, Francis Ernest Blanchard.	Military Clerk ..	J. 10-1-10.
Hira Singh ..	Cashier, U. S Club ..	I. 13-1-08.
Hitchins, Charles Tatham ...	Lieutenant, H.E.I.C. Service ...	I. 15-9-56.
Hobson, Henry ..	Chemist ..	I. 21-7-68.
Hodder, William ..	School Master ..	J. 13-6-87.
Hoff, Frederick Cornelius ...	Clerk ..	J. 11-8-90.
Hoff, William Hale ...	Ditto ..	J. 16-8-49.
Hoghton, William Alexander ..	Sergeant, H.E.I.C. Service ..	I. 17-7-52.
		Rj. 14-11-53.
Holland, Robert Erskine ..	I. C. S. ..	J. 10-7-05.
Holliday, Clifford Howard ..	Optician ..	I. 12-5-24.
Hollis, Leslie Seymour ..	Warrant Officer I.A.S.C. ..	J. 13-8-23.
Holloway, Percy John ..	Comptroller's Assistant, H. E. the Viceroy's Household.	J. 12-7-26.
Holroyd, George ...	Captain, H.E.I.C. Service ...	J. 18-7-53.
Hopkins, Joseph ..	Controller of Accts. ..	I. 4-10-75.
		Rj. 5-5-79.
Horsey, Thomas Frederick Charles.	Military Clerk ..	J. 15-12-04.
Hoskyn John Cunningham Moore	Captain, I. A. ...	J. 7-6-05.
Hossenlop, Robert Leon ..	Hotel, Proprietor ..	I. 11-3-95.
Howatson, Frederick Pitt Alexander.	Clerk ..	J. 1-5-82.
Howell, Llewellyn James ..	Captain, I. S. C. ..	J. 8-6-96.
Howey, John Robe ..	Military Clerk ..	I. 12-6-11.
Huff, Albert William ..	Military Clerk ...	J. 10-5-20.
Hughes, Reginald Tharle ...	Military Clerk ..	J. 11-2-01.
Hughes, Robert William ..	Clerk ..	J. 8-3-09.
Hume-Spry, Will Edmund ..	Captain, Indian Army ..	J. 10-7-11.
		Rj. 8-5-22
Humm, Percy Stanley ..	Captain, Dental Surgeon ..	J. 8-12-19.
Humphrey, Francis Allen Walker	Draper ..	I. 8-6-08.
		Rj. 9-7-23.
Humphrey, Alfred Frederick ..	Military Clerk ..	J. 13-8-06.
		Rj. 10-8-08.
Hunt, George Archibald ...	Dy. Superintendent of Telegraphs.	I. 9-8-20.
		Rj. 14-12-25.
Hunter, Harry Renfrew ..	Dental Surgeon ...	J. 16-6-14.
Hussey, Henry ..	Lieut. Inspector of Army Schools.	I. 11-10-15.
Hynd, W. T. ..	Merchant ..	J. 11-5-96.
Inayat Ali Khan Sahib ..	Nill ..	I. 15-8-79.
Ingle, Henry Charles ..	Staff-Sergeant R.A.S.C. ..	J. 8 9-24.
Inglis, William Malcolm ..	No record ..	J. 1-6-63.
Ingram, Benjamin ..	Military Clerk ..	J. 14-10-01.
		Rj. 14-8-05.
Innes, Peter ..	Colonel, H.E.I.C. Service ..	Rj. 16-6-56.
Ireland, Harry Robert ..	Telegraph Master ..	J. 12-6-22.
Irwin, Henry ..	Civil Engineer ..	J. 23-4-83.

Names.	Profession or Occupation.	Date.
Ishar Das Puri	Clerk	J. 10-6-13.
Ishwar Das	Of Kapurthala State	I. 13-8-88.
Ivan Chen	Special Plenipotentiary of the Republic of China, China-Thibet Conference	I. 3-6-14.
Jackson, R. W. H.	Captain R.A.M.C.	J. 8-7-01.
Jackson, Sydney Crosby	Captain H.M.S.	J. 20-6-53.
Jackson, Thomas Henry	Staff-Sergeant I.A.O.C.	J. 14-12-25.
Jacob, Alexander Malcolm	Jeweller	J. 16-6-79.
		Rj. 10-10-87.
Jaikishen Kapur	Clerk	J. 12-8-07.
Jal Framjee Masters	Clerk	I. 10-3-24.
James, Abraham	Clerk	J. 14-5-83.
James, Arthur Harvey	Journalist	I 8-6-96.
James, Charles Henry	Civil Surgeon	J. 10-8-14.
James, Edward Bertram	Accountant, M.W.S.	J. 14-5-06.
James, George Atkinson	Accountant, P.W.D.	I. 14-8-82.
James, Stanlake	Member of the Roy. Col. of Surgeons	I. 14-6-97.
Jameson, Thomas	Military Clerk	I. 4-8-68.
		Rj. 21-4-73.
Jefford, Charles Victor	Military Clerk	J. 12-11-17.
Jeffrey, George	Merchant	J. 8-5-50.
Jeffrey, George	Captain H.M's. Service	J. 21-5-55.
Jenn, William Henry	Musician	I. 14-11-98.
John, E. Rochfort	Assistant Supdt Punjab Police	I. 5-10-95.
John, Peter Sophocles	Bar-at-Law	J. 9-9-95.
Johnson, Edgar Osborne	Lieut. I.M.D.	J. 10-9-23.
Johnson, Richard	Government Contractor	J. 11-5-85.
Johnston, David E.	Secretary Municipal Comtee.	J. 13-6-04.
Johnstone, Eustace Martin	Octroi Superintendent	I. 11-2-07.
Jones, Alexander	Clerk	I. 21-8-71.
Jones, Harry Harvey	Major Indian Army	J. 10-7-11.
Jones, Harry Reynold	Military Clerk	J. 8-2-15.
Jones, Lewis John Fillies	Lieut. H. M's. Service	I. 4-7-59.
Jones-Mortimer Lambton Alex	Captain, Somerset L.I..	J. 13-6-04.
Jones, Robert	Merchant's Assistant	I. 26-7-09.
Jones, William	Printer	J. 9 1-99.
Joseph, Arthur Frederick	Schoolmaster	J. 9-9-12.
Jowett, Thomas John	Chemist	I. 18-1-69.
Kaikhushro Maneksha Mistri	Private Secretary to H.H. the Maharaja of Patiala	I. 17-7-14.
Kaishree Singh, H.H. Maharao of Sirohee.		I. 14-8-99.
Kazi Ghulam Rabbani	Ex. Asst. Comr.	J. 22-6-08.
Keki Dinshaw Heerjeebhoy Framjee	Merchant	I. 13-8-23.
Kelly, William	Accountant P. W. D.	J. 11-6-00.
Kemp, James	Tailor's Cutter	J. 14-5-17.
		Rj. 8-6-25.
Kemp, Walter Henry	Vety, Major. C.V.D.	I. 14-6-97.
Kennard, Albert	Sergeant Major, R. A.	I. 8-10-00.
Kent, H.	Jeweller	J. 12-6-99.
Kerr, Charles William Ernest	Asstt. Surgeon, S. M. D.	J. 10-4-05.
Kevan, Peter Charles	Military Pensioner	J. 13-12-20.
Key, Frank Llewellyn	School Master	I. 16-11-91.
Kherod Nath Mitter	Clerk	I. 12-8-01.

Names.	Profession or Occupation.	Date.
King Thomas ...	(See Konigs) ..	..
King-Harman, Montague Jocelyn	Colonel I. A. ..	J. 13-6-92.
Kishen Singh ..	Aide-de-Camp to H. H. the Maharaja of Patiala ..	I. 17-7-14.
Kitchener, Herbert, Horatio, *Viscount.*	General, Commander-in-Chief in India.	J. 13-4-03.
Knowles, Thomas William ..	Engineer ..	J. 4-8-62.
Knowles, Charles James ...	Clerk ...	I. 8-6-08.
Konigs, Julius, *Alias* Thomas King.	Military Clerk ...	I. 15-5-82.
Korper, George B. ..	Ditto ..	J. 5-9-81.
Kramer, Wana ..	Director of Physical Training Patiala State ..	I. 13-7-14.
Kuch Behar ..	H. H. the Maharaja (See Nripendra Narayan),	..
Laing, James ..	Merchant ..	9-9-01.
Lambert, Henry McLaren ..	Captain, 1st Dragoon ..	I. 11-7-04.
Lampat, Percy ..	Electrical Engr. ..	I. 11-6-00.
Landseer, George ..	Artist ..	J. 4-8-62.
		Rj. 15-7-72.
Lang, John ..	Editor, Moff'lite Paper ..	J. 5-6-50.
Lascelles, the Hon'ble C. G. ..	Lieutenant, H. M's. Service ..	I. 20-9-75.
Lawrence, Alexander Samuel ...	Clerk ...	J. 7-6-05.
Lawrence, Alfred Frederick ...	Warrant Officer H. E. the Viceroy's Band.	I. 22-11-09.
Lawson, Ernest Fenton ..	Jeweller ..	I. 14-8-11.
Leach, John ..	Lieutenant, R. H. A. ..	I. 31-7-77.
Leech, William Henry ..	Sergeant Somerset L. I. ..	I. 1-11-95.
Lee-Baker, Leonard Humphrey ..	Clerk in Holy Orders ..	J 12-6-22.
Leeson, Arthur ...	Warrant Officer I.A.O.C. ..	J. 9.8-26.
Legh, Herbert Cuthbert ..	Captain, King's Royal Rifles ..	J. 9-10-88.
Leigh, Frank ..	Asst Secretary, Punjab Govt. ..	I. 21-7-86.
		Rj. 9-7-88.
		Rj. 9-7-94.
		Rj. 10-8-96.
LeMaistre, George Harry ..	Civil Engineer ..	J. 14-6-97.
Lemarchand, Charles Heyman ..	D. S. of Police ..	J. 8-4-89.
Lemon, William ..	Clerk ..	I. 11-7 59.
Lennox, James ..	Military Clerk ..	I. 8-8-87.
		Rj. 8-10-94.
		Rj. 13-2-05.
Lennox, William ..	Assistant, Thacker Spink & Co.	I. 9-7-06.
Levinge, Charles Hugh ..	Captain late 93rd Foot ..	J 4-5-63.
Lewsey, Thomas Lionel ..	Photographer ..	J. 8-3-69.
Lewsey, William Russell ..	Clerk ..	I. 19-5-56.
		Rj. 21-4-62.
Lewis, Edgar Samuel ..	Punjab Civil Service ..	I. 8-8-21.
Lewis, Thomas Oddian ..	Military Clerk ..	J. 10-2-19.
Liddell. Silas Hiscutt ..	Printer ..	I. 13-10-13.
Line, Richard ..	Electrical Engineer ..	J. 12-12-21.
Line, Robert Samuel ..	Musician, H.E. the Viceroy's Orchestra.	J. 13-9-26.
Linford, Wilberforce ..	Sergt. Instructor, Simla Volunteers. ..	J. 10-2-02.
Litchfield, John William ..	Condr. Comst Deptt ..	J. 14-9-91.

Names.	Profession or Occupation.	Date.
Litster, Archibald	Military Clerk	J. 18-8-62.
		Rj. 3-7-65.
		Rj. 7-6-69.
		Rj. 2-4.77.
		Rj. 21-4-79.
Lloyd, Thomas William	ditto	J. 13-5-01.
Lock, Edgar Samuel	Military Clerk	I. 12-11-17.
Loggie, James	Draper	J. 13-4 96.
Longridge, James Atkinson	Captain I. A.	J. 10-4-05.
Lorimer, John Gordon	I C. S.	J. 13-11-99.
Low, Robert Cunliffe	Lieutenant, Indian Army	I. 16-8-59.
Luard, Peter William	Major, Indian Army	I. 10-8-59.
Luck, George	General, H. M's. Service	J. 13-8-88.
Lukis, Charles Pardy	Major, I. M. S.	I. 5-8-99.
		Rj. 28-6-09.
Lumgair, David Herbert	Band Master, Garhwal Rifles	I. 11-8-02.
Lundy, Edwin Arthur	Surgeon Dentist	J. 10-9-94.
Lynch, Michael	Clerk	I. 21-5-66.
Lyons, Alexander	Sub Medical Dept.	I. 24-6.63.
Lyster, Harry Hamon	Captain, H. M's Service	J. 21-7-62.
MacCall, Henry Blackwood	Captain, 60th R. Rifles	J. 17-6-78.
Macdonald, Robert Graham	Clerk	I. 3-9-66.
		Rj. 9-7-83.
Mack, Herr William	Musician	..
Mackenzie, Alexander Kincard Johnston Canning.	Lieutenant, H.E.I.C. Service	I 20-9-58.
Mackenzie, Alexander Robert Davidson.	Colonel, I A.	J. 13-8-94.
Mackenzie, Francis James Napier	Lieutenant, H.M's. Service	J. 4-7-59.
Mackenzie, James	Lieut.-Col. H.E.I.C. Service	J. 13-4-53.
		Rj. 1-1-56.
Mackinnon, Walter	Architect	I. 10-2-02.
Macleay, James Ronald	Lieutenant, R A.	J. 20-6-59.
		Rj. 20-5-61.
		Rj. 17-8-63.
Macleod, Charles Higgot	Clerk	J. 4-5-63.
		Rj. 21-8-71.
		Rj. 19-6-76.
Macnab, Allan James	Major, I.M.S.	J. 7-6-05.
Maconchy, Ernest William Stuart King.	Colonel, Indian Army	J. 14-6-09.
Maconochie, Alexander Francis	I.C.S.	I. 5-6-95.
Maconochie, Edward	I.C.S.	J. 12-9-98.
Macpherson, Duncan	Lieutenant, H. M's. Service	J. 4-7-59.
Maelzer, Reginald Arnold	Electrical Engineer	I. 12-7-20.
Magson, Charles	Struct Engineer	I. 11-4-27.
Maguay, Christopher	Lieutenant, 22nd N.I.	I. 4-10-51.
Mahomed Pir Buksh	Barrister-at-Law	J. 9 7-00.
Maiden, Charles Bowers	Postmaster	J. 13-5-12.
Mainwaring Edward Phillipson	Lieutenant, H.M's. Service	I. 1-12-62.
Maitland, Pelham James	Colonel, B.S.C.	I. 12-10 91.
Man Mohan	Banker	J. 14-9-14.
Mandy, George	Merchant	I. 20-5-61.
Manley, Clifford	Military Clerk	I. 21-5-77.
		Rj. 1-5-82.
Mansfield, Leopold Albert Ernest.	Military Clerk	I. 11-9-93.
Manuel, John	Clerk	I. 7-6-69.
		Rj. 19-6-76.

Names.	Profession or Occupation.	Date.
Manuel, Wilton ..	Clerk ..	I. 17-10-87.
Marckman, George John	Military Clerk ..	J. 18-4-81.
Marcoolyn, Henry John	Military Clerk ..	I. 14-3-92.
		Rj. 8-10-00.
Marriott, Edward Frere	Major, I.S.C. ..	I. 8-3-97.
Marsden, Charles John	Military Clerk ..	J. 17-6-72
		Rj. 20-5-78.
Marsb, Thomas ..	Manager, Murree Brewery ..	I. 21-5-66.
Marshall, C.H.T. ..	Colonel, B.S.C. ..	J. 10-9-88.
Marshall, George W. ..	Clerk ..	J. 13-6-04.
		Rj. 12-10-08.
Marshall, Percy Harold ..	Military Clerk ..	J. 10-5-09.
		Rj. 12-5-15.
Martin, Algernon Shelton St. ..	Engineer	J. 12-11-23.
Martin, William Jeremiah Phillips	Assistant Surgeon, I.S.M.D. ..	J. 8-9-13.
Massy, Harry Stanley ..	Lieutenant, 19th B.L. ..	J. 3-6-78
		Rj. 11-6-83.
Masters, J. F. (See Jal;Framjee Masters).		..
Masters, S F. (See Shavak Framjee Masters).		..
Matheson, Frederick John ..	Military Clerk	J. 11-10-20.
Mathews, A.H. ..	Secretary Simla Bank ..	J. 12-10-49.
Mathews, Frederick William ..	Asst. Surgeon, S.M.D. ..	J. 13-5-07.
Maula Bakhsh ..	Attache, F. & P. Dept. ..	I. 10-7-16.
Maxwell, John Harley ..	Lieutenant, H. E.I.C. Service ..	I. 23-5-53.
		Rj. 16-6-56.
Maxwell, Thomas Colville ..	Actor and Vocalist ..	I. 9-2-14.
May, Alexander, George Henry	Engineer ..	J. 12-4-09.
Mayer, George Hugh ..	Sergt. 1/4th Devon Regiment ..	I. 9-10-16.
McAllister, Robert Hastings ..	Clerk ..	J. 8-6-85.
McCarthy, Washington ..	Merchant's Clerk	..
McCarthy, William Thomas ..	Military Clerk ..	J. 11-3-12.
		Rj. 13-9-20.
McDermott, John ..	Military Clerk ..	J. 20 9-80.
		Rj. 8-6-85.
		Rj. 13-5-89.
McGowan, William Henry ..	Post Master ..	I. 21-8-52.
McGregor, Duncan ..	Municipal Overseer ..	I. 19-7-80.
		Rj. 13-7-85.
McGregor, Robert Lewis Grant .	Captain, H. M's. Service ..	I. 2-9-62.
McGregor-Cheers, John ..	Military Clerk ..	J. 14-5-00.
		Rj. 13-1-02.
McIntyre, Peter ..	Military Clerk ..	J. 27-6-10.
McKay, John ..	Military Mechanist, R.E. ..	J. 10-6-13.
McMahon, Arthur Henry ..	Colonel, Indian Army ..	J. 12-6-11.
McRae, Collin Stuart ..	Military Clerk ..	I. 19-4-75.
Meakin, Harry George ..	Brewer ..	I. 21-8-71.
Meema Mull ..	Clerk ..	J. 12-5-84.
Mela Ram ..	Assistant Surgeon S.M.D. ..	J. 9-1-05.
Mendies, Arthur Gerald ..	Assistant Office of Chief Controller of Stores.	I. 9-7-23.
Menne, Carl Joseph ..	Secretary to Imperial German Consulate General.	I. 12-6-11.
Meston, James Scorgie ..	I.C.S. ..	J. 9-10-06.
Metcalfe, Edward ..	Lieutenant, H. M's. Service ..	J. 2-9-62.
Metcalfe, J. ..	Captain A.D.C. to Gov. Genl. ..	J. 8-8-49.
Michael, John Adolphus ..	Govt. Telegraph Department ..	I. 1-6-06
Michell, George Bruce ..	Military Officer Major, S. and Camel Corps	Rj. 8-8-49.

Names.	Profession or Occupation.	Date.
Michell, George Martin ..	Batty. Sergeant Major, R.A. ..	I. 16-9-89.
Miles, C.W. ..	Lieut. 23rd N.I. ..	J. 22-8-49.
Miller, Hon'ble Sir Alexander Edward.	Member of Council ..	I. 23-5-92.
Millington, Victor Cowper ..	Chauffeur, Viceregal Lodge ..	J. 14-5-17.
Mills, Daniel Timothy ..	Sub-Medical Department ..	J. 12-7-86.
Milne, Frederick Latour ..	Electrical Engineer ..	J. 11-3-12.
Minto, Archibald Henry ..	Assistant Indian Stores Dept. ..	I. 12-10-25.
Mitchell, Cyril ..	Brewer ..	J. 11-2-07.
Mitchell, Peter ..	Clerk ..	I. 21-5-66.
Mitchell, William ...	Engineer ..	J. 14-4-02.
Mitchell, William Marcus ...	Sub-Medical Department ..	J. 18-1-69.
		Rj. 21-6-80.
Moffat, J. D. ..	Captain, 11th L.C. ..	J. 8-8-49.
Mohsin Ali ..	Dist. I. of Police ..	J. 14-8-82.
Molyneux Edward ..	No record ..	J. 1-6-63.
Monckton, Henry ..	I. C. S. ..	J. 26-6-52.
Monckton, Oliver Paul ..	Engineer ..	I. 10-9-06.
Money, George Edward ..	Lieut.-Col. I. S. C. ..	J. 14-10-95.
Monro, George ..	Military Clerk ..	J. 12-2-00.
Monro, Seymour Charles Hale ..	Lieutenant 72 Highlrs. ..	I. 2-9-78.
Montgomery, Charles Lyons ..	Lieutenant H.E.I.C. Service ...	J. 21-8-52.
Montgomery, Robert Armidal Kerr.	Lieutenant R.H.A. ...	I. 22-9-88.
Moody, Alfred Edward ..	Military Clerk ..	J. 11-10-09.
Moody William Ernest .	Major I.M.D. ..	J. 8-2-26.
Moorland, John ..	Colonel B.S.C. ..	J. 5-9-70.
Moorman, Richard ..	Clerk ..	I. 18-5-63.
More Lancelot Paxton ..	Lt. Col. R.A.M C. ..	J. 11-10-15.
Morrell, William ..	Steward Bishop Cotton School	J. 12-8-95.
		Rj. 11-4-98.
Morris, Thomas ..	Merchant ..	I. 3-5-69.
Morris, Thomas Major ..	Military Clerk ..	I. 8-9-19.
Morris, Arthur ..	Municipal Overseer ..	J. 9-5-92.
		Rj. 14-5-94.
Morrow, Charles Thomas ..	Warrant Officer, I.M.L. ..	I. 14-5-17.
Moss, Benjamin Hugh ..	Overseer, P.W.D. ..	I. 10-10-04.
		Rj. 13-5-18.
Muller-Desroches, Jean Ignace	Professor of Languages ..	I. 27-9-09.
Mullins, William ..	Telegraph Master ..	J. 11-5-91.
		Rj. 13-6-98.
Murray, Charles John ..	Captain, I.M.C. ..	I. 23-11-18.
Murray, Thomas ..	Clerk ..	I. 23-5-53.
Murray, Kenneth ..	Merchant ..	J. 29-5-65.
Mutimer, Jack ..	Military Clerk ..	J. 12-8-12.
Myatt, Arthur Egbert ..	Soldier ..	J. 14-9-96.
Myers, Benjamin ..	Clerk ..	I. 21-8-65.
Myers, J. E. ..	Overseer P. W. D. ..	J. 6-9-80.
Nangle, Montague Claude ..	Captain, I. A. ..	I. 13-8-06.
Narayandas Talwar ..	Inspector of Post Offices ..	I. 14-7-13.
Napier, George S. Frederick ..	Captain Oxford L. I. ...	J. 11-5-96.
Nembhard, John Frederick ..	Major H.E.I.C. Service ..	16-6-53.
Newland, Frederick ...	Draper's Manager ..	I. 10-12-23.
Newman, Felix Lawrence. ..	Military Clerk ..	J. 11-5-03.
Newman, Water Reginald ..	Clerk ..	I. 5 7-66.
		Rj. 7-8-71.
Nicholetts, H. S. ..	Telegraph Dept. ..	I. 20-5-61.
Nickels, Thomas ..	Barrister-at-Law ..	J. 13-8-06.

Names.	Profession or Occupation.	Date.
Nirmal Chunder Sen ..	Private Secretary to Maharaja Kuch Behar.	J. 9-7-00.
Nixon, Edward Gladstone ..	Sergeant R. A. ..	I. 9-9-89.
Noel-Paton, Frederick ..	D. G. of Commercial Intelligence.	J. 7-6-05.
Nowell, Frederick ..	Steward to H. E. the Viceroy.	I. 10-10-87.
Nripendra Narayan, Maharaja Kuch Behar.	......	J. 10-9-83.
Oakes, Edward ..	Lieutenant H. E. I.C. Service	J. 22-5-51.
O'Connor, Edward Treston ..	School Master ..	I. 24-6-65.
O'Connor, Malcolm S. Scott ..	Asst. Secretary Railway Board.	J. 11-6-06.
O'Connor, Mark ..	Clerk ..	I. 5-7-66.
O'Conor, James Edward ..	Under Secretary to Government Finance Dept. ..	J. 5-8-67.
		Rj. 21-8-71.
		Rj. 13-8-94.
Ogden, William ..	Accountant P. W. D. ..	I. 3-6-78.
Okhoy Coomar Roy ..	Clerk ..	J. 9-9-95.
Oldfield, Henry Ambrose ..	Residency Surgeon Nepaul ..	J. 16-8-49.
Otter, Charles James ..	Major H. M. S. ..	J. 7-7-51.
Ottley, John W. ..	Captain R. E. ..	J. 15-7-78.
Ottley, William John ..	Captain I. S. C. ..	I. 12-8-01.
Otto, Bertram Charles William.	Clerk ..	I. 10-7-16.
Owen, Charles Arthur ..	Asst. Surgeon I. M. S. ..	I. 11-11-95.
		Rj. 14-6-20.
Owen, Charles William ..	Major I. M. S. ..	J. 8-8-92.
Paige, Reginald Herbert ..	Draper ..	I. 13-8-06.
Palin, Loranst, Frederick ..	Musician ..	I. 16-9-62.
Palmer, Sir Arthur Power ..	General, C.-in-C. in India. ..	J. 10-6 01.
Palmer, Barry ..	Military Surgeon ..	J. 13-8-83.
Palmer, Henry ..	Major H. E. I. C. service ..	J. 4-7-53.
Palmer, ..	..	
Palmer, Ropert Chetwynd ..	Journalist ..	J. 11-9-16.
Park, Gabriel, Frederick William Jacob.	Merchant ..	I. 20-8-55.
Parker, Edwin Woodall ..	District Judge ..	J. 8-8-87.
		Rj. 11-7-98.
Parker, George Robinson ..	Tailor ..	I. 12-11-17.
Parkes, Thomas ..	Sergeant R. A. ..	I. 22-9-90.
Parsons, Clement, George ..	Captain. I. S. C. ..	J. 10-7-99.
Patiala, H. H. the Maharaja of (See Bhupindar Singh Mahindar.)		
Patterson, Alexander, Bleakley.	Commissioner of Salt Revenues.	J. 10-9-94.
Patterson, Arthur Robert ..	Captain I. S. M. D. ..	I. 9-4-17.
Paxton, Ralph Ernest ..	Assistant Parke, Davis & Co. ..	J. 9-10-06.
Peachey, Lional Richard ..	Mechanical Engineer ..	I. 14-2-10.
Pears, Stewart, E. ..	I.C.S. ..	J. 13-8-00.
Pearson, Alfred ..	Military Officer ..	I. 22-8-49.
		Rj. 5-6-51.
Pearson Elof ..	Tailor's Cutter ..	I. 11-8-02.
Pease, Henry Thomas, C.I.E. ..	Colonel, Civil Vety. Dept. ..	J. 9-9-07.
		Rj. 26-7-09.
Pemberton, Duncan Scott ..	Lieutenant, H.E.I.C. Service ..	I. 2-8-58.
Pepper, Henry ..	Military Clerk ..	J. 13-1-02.
Perry, Francis ..	Clerk ..	I. 17-9-51.
		Rj. 14-11-53.
Pertab Singh ..	Civil Service ..	J. 11-7-98.
		Rj. 26-7-09.

Names.	Profession or Occupation.	Date.
Peyton, Algernon, F.	Lieutenant 3rd Hussars	I. 31-7-77.
Perushottam Sinha	Clerk	J. 9-10-11.
Phelps, Arthur Austin	Auctioneer and Estate Agent	J. 11-8-13.
Phelps, Harry Richbell	Tailor	I. 18-9-06.
Phelps, John Isaac	Tailor	I. 2-9-68.
		Rj. 20-9-75.
		Rj. 8-10-83.
Philipe, George William deRhe	Clerk	J. 9-5-92.
Phool Chand, Lala	Store Keeper, U S. Club	I. 13-10-84.
Pilcher Frederick Jones	Asst Secy. Army Temperance Association.	J. 13-5-95.
Pilcher, Victor George	Sergeant R.A.	I. 9 4-00.
Piper, Charles Frederick	Merchant's Assistant	J. 12-10-85.
Pitman, Frederick Henry	Tailor's Cutter	I. 11-4-21.
Pitts, Thomas Alwyne	Military Clerk	J. 9-12-18.
Plowden, Henry Gordon Chicheley.	Captain 11th I.C.	J. 12-10-49.
Pluck, Harry	Military Clerk	J. 10-4-11.
Pogson, John Frederick	Lieutenant Invalid Estabt.	Rj. 3-9-51.
		Rj. 27-5-66.
Polacek, Camillo Karl	Photographer	J. 14-4-02.
Polden, Robert James	Military Surgeon	I. 15-5-82.
Poole, George Edward	Sub-Medical Department	Rj. 8-8-49.
		Rj. 16-8-58.
Porter, Geoffrey Morehead	Lieutenant R.E.	I. 20-8-77.
Porter, F.	Assistant Rankeu & Co.	J. 11-6-00.
Porter, Joseph	Clerk	I. 10-12-94.
Powell, Francis Graham	Captain H.M's. Service	J. 2-9-62
Power, James Otway Bleuerhasset	Clerk	I. 9-8-86.
		Rj 9-6-90.
		Rj. 8-8-92.
Pratt, D.	Lieutenant 22nd N.I.	I 17-9-51.
Pregno, Caesar	Hotel Manager	J. 19-12-06.
		Rj. 10-7-11.
Press, Frederick Nimrod	Military Clerk	I. 10-8-96
		Rj. 12-10-03
		Rj. 15-6-21.
Price, Arthur Roland	Electrical Engineer	J. 16-6-14.
Prinsep, the Hon. Sir H.T.	Judge of High Court Calcutta	J. 13-7-96.
Prior, Charles James	Military Clerk	J. 13-6-10.
Probodh Chandra Mukherjee	Clerk	I. 22-8-11.
Pruce, Frederick Jervis	Clerk	J. 11-7-98.
Pryce, Athelstone Robert	Captain 13th Hussars	I. 31-7-77.
Pye, James	Warrant Officer P.W.D.	J. 12-12-21.
Pymm, Russell Austin	Hair Dresser	I. 12-10-85
		Rj. 13-5-89.
Quarry, Frederick William	Pleader	J. 1-2-69.
Quick, Leopold, E.	Jeweller	J. 8-7-89.
Quigley, Andrew Lindsay Kennedy.	Clerk	J. 1-10-60.
..	..	Rj. 1-4-63.
..	..	Rj. 1-5-76.
Quigley, Joseph	Sergeant M W.S.	I. 13-7-03.
Quinnell, Richard James	Sub-Med. Dept.	I. 28-8-54.
Rae, Ernest Alfred	Engineer	J. 12-4-09.
Radcliffe, Septimus, Augustus Howlet.	Merchant	I. 5-9-70.

Names.	Profession or Occupation.	Date.
Radha Kishen	Clerk	J. 12-11-94.
Raj Coomar Dutt	Clerk	I. 13-9-86.
Raleigh, Adrian Gifford	Lieut. 2nd Battn. Leicestershire Regiment.	I. 11-11-20.
Ralph, James	Overseer P.W.D.	J. 1-5-82.
Ram Ratan Puri	Clerk	J. 8-7-95.
Ramji Das	Clerk	J. 12-8-12.
Ramsay, Alexander	Merchant	I. 18-8-68.
Ramsay James	Major H.E.I.C. service	J. 8-8-49.
Randall, Robert John	Military Clerk	I. 12-8-18.
Rawlins, Thomas, W.	I.C.S.	J. 6-8-77.
Rawlinson, Henry Seymour	Lieutenant A.D.C. to C.in C.	J. 9-10-88.
Read, Frank Joseph	Jeweller	J. 11-8-13.
Reader, John	Warrant Officer I.O.D.	I. 10-7-22.
Rebeiro, John Dolby	Pleader	I. 18-7-81.
Reeves-Brown, Gerald	Chemist	I. 7-6-07. Rj. 14-5-17.
Reinhold, Charles	Merchant	I. 3-8-74.
Rennick, Frank Robert	Lieutenant, I.A.	I. 16-11-91.
Revnell Revd Arthur Jesse	Wesleyan Minister and Superintending Wesleyan Chaplain in India.	I. 9-8-26.
Reynolds, Harry Lewis	Military Clerk	I. 12-5-02. Rj. 9-10-06.
Richardson, Herbert	Military Clerk	J. 9-12-18.
Richardson, Ralph	Warrant Officer J.O.D.	J. 12-6-22.
Riches, Charles	Soldier	J. 10-8-96.
Riddell, Henry Philip Archibald Buchanan.	I.C.S.	Rj. 8-8-49.
Rippon, Thomas Stanley	R.A.M.C. Medical Staff R.A.F.	J. 13-9-20.
Rivers, George Charles	Commercial Accountant	I. 1-9-73.
Robberds, Revd Frederick	Clerk in Holy Orders.	J. 10-6-67.
Robertson, Arthur	Clerk	J. 20-6-64.
Robertson, Bertram James	Military Clerk	J. 10-5-15. Rj. 12-11-17.
Robertson, John	Military Clerk	J. 19-4-75. Rj. 8-2-92. Rj. 13-4-96.
Robertson, Roderick	Captain, 70th B.I.	J. 5-6-51.
Robertson, William	I.C.S.	I. 16-8-5.
Robinson, Henry Mould Revd.	School Master	J. 12-7-86.
Robinson, William Ernest	Telegraph Engineer	J 14-4-24.
Rochelle, William	Sergeant R.A.	I. 8-7-89.
Rocke, Cyril Edmund Alan Spencer.	Captain I.A.	J. 8--913.
Rodgers, James Randolph	Assistant Foreign and Political Dept.	I. 10-7-16.
Rodgers, Rivers Thomas	Asst. Surgeon, S.M.D.	J. 10-9-00.
Rogers Edward Frederick Bright	Clerk	I. 11-7 21.
Rogers, Felix Deeble	Military Clerk	J. 11-10-20.
Rogers, T.	Military Clerk	J. 11-3-95.
Rose, Charles Archibald Walker	H.M. Consular Service	I. 11-5-14.
Rose, George William	Chemist	J. 8-6-91.
Rose, Horace Arthur	I.C.S.	J. 13-1-02.
Rose, Harcourt Ranking	Captain I.A.	J. 3-9-77.
Rose, John	Sergeant R.A.	I. 1-6-06.
Rosetti, Luigi	Musician	J. 12-7-86.
Ross, Alfred Newton	Assistant Surgeon, I.S.M.D.	I. 23-6-17.
Ross, James Adolphus	Cornet 5 L.C.	I. 17-10-49.
Rosser, John Campbell	Military Clerk	J. 28-6-09
Rotton, Arthur	Lieutenant H.E.I.C. Service	J. 10-9-58.

Names.	Profession or Occupation.	Date.
Rowland, Henry	Military Clerk	J. 10-5-09.
Rowley, William Henry	Sergeant R. A.	I. 10-10-87.
Roy, G. K.	(See Gouri Kant Roy)	...
Roy, O. C.	(See Ookhoy Coomar Roy)	...
Royston, Charles, Philip Yorke Viscount.	Lieutenant H. M's. service	I. 23-5-59.
Rubenstein, Maurice	Hairdresser	J. 8-9-13. Rj. 11-6-17.
Rudolf, Norman Scott	Chemist	I. 12-6-99.
Ruegg, Alfred James	Military Clerk	J. 8-4-01.
Russell, Henry George	Manager Messrs. (Kellner and Coy.	J. 10-2-13. Rj. 11-5-25.
Russell, Maurice John	Merchant	I. 10-8-85.
Russell, William Albert	Principal Vety. Surgeon	J. 11-5-91.
Russell-Stuart Albert Edward	Bandmaster	I. 8-2-09.
Rutledge, David	Clerk	I. 8-7-89.
Ruxton, George Percy	Warrant Officer Supply and Transport Corps.	I. 9-10-06.
Ryan, Henry Edward	Clerk	I. 18-8-68.
Sams, Herbert Arthur	I. C. S.	I. 12-8-01.
Samuels, Samuel	Loco Foreman S.K.S. Railway	J. 8-5-05.
Sandbach, Arthur Edward	Lieut.-Col. R.E.	J. 13-3-99.
Sanders, Revd. Montagu Charles	Chaplain Church of England	J. 14-3-98.
Sanderson, Thomes Ray	Warrant Officer, I.O.D.	I. 10-7-22.
Sanderson, R. W.	Clerk	J. 8-6-96. Rj. 13-8-00.
Sanford, George Batthyany	Major, I.A.	J. 9-5-10.
Sanford George Edward Langham Somerset.	Lieut.-Col. R.E.	I. 19-7-80.
Sarel, Henry Andrew	Colonel H. M's. Service	J. 21-7-62.
Sartorius, Reginald W. V.C.C.M.G.	Major B. S. C.	J. 4-10-75. Rj. 16-7-77.
Saunders, Charles John Godfrey	Clerk in Holy Orders	J. 13-11-22.
Saville, William James	Army Schoolmaster	J. 13-5-18.
Scatcherd, John Frederick	Sanitary Engineer	J. 10-11-24.
Schofield, Arthur Bernard	Military Clerk	I. 14-7-19.
Schrodea, Earnst	School Master	I. 13-9-97.
Schwaiger, Imre Geo Maria	Merchant	J. 11-5-96.
Scott Archibald	Sub-Engineer P.W.D.	J. 6-6-82.
Scott, James	Clerk	J. 10-8-85. Rj. 13-5-95.
Scott, Malcolm de Burgh	Major R. A. S C.	J. 11-4-21.
Sealy, Philip Temple	Captain, R. A. S. C.	J. 11-4-21.
Seddons, J. H.	Draper's Asst.	J. 14-5-00.
Seide, Charles Herr	Band Master Viceroy's Band	J. 21-6.75.
Sellors, Samuel Robert	Civil Engineer	J. 14-11-92. Rj. 9-7-94.
Sen, N. C.	(See Nirmal Chunder Sen.)	
Shanker Dayal	Vakil Patiala State	I. 13-7-91.
Shavak Framjee Masters	Confectioner's Manager	I. 12-1-25.
Shaw, Ernest	Accountant	J. 9-9-12.
Shaw, Ernest Reginald	Jeweller	I. 8-9-24.
Shaw, Lindsay John	Military Clerk	I. 14-9-91.
Shearcroft, Reginald James	Military Clerk	J. 8-9-19.
Shearer, Johnston	Surgeon Major I. M. S.	J. 13-1-96.
Shepherd, Robert Stephen McGregor.	Journalist	I. 10-7-99.
Sheppard, James	Military Clerk	I. 13-10-19.
Sherer, Joseph Ford	Lieutenant H. E. I C. Service	I. 13-8-51.

Names.	Profession or Occupation.	Date.
Showell, George Washington	Bank Clerk	I. 19-4-75. Rj. 16-4-77.
Shute, Arthur Fitzgerald	Civil Engineer	I. 14-7-02.
Sibold, Rudolph	Professor of Music	J. 19-6-54.
Sills, Gerald Charles	Captain, British Service	I. 10-1-21.
Simpson, Archibald	Colour Sergt. K. O. S. B-	I. 11-5-91.
Simpson, Arthur Lind	Banker	J. 10-1-21.
Simpson, Benjamin	Military Clerk	J. 13-7-85. as serving Bro.
Simpson, Charles Frederick	Military Officer	I. 4-10-51.
Simpson, Edward James	Captain H. E. I. C. Service	J. 8-8-49.
Sinclair, J. Decoury	Captain H. M's Service	J. 8-8-49.
Singleton, William	Overseer P. W. D.	J. 16-8-80.
Sital Singh	Clerk	J. 12-8-12.
Smallwood, Frank Graham	Captain R. A.	J. 12-8-01.
Smith, Charles	Sergeant H. E. the Viceroy's Band.	J. 13-7-96.
Smith, Charles	Military Clerk	J. 12-1-14. Rj. 13-5-18.
Smith, Harry	Military Clerk	I. 5-6-65.
Smith, Henry Coape	Ensign H. E. I. C. Service	I. 20-10-56.
Smith, James	Overseer P. W. D.	J. 10-5-86.
Smith, John Colpoy	Military Surgeon	J. 5-6-51.
Smith, Walter	Civil Engineer	J. 14-5-83.
Smith, Walter	Military Clerk	I. 9-4-06.
Smith, William	Dairy Expert	I 28-6-09.
Smyth, Thomas Cartwright	Revd. Doctor	J. 7-9-63.
Smyth, James Dutton	Lieut. 98th Foot	J. 16-8-49.
Smyth, Robert Allan	Cornet 7 D. Gds.	I. 1-6-63.
Smythe, Robert Sparrow	Theatrical Manager	I. 24-6-65.
Snodgrass, John	Major H. M's. 96 Foot	J. 7-8-52.
Sooboda, Alexander	Artist (Painter)	I. 17-7-54.
Sorrie, Peter	Military Clerk	J. 19-4-75.
Sparkes, Thomas George	Military Clerk	I. 12-8-95. Rj. 3-3-99.
Sprague, Thomas Actwell	Sergeant, 1/5th Somerset Regt.	I. 1-5-17.
Spur, Thomas	Supervisor P.W.D.	J. 16-10-76.
Stagg, Joseph Elias	Merchant's Assistant	I. 4-7-70.
Stansfeld, Henry Hamer	Colonel B. S. C.	J. 15-5-76.
Steffen, Charles Henry Louis	Hotel Manager	I. 13-10-24.
Steiner, Frederic	Asst. Manager Cecil Hotel	I. 11-7-21.
Stephen, William	Clerk	J. 16-4-77. Rj. 15-5-82.
Stephens, Bertie Edwin	Clerk	J. 16-6-14.
Stewart, Robert Dalrymple	Lieutenant H M's. Service	J. 11-7-50.
Stevens, Charles Osmond Hibbert	Driver, Kalka Simla Railway	J. 14-2-21.
Stevens, Robert Patrick	Sergeant 1/6th East Surrey Regt.	I. 13-11-16.
Stewart, Alexander McLeod	Lieut., Genl. List Infantry	J. 6-7-63.
Stewart, George Cosmo.	Captain R A.	J. 10-9-06.
Stewart, John	Asst. Supdt. of Telegraphs	J. 13-8-94. Rj 12-6-99.
Stirling John McNeish	Warrant Officer I.M D.	J. 8-3-26.
Stoddard, Alfred Ernest	Clerk	J. 11-5-96.
Stokes, William Allan	Captain E.R.	
Stooks. Gerald Summer	School Master	I. 11-11-07.
Stowell, Walter Frederick	Clerk	I. 14-3-92.
Stranack, E. F.	Banker	J. 19-5-79.
Stuart, Charles	Clerk	I. 27-5-66.
Suffolk, Henry Molyneux Howard, Earl of,	A.D.C. to H.E. the Viceroy	I. 12-6-99.

Names.		Profession or Occupation.		Date
Sullivan, Owen Charles	..	Commission Agent	..	I. 14-4-02. Rj. 13-6-04. Rj. 8-3-09.
Sullivan, James	..	Hospital Steward		J. 18-5-54.
Summers, Ambrose	..	Hair Dresser		I. 1-7-72.
Sunder Lall Pathuk	..	Conservator of Forests Patiala State.		I. 14-10-89.
Surendrnath Mozoomda		Civil Assistant Surgeon	..	J. 14-8-11.
Swales, William Henry	..	Tailor		I. 12-9-88.
Swanyne, Eric John Eagles	..	Captain I.S.C.	..	I. 11-3-95.
Sweet, George William	..	Ex. M. W. Accounts	..	J. 14-4-90.
Swinton, Charles Vivian	..	Captain H.E.I.C. Service	..	J. 16-5-53
Syed Amir Ali	..	Dy. Inspector of Police	..	I. 9-7-83.
Syed Mohamedah Imam	..	Barrister-at-Law Member of Council.		J. 14-8-11.
Symes, Edward Walton		Chemist	..	I. 1-2-69.
Talbot, George Richard	..	Major 2nd En. Ben. Fus.		J. 27-7-52.
Tanner, Godfrey Dickson	..	Assistant Thacker Spink & Co.		J. 12-8-07.
Tapp, Henry Thomas	..	House Agent		Rj. 1850†.
Tara Charau	..	Private Secretary to H.H. the Maharaj Rana of Dholpur.		J. 9-8-15.
Taunton, George Edward	..	Military Clerk		J. 23-4-83.
Tayler, William Edward	..	Conductor, I.A.O.C.	..	J. 12-4-26.
Taylor, David	..	Horse Trainer		J. 11-5-96.
Taylor, Thomas	..	Military Clerk		I. 8-2-04.
Teeling, Charles O'Hagan	..	Clerk		I. 27-9-09.
Tellery, Anton	..	Merchant	..	J. 28-6-09.
Tellery, Frank Ignatius	..	Architect		I. 8-7-07.
Temple, Algar Bowdoin	..	Ensign 49 B.I.		I. 2-10-54.
Temple Bernard	..	Journalist	..	J. 14-7-02.
TenBrocke, Anthony Henry	..	Clerk		I. 4-9-71.
Terry, Thomas William	..	Sub-Conductor, I.M.L.		I. 12-9-18.
Thakur Surat Singh	..	Clerk		J. 12-5-13.
Thomason, Archibald Fawcett	..	Captain I.A.		I. 13-8-06
Thompson, John Stanley		Lieutenant 1/7th Rajputs	..	J. 13-10-19.
Thomson, George William		Lieutenant R.A.		I. 19-6-65.
Thornhill, Bensley		Civil Engineer	..	I. 9-9-01.
Thornton, Hector James		Govt. Tel. Dept.		I. 28-9-07.
Thorpe, Edward Courteney	..	Military Surgeon	..	I. 17-7-51. Rj. 18-7-70.
Thrope, Joseph Mathew	..	Proprietor, Station Press	..	I. 8-2-09.
Tibbetts, Henry William	..	Hospital Steward		J. 16-10-54.
Tilley, Christopher Robert	..	Gunmaker's Asst.		J. 9-5-04.
Tinson, John	..	Sanitary Engineer	..	J. 10-5-09. Rj. 8-7-12.
Tissendie, Walter Seymour	..	Clerk	..	J. 25-5-08. Rj. 23-8-09.
Todhunter, William Philip	..	Sergeant, I.M.L.		I. 14-5-17.
Tomkyns, Alexander Pakington		Surgeon H.E.I.C. Service	..	I. 20 10-56.
Topple, Edward John	..	Clerk		I. 17-5-75.
Towelle, William Joseph Martin		Merchant		I. 2-8-75. Rj. 10-6-95.
Townley, George	..	Merchant	..	I. 4-7-81. Rj. 9-3-08.
Treglown, Sydney	..	Tailor		J. 8-5-05. Rj. 14-5-88.
Trevelyan, H.A.	..	No record	..	J. 20-5-61.
Trower, Frederick Courtney	..	Captain H. M's. Service	..	
Tucker, Samuel Reeve	..	Military Surgeon	..	I. 19-6-50.

Names.	Profession or Occupation.	Date.
Tufnell, Carlton F.	Civil Engineer	J. 14-5-83.
Turnbull, Joseph	Sergeant R.A.	J. 14-5-06.
Turner, Agustus Henry	Major I.A.	J. 14-5-83.
Turner, F.M.	No record	J. 1-9-79.
Turner, Norman Francis	Lieutenant British Service	I 11-4-21.
Tyrrell, C.R	Major R.A.M.C.	J. 9-4-00.
Udaibhan Singh	Maharaja Rana of Dholpur	J. 9-8-15.
Unwin, George	Military Clerk	J. 16-4-14.
Upton, Henry Edward Montague Dorrington, Clotsworthy.	Lieutenant 60th Rifles.	I. 5-8-78.
Vanek, Joseph	Professor of Magic	J. 15-5-76.
Vaughan, Edward Gyles	Captain I.A.	I. 13-6-04.
Vaughan, Sidney George	Soldier	J. 10-8-96.
		Rj. 11-10-20.
Veasey, Thomas Walter	Staff Sergeant I.A.O.C.	J. 14-4-24.
Verney, Arthur James	Stud Groom	J. 10-7-05.
Vibart. Edmund Charles	Lieutenant 11 B.I.	I. 29-8-49.
Vincent, Arthur Hare	Lieutenant H. M's. Service	I. 2-9-62.
Vivian, Francis Daniel	Merchant	I. 3-9-51.
		Rj. 19-5-56.
Vogt, Carl Frederick William Rudolf.	Manager Messrs Hanhart & Co. Jewellers.	J 13-6-98.
Vyall, Henry Edwin	Clerk	J. 15-7-72.
Wade, Richard	Band Master 10th Hussars	J. 16-5-08.
Wahab, Henry John	Captain H.M's Service	J. 7-7-62.
Wakefield, William Samuel	Merchant	J. 17-6-72.
		Rj. 15-6-74.
Walker, George	No record	J. 10-4-05.
Walker, James Lewis	Banker	J. 19-4-75.
		Rj. 8-9-84.
		Rj. 9-8-86.
Walker, James William	Army Schoolmaster	J 11-3-18.
Walker, John	Clerk Simla Bank	I. 16-8-49.
		J. 21-7-56.
Wallace, Annesley Frederick	Merchant	I. 11-6-61.
Wallace, George	Clerk	J. 5-8-72.
Wallace, Frank Ellerslie	Assistant Private Secy. to Maharaj Rana of Dholepur.	I. 20-8-91.
Waller, George Holland	Military Clerk	I. 6-7-63.
Wallis, Beresford Gahan	Executive Engr. P.W.D.	J. 14-9-91.
Walfis, Joseph William	Military Clerk	J. 10-3-19.
Walmsley, Edwin	Military Clerk	J. 13-7-85.
Walters, Elijah	Soldier	I. 21-8-65.
		Rj. 17-6-72.
Walther, Carl	Professor of Music	I. 14-9-91.
Wanstall, Charles	W. O. Const. Department	J. 14-3-92.
Ward, Frederick Herbert Tetley	Assistant Home Department	I. 28-6-20.
Ward, George	Lieutenant H.E.I.C. Service	I. 24 9-53.
Warde, Ellis Burroughes	Soldier H. M's. Army	I. 15-8-61.
Warde, Leonard Ward	Clerk	I. 20-8-18.
Warden, Alfred Walter	Captain, I. S. C.	i. 5-8-99.
Warneford, Reginald William H.	Civil Engineer	J. 11-8-02.
Warner, Charles Mark Ernest	Assistant Surgeon, I.S M.D.	J. 13-11-16.
Warren, Charles	Captain, H. M's. Service	J. 20-6-60.
Warren, Stanley Samuel	Master Tailor	I. 10-8-25.

Names.	Profession or Occupation.	Date.
Watson, Edward	Hair Dresser	J. 7-7-73.
Watson, Richard	Merchant	I. 20-6-82.
		Rj. 10-9-94.
Watts, Harry	Military Clerk	I. 12-6-99.
Watts, Herbert, Ponsonby	Captain I. A.	I. 10-9-06.
Waugh Robert Travers	Military Clerk	I. 9-4-06.
Waugh Thomas George Bertam	Military Clerk	J. 11-5-96.
Webber, Joseph	Head Master Christ Church School.	J. 14-6-97.
Webber, Stanley Thomas	Bandmaster, Seaforth Highlanders.	I, 14-7-24.
Webster, Charles Thomas	Sergeant R. A.	I. 12-8-89.
Welch, Charles Trevor	Captain, I.A.R.O	I. 11-10-20.
Welch, George Job	House Agent and Contractor.	J. 11-10-97.
		Rj. 14-5-06.
Welch, George Henry	Clerk	J. 26-7-09.
Weldon, Most Revd. Bishop	Bishop of Calcutta	
Wells, William George	Dy. Examiner Military Accounts Department.	I. 30-9-10.
Welner, Hugh Ernest	Assistant, Foreign and Political Department.	I. 10-7-16.
Werge, William	Military Officer	I. 3-7-52.
West J.I.	Manager, Church Missionary Society.	J. 8-6-96.
Western, Charles Maximilian Thomas.	Captain, I.A.	I. 12-2-12.
		J. 13-9-20.
Weston, William	Military Clerk	Rj. 11-1-26.
West, J. I.	Manager, Church Missionary Society.	J. 8-6-96.
Westrap, Albert James	Govt. Telegraph Department.	I. 13 6-04.
Wheatley, George	Assistant, Army Headquarters	J. 10-10-21.
Wheeler, F.	Sergeant Major Simla Volunteer Rifles.	J. 10-4-05.
Whetham, Lewis Charles	Military Clerk	I. 22-8-17.
Whish, Martin Boileau	Captain H. E. I. C. Service	J. 4-7-53.
White Benjamin Joseph	Tailor	I. 7-8-54.
White Charles	Civil Engineer	J. 11-6-00.
White, Daniel Richard	Asst. Engineer P. W. D.	J. 14-9-85.
White, Edward John	Captain H. E. I. C. Service	J. 4-8-56.
White, John	Clerk	I. 4-8-68.
White, William Arthur John	Sergeant Clerk, Royal Air Force	I. 12-5-24.
Whitehouse. James Ernest	Engineer M. W. S.	J. 13-11-05.
Whitelaw, Henry	Military Clerk	I. 12-4-20.
Whiteley, David	Military Clerk	I. 15-3-69.
Whitlock, Arthur Edward	Schoolmaster	J. 11-9-16.
Wibley, Charles Thomas	Firm of Messrs. Cooke & Kelvey.	J. 10-7-05.
Wickes, Charles H.	Clerk	J. 7-6-80.
Wickham, William Allan	Military Clerk	J. 11-8-84.
Wickham, William James Richard.	Lieut.-Colonel I. S. C.	J. 8-6-03.
Widger, George William Broadwood.	Military Clerk	I. 11-5-14.
		Rj. 14-7-19.
Wiffen. Charles Edward	Tailor's Cutter	I. 8-6-03.
		Rj. 27-4-08.
Wigg, Charles	Assistant Callan & Co.	J. 29-5-65.
Wigley, Frederick George	Barrister-at Law	J. 11-4-92.
Wigstrom, R. B.	Assistant Surgeon, 14th Dragoons.	J. 8-8-49.
Wilden, Herbert Reeve	Sergt. Farrier R. A.	I. 9-10-93.

Names.	Profession or Occupation.	Date.
Wilkinson, James Elworthy ..	Military Clerk ..	J. 10-8-91.
Wilks, Bertie Sinclair ..	Clerk ..	I. 9-4-17.
Williams, Charles Beynon ..	Civil Engineer ..	I. 1-9-02.
Williams, Edward Vincent ..	Military Clerk	I. 11-8-19.
Williams, Henry ..	Professor Music ..	I. 19-7-75.
Williams, Joseph Alfred ..	Clerk ..	I. 11-4-92.
Williams George ..	I. C. S. ..	J. 6-9-69.
Williams, George Lloyd ..	Captain, 24th Foot ..	J. 8-8-49.
Williamson, Ernest ..	Staff Sergeant, I. M. I. ..	1 4-8-16.
Wills, Charles Edward ..	Clerk ..	J. 25-5-08.
		Rj. 10-1.21.
Willson, William Cater ..	Military Clerk ..	I. 6-7-63.
		Rj. 19-4-75.
Wilsey, Edward Owen Willasey	Clerk ..	I. 13-6-98.
Wilson, Arthur Bakewell ..	Clerk ..	I. 9-4-94.
		Rj 12-6-99.
Wilson, Andrew Hogarth ..	Chemist ..	I. 29-8-04.
		Rj. 13-12-5.
Wilson, George ..	Military Clerk ..	I. 1-6-06.
		Rj. 12-6-99.
		Rj. 10-6-13.
Wilson, Jarvie Webb ..	Captain, I. A. ..	1. 12-7-20.
Wilson, Stuart ..	Clerk ..	I. 24-4-99.
		Rj. 12-10-08.
Wilson, William Henry ..	Agent .	J. 6-6-64.
Wilson, William, T. ..	Architect ..	J. 11-5-85.
Wilsone, Arthur Henry ..	Clerk ..	I. 14-9-85.
Winn, George Franklin ..	Clerk ..	J. 10-6-95.
Winning, Robert Reginald ..	School Master ..	I. 11-12-15.
Wolseley, Richard ..	Surgeon R.A.M.C. ..	J. 14-5-82.
Wood, Samuel George ..	Clerk ..	I. 4-9-71.
		Rj. 20-6-81.
Wood, Thomas ..	School Master ..	I. 2-5-53.
Woodington, Oliver ..	Assistant Messrs. Watts & Co.	I. 8-6-96.
Woodcock, Reoben Wilfred ..	Steward and Caterer ..	J. 10-5-26.
Woodthorpe, Robert Gossett ..	Colonel R. E. ..	I. 11-8-90.
Woodward, Oscar ..	Supdt. Kellner's Refreshment rooms.	J. 11-5-96.
Wright, Cecil Francis Salisbury	Clerk ..	I. 13-7-85.
		Rj. 13-4-91
Wright, James ..	Quarter-Master Sergt. R. A. ..	I. 12-10-96.
Yarde Buller, the Hon. John Reginald Lopes.	Captain, Scots Guards ..	J. 11-8-02.
Yates, William Henry ..	Surgeon, I. M. S. ..	J. 22-6-68.
Yeatman Biggs, Arthur Godolphin.	Colonel, R.A. ..	J. 12-2-94.
Young, Harry Norman ..	Captain, I A. ..	J. 14-5-06.
Young. James ..	Lieutenant, 4th N.I. ..	I. 16-8-49.

www.ingramcontent.com/pod-product-compliance
Lightning Source LLC
Chambersburg PA
CBHW080206300326
41934CB00038B/3369